PENGUIN BOOKS

CUT STONES AND CROSSROADS

RONALD WRIGHT was born in England and now lives in Ontario. His award-winning books include *Stolen Continents* and *Time Among the Maya*. His recent novel, *A Scientific Romance*, won Britain's David Higham Prize for Fiction and was chosen a book of the year by the *Globe and Mail*, the *Sunday Times* and the *New York Times*. His new novel, *Henderson's Spear*, will be published shortly.

Books by Ronald Wright

FICTION

Henderson's Spear
A Scientific Romance

HISTORY

Stolen Continents

TRAVEL

Time Among the Maya
On Fiji Islands
Cut Stones and Crossroads
Quechua Phrasebook

ESSAYS

Home and Away

CUT STONES AND CROSSROADS

A JOURNEY IN THE TWO WORLDS OF PERU

RONALD WRIGHT

PENGUIN BOOKS

PENGUIN BOOKS
Published by the Penguin Group
Penguin Books Canada Ltd, 10 Alcorn Avenue, Toronto, Ontario, Canada M4V 3B2
Penguin Books Ltd, 27 Wrights Lane, London W8 5TZ, England
Penguin Putnam Inc., 375 Hudson Street, New York, New York 10014, U.S.A.
Penguin Books Australia Ltd, Ringwood, Victoria, Australia
Penguin Books (NZ) Ltd, cnr Rosedale and Airborne Roads, Albany, Auckland 1310,
New Zealand

Penguin Books Ltd, Registered Offices: Harmondsworth, Middlesex, England

First published in the United States of America by Viking Penguin Inc., 1984
Published in Penguin Books, 1986

Published in this edition, 2001

1 3 5 7 9 10 8 6 4 2

Maps by Sharon Thorpe

Manufactured in Canada

CANADIAN CATALOGUING IN PUBLICATION DATA

Wright, Ronald
Cut stones and crossroads: a journey in Peru

ISBN 0-14-100026-0

1. Peru – Description and travel – 1981 – . 2. Incas – Social life and customs.
3. Incas – Architecture. 4. Wright, Ronald – Journeys – Peru. I. Title

F3425.W75 2001   918.504'633   C00-932489-5

Visit Penguin Canada's website at www.penguin.ca

TAYTAMAMAYMAN
TO MY PARENTS

CONTENTS

CUT STONES AND CROSSROADS   1

AFTERWORD   211

CHRONOLOGY   215

NOTE ON RUNASIMI PRONUNCIATION   219

GLOSSARY   221

SOURCE NOTES   230

BIBLIOGRAPHY   233

INDEX   239

MAPS

    THE INCA EMPIRE, C. 1525   ix

    AUTHOR'S ROUTE   x

    PLAN OF CUSCO   xi

ILLUSTRATIONS FOLLOW PAGE   112

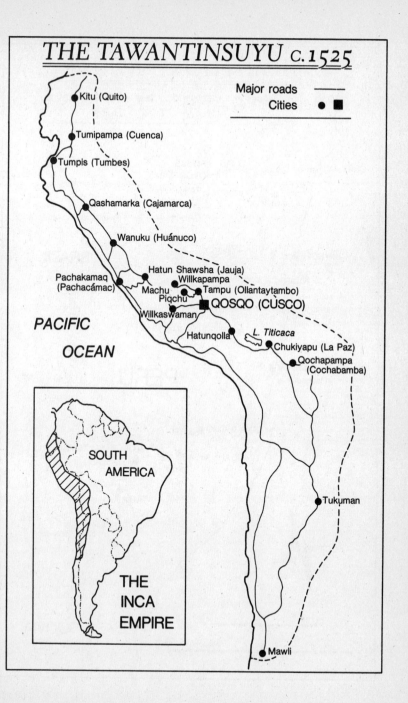

THE TAWANTINSUYU c.1525

Major roads ———
Cities ● ■

Kitu (Quito)

Tumipampa (Cuenca)

Tumpis (Tumbes)

Qashamarka (Cajamarca)

Wanuku (Huánuco)

Hatun Shawsha (Jauja)
Willkapampa
Pachakamaq
(Pachacámac)
Machu   Tampu (Ollantaytambo)
Piqchu
Willkaswaman   QOSQO (CUSCO)

Hatunqolla   L. Titicaca
            Chukiyapu (La Paz)
            Qochapampa
            (Cochabamba)

PACIFIC

OCEAN

SOUTH
AMERICA

THE
INCA
EMPIRE

Tukuman

Mawli

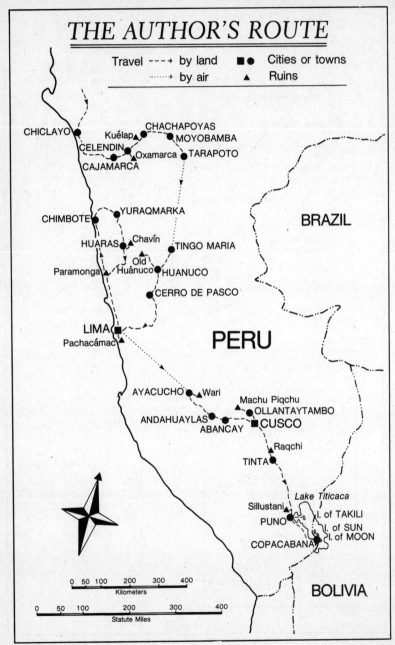

THE AUTHOR'S ROUTE

Travel ----→ by land   ■ ● Cities or towns
        ·······→ by air   ▲ Ruins

CHICLAYO

CHACHAPOYAS
Kuélap▲
CELENDIN   MOYOBAMBA
            ▲Oxamarca   TARAPOTO
CAJAMARCA

BRAZIL

CHIMBOTE   YURAQMARKA

HUARAS   ●Chavín
          ▲   TINGO MARIA
          Old
Paramonga▲ Huánuco HUANUCO
          CERRO DE PASCO

LIMA
Pachacámac▲

PERU

            AYACUCHO● ▲Wari
                        Machu Piqchu
                        ▲ OLLANTAYTAMBO
ANDAHUAYLAS   CUSCO
        ABANCAY

                    Raqchi
            TINTA

                    Lake Titicaca
            Sillustani
                        I. of TAKILI
            PUNO   I. of SUN
                        I. of MOON
            COPACABANA

                    BOLIVIA

0 50 100 200 300 400
        Kilometers

0 50 100 200 300 400
        Statute Miles

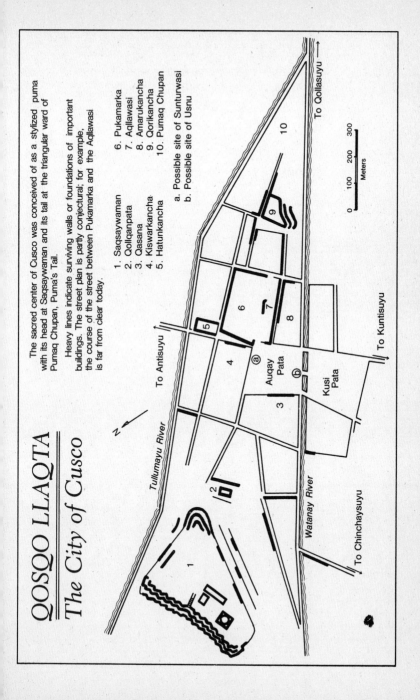

QOSQO LLAQTA
The City of Cusco

The sacred center of Cusco was conceived of as a stylized puma with its head at Saqsaywaman and its tail at the triangular ward of Pumaq Chupan, Puma's Tail.

Heavy lines indicate surviving walls or foundations of important buildings. The street plan is partly conjectural; for example, the course of the street between Pukamarka and the Aqllawasi is far from clear today.

1. Saqsaywaman
2. Qollqanpata
3. Qasana
4. Kiswarkancha
5. Hatunkancha
6. Pukamarka
7. Aqllawasi
8. Amarukancha
9. Qorikancha
10. Pumaq Chupan

a. Possible site of Sunturwasi
b. Possible site of Usnu

To Antisuyu

Tullumayu River

Auqay Pata

Kusi Pata

Watanay River

To Chinchaysuyu

To Kuntisuyu

To Qollasuyu

0 100 200 300
Meters

CUT STONES
AND
CROSSROADS

= 1 =

CHICLAYO, PERU
Last night I picked a bad hotel. The rooms were mere plywood cubicles in a large ward, and in the mattress there were leggy things like silverfish. A drunken couple made love noisily for hours; at about two o'clock this morning I heard: "Ay, kiss me, Pedro, kiss me"—long silence—"now the other one."

———

These coastal towns are garish and shabby; they always smell of urine and rotting fish. The rainless climate allows a steady accumulation of filth that dries and shrivels but is never washed away. I forget the bad side of this country between visits, and it makes for hard beginnings.

Today is my thirtieth birthday. I shall go to Cajamarca by *colectivo* limousine—damn the expense.

7:00 A.M.
An hour south of Chiclayo; the driver stops for breakfast at a roadside restaurant in the desert. The air is cool and the smells have not yet woken. Deserts are lovely only at dawn and dusk.

Yesterday I was in jungle and banana groves, but at the frontier between Ecuador and Peru the climate changes abruptly—as though nature were trying to imitate cartography. Except for some small and widely separated valleys, the Pacific littoral from here to Chile is a naked beach on which nothing grows, nothing decays, and nothing moves but dunes and the dilapidated trucks that ply the Pan-American Highway.

The men at the service station fuss over the old Dodge and call our driver "gringo" because of the European cast to his features. In Mexico that word would start a fight, but in race-conscious Peru it is taken as a compliment. Nobody is called *indio* except as the gravest of insults; however, a person with Indian looks can be nicknamed *chino* (Chinaman) without offense.

CHINO, EL PUEBLO ESTA CONTIGO! ("Chino, the people are with you!") has not yet faded from a wall: President Velasco, who died two years ago, was a chino.

Another hour southbound on the Panamericana (rippled asphalt; width, twenty feet; length in Peru, two thousand miles) and the colectivo turns east toward the mountains, on a road that follows the Jequetepeque River to its source. The road is shimmering in the heat like a strip of celluloid. The driver overtakes a truck and almost fails to see an approaching car half hidden in a mirage. I'm glad now to be sitting in the back. (I had wanted a front seat beside the slender girl, but instead I have her mother—large and sweaty—for company.)

The irrigation here is impressive. The whole valley floor is leveled in terraced rice paddies and maize fields. By careful management a vast area is fed by a rather meager flow of water. The system must have ancient origins: when our road left the Panamericana we passed the extensive mud ruins of Pacatnamú, where the Mochica and Chimú kept large populations before the time of the Incas.

11:00 A.M.
The irrigated valley has narrowed to a rocky gorge, and we are leaving the desert. The hills are sparsely clothed in cactus and scrub sustained by the moisture of clouds that sometimes form here in the night.

The air is cold now; icy drafts from beneath the ill-fitting door stab my legs; the señora is delightfully warm.

Just before the pass, at about thirteen thousand feet, the paving ends. The car jounces and an exhaust pipe clatters onto the road. We get out while the driver repairs it unconvincingly with a piece of wire found in the ditch. I am feeling *soroche* (altitude sickness)—a wringing headache and a fragile sense of reality, like a tequila hangover.

The señora produces a hip flask from somewhere on her person:

"Have some *pisco* for the cold, mister?"

"No, thank you. Very kind." Until one is accustomed, alcohol has triple its usual effect at these heights, and pisco (raw grape spirit) is an unsubtle drink at the best of times.

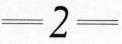

CAJAMARCA—9,000 FEET

From four years ago, I remember a white city in green countryside, but now the hills are brown and gray, and only the valley floor is lush. It is the beginning of the wet season; the rains are late.

This hotel is better: a proper room and private bath. But the walls need painting—there are vertical snail tracks beside the bed: I wish Latin Americans wouldn't spit. "Hot water at all hours," claims the management, but only a chill trickle runs from the shower. Fortunately, in Cajamarca there's an alternative.

Twenty minutes on a minibus caught in the plaza and I am at the Baños del Inca (Inca's Baths) hot springs. An attendant takes me down a steamy corridor which has rows of doors on either side. Laughter and splashing can be heard. There is no communal pool but the private rooms are large enough for parties.

My room has tiled walls, a window up high, and a sunken tank occupying most of the floor. The water is hot and abundant, slightly sulphurous; I fill the tank to a depth of three feet and float. Bliss. I left Canada only two weeks ago; already a tub (unattainable on this continent of dank showers) has become a luxury.

In a run-down older section of the spa is a tank exhibited as a genuine Inca bath. It is about ten feet square, crudely made of rough stones and cement, and quite unlike any Inca work I have seen. Perhaps it dates from a different ancient period; most likely it's a modern fabrication.

Pizarro's secretary saw Inka Atau Wallpa's establishment at the hot springs and has left this description:

> It consisted of four rooms built around a courtyard in which was a tank fed by water from a pipe. This water, which was so hot that it burnt the hand . . . was joined on the way by cold water in another pipe, the two running into the tank together. . . . The pipe was large and made of stone. . . .
>
> The apartment in which Atahuallpa spent the day was a gallery looking down on a garden, and beside it was the room in which he slept, which had a window facing the courtyard and the tank. . . . The walls were plastered with a red bitumen finer than ochre, which was very bright. The wood used for the roofing of the house

was stained with the same dye. The other room in front consisted of four bell-shaped vaults joined into one, and was washed with snow-white lime.

The Inca was fasting here and nursing a war wound in the waters when he received disturbing news. Waman Puma, a sixteenth-century native chronicler, recorded how the foreigners were first described to the ruler of Peru:

> There are [coming] men who never sleep and who eat silver and gold, as do their beasts who wear sandals of silver. And every night each of these men speaks with certain symbols; and they are all enshrouded from head to foot, with their faces completely covered in wool, so that all that can be seen are their eyes.

It was November 1532.

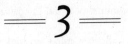

== 3 ==

6:00 A.M.

With morning comes the prehistoric sound of flutes and drum. Above a lilting melody a trumpet wails. Louder. A parade?

From the window I can see a dozen Indians, traditionally dressed in ponchos and homespun breeches, advancing solemnly up the street. One has a large drum, others flutes; two are carrying extraordinary *cornetas*—bamboo tubes twelve feet long, flared with tin at the ends. The sound of these is somewhere between that of a bugle and of an alpine horn. A man without an instrument is lighting and scattering powerful fireworks, which echo like gunshots in the narrow street.

The men seem oblivious of the waking town around them. They march like ghosts, with a compulsion that may date from when Cajamarca was an Inca city. I half expect to see them disappear or pass through a wall. Their self-absorption tells me this is not a parade for spectators. I am witnessing a private ritual: the twentieth century intruding on the sixteenth.

Something more familiar wakes me a second time an hour later: *She loves you, yeah, yeah, yeah* . . . Beatles in Cajamarca?

The teenage boy mopping the passage outside my room is singing along: "*Chi lub yo . . .*"

What was the procession, I ask.

"Those were Indians from the hills. They come here sometimes."

"What were they celebrating?"

"A fiesta."

"Which fiesta?"

"I don't know"—as if to say: I don't want to know; don't ask me; I'm not an Indian from the hills.

"*Chi lub yo . . .*"

And then, worst of all, the station break: *In Cajamarca, you are listening to . . . Radio Atahuallpa!*

Breakfast, always a problem in Peru: a greasy fried egg in a stale bun and weak, tepid coffee at a café on the square.

Cajamarca's plaza is one of the most delightful in South America. Tall, leafy trees shade benches amid flower beds tended meticulously in the English way. There are ornamental shrubs and hedges cut in striking shapes: a man riding a llama, a Peruvian shield, a whole family of llamas, and, most surprising of all, huge bushy heads cut in imitation of stone originals from the ancient ruins of Chavín: grotesque leering faces, wizened and with feline fangs, rendered oddly charming in the well-trimmed shrubbery. A tranquil place, hard to reconcile with the violence that took place here on the evening of November 16, 1532, when several thousand unarmed retainers were killed in cold blood and Atau Wallpa was pulled from his litter by the hair.

The only injury on the Spanish side was a cut suffered by Pizarro himself as he parried another Spaniard's blow intended for the Inca.

There is no commemoration of these events in the Cajamarca of today. No statue recalls Atau Wallpa, no plaque the thousands who died. It is as though nothing happened.

A comparison is in order: in Tlaltelolco, Mexico City, where the Aztec nation fell, this inscription has been erected near the ruins of a pyramid:

13th of August 1521

Heroically defended by Cuauhtémoc, Tlaltelolco fell into the power of Hernán Cortés. It was neither triumph nor defeat, but the painful birth of the mixed people which is the Mexico of today.

Peru, unlike Mexico, is still a nation divided: a land of conquered and conqueror. There is no such philosophical view of the past. Pizarro's statue still stands in the center of Lima (despite efforts to remove it during the Velasco regime) and his shriveled remains in the cathedral are still venerated by many *criollos*, Peruvians of Spanish descent.

Meanwhile in the mountains, on certain days, the Indians remember their dead *Inka*—their king—in orally transmitted poems and plays about the Conquest. These lines in Runasimi (the Inca language, also known as Quechua) are from *Atau Wallpa Wañuy* (*The Death of Atau Wallpa*), an epic lament first written down in the eighteenth century:

Phuyu phuyulla	Like a great cloud
Wiraqochami	The *Wiraqochas* [Whites]
Qorita nispa	Demanding gold
Tunt'arirqami.	Have invaded us.
Inka Yayata	After seizing
Hap'ikuchispa,	Our Father Inca,
Siripayaspa,	After deceiving him,
Wañuchirqami.	They have put him to death.
Puma sonqowan,	He with the heart of a puma,
Atoq makiwan,	The powers of a fox,
Llamata hina	They have killed
Tukuchirqami.	As if he were a llama.
Runtuq urmaspa,	Hail is falling,
Illapantaspa,	Lightning strikes,
Inti haykuspa;	The sun is sinking;
Tutayarqami.	It has become forever night.

=====

Not far from the plaza is the so-called Ransom Room, which Atau Wallpa supposedly filled with treasure in a futile bid to buy his freedom from the men who "eat gold." The Incas, with no concept of money or private wealth, did believe at first that the Spaniards ate precious metals, or were suffering from a disease for which gold was the only cure. No other explanation seemed to justify the lengths to which the invaders were prepared to go in order to obtain it.

The room is all that remains of the once extensive Inca buildings in Cajamarca. It is well made of stone blocks fitted precisely together without mortar in the classic imperial style. The walls slope inward, strengthening the corners against earthquakes by applying a slight preload, and giving the building a characteristically squat, massive appearance. This perspective is skillfully turned into a virtue by being echoed in the trapezoidal form of the doors and niches—the leitmotif of Inca architecture.

The Ransom Room has survived because it belonged during the colonial period to the Astopilco family, *kurakas* (native nobles in the Spanish administration) who were loath to pull down their ancestral buildings.

But it has suffered over the years: three doorways have been rudely hacked through one of the walls, and a line reputed to show the height of the treasure pile has been painted, or at least retouched, around the inside.

In fact, there is no evidence that this was the treasure chamber, though it may have been where Atau Wallpa himself was kept.

There is a little garden in the courtyard outside the room, with a tall San Pedro cactus and other local plants. I imagine the Inca here, a fallen eagle, but an able and resourceful man who spent his captivity learning what he could about the strange people who had overthrown him. Alonso de Guzmán recalled:

Atahuallpa was so intelligent that in twenty days he understood Spanish and learnt to play chess and cards. . . . He learnt many things. . . . He was greatly astonished at the Christian way of communicating by writing [and] asked a man to write down certain words at his dictation, and then asked another man privately to read them, and thus he learnt to understand this marvel.

When the time came to get rid of the Inca, and he was confronted with the trumped-up charges to justify his execution, Pizarro's secretary records the following exchange:

The Governor [Pizarro] then spoke to Atahuallpa: "What treason is this you have been plotting against me? I have treated you honourably as a brother and have trusted your word."

"Are you mocking me?" Atahuallpa replied. "You are always making jokes at my expense. How can I and all my people possibly cause any anxiety to valiant men like you?"

The readiness of his wit surprised those Spaniards who heard his conversation in captivity. They were amazed to find so much intelligence in a savage.

A gloom has settled on me in this place. I leave to see the last station on Atau Wallpa's Calvary.

At the ruined church of Belén (Bethlehem) two teenage girls point out the woman with four breasts. There she is, prominent in the riot of Indo-

Baroque sculpture, her naked bust with four pendulous breasts, one pair below the other. I can't decide whether the carving is humorous or shows a snickering fascination with deformity. The girls don't know its history, but their laughter lifts my mood.

———

A long flight of formal steps leads halfway up the hill of Santa Apolonia to a fussy Catholic shrine—the basilica of the saint. I am interested in seeing the much older shrine on the summit.

The steepest part of the hill is climbed by a spiral stair, at least partly ancient, and probably the place where Pedro de Candía lay hidden with the cannon that signaled the start of the massacre in the square below.

The plaza is visible from here as a patch of greenery and two church towers awash in a choppy sea of terracotta roofs.

The shrine itself, like so many in Peru, is a natural rock outcrop into which has been carved a bewildering collection of geometrical and curvilinear forms: basins, planes, niches, steps, and channels. The earliest work here is thought to date back to Chavín times (c. 500 B.C.), with modification by the Incas two thousand years later, and some fanciful nineteenth-century tinkering. At the very top is a sculpture resembling a seat, much weathered and defaced. It may have been the bowl of a sacred fountain, or a receptacle for the sacrificial beer beloved by Peruvian deities and priests.

A small boy offers me "an explanation of the ruins" in the hope of a tip.

"There's a tunnel all the way from here to Cusco!" he begins. (Cusco, the Inca capital, is about a thousand miles away.)

"Oh. Where is the entrance?"

"Nobody knows. It's been blocked up. But it goes right under here." He stamps his bare foot emphatically on the hapless Inca's Seat.

All over Peru, Ecuador, and Bolivia there are tales of tunnels leading to Cusco or linking ancient monuments. The myth is probably a survival of a *seqe* (or *ceque*) system—a web of imaginary lines intersecting the *wak'as*, the major shrines in the empire, and converging on Cusco. Some seqe systems were actually laid out where terrain permitted; the famed lines of Nazca (Von Däniken's airfields) in the southern desert are probably a series of such networks superimposed.

When one combines the seqe concept with the elaborate Peruvian underworld and the fact that some bedrock shrines do have subterranean labyrinths for the placement of offerings, one has all the makings of the modern belief in tunnels to Cusco.

"There is also gold," says the boy.

This belief is far more dangerous: it has resulted in untold destruction by avaricious treasure-seekers. Gold fever has been endemic in Peru since the Europeans arrived; even today, enough small pieces of the metal are occasionally found to cause sporadic outbreaks of the disease.

"What is this place called?" I ask.

"The Inca's Seat."

"But what is it in Runasimi?"

"Inka Kunka."

Tiyana is the word for seat, so this is surprising. But then I remember that *kunka* means neck, and that Atau Wallpa was killed by the garrotte.

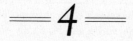

Luís is a Cajamarcan with an interest in cinematography, which he studies in Lima. At the moment he is home on holidays. He is as fascinated by the gringo world as I am by Peru, and invites me to meet his mother, a kindly, devout woman who teaches in a village school. She makes us a sumptuous Peruvian meal: raw fish *ceviche*; potato soup; a huge mound of rice on which repose the limbs of a roast guinea pig.

Over the meal, Luís describes a satirical film he made at the Lima zoo with his fellow students. The campaign song of a political party—*Happiness with APRA, the only solution*—was set to footage of a monkey vigorously masturbating. We all laugh. There is no shyness between mother, son, and stranger.

Luís offers to guide me to the Cumbe Mayo tomorrow.

Our walk began at the Inca's Seat, where we met after breakfast, and takes us through the squatter settlement on the hills above the city. The dogs here are fierce and cowardly—always a dangerous combination.

They used to call these slums *barriadas*, but now there is a new euphemism: *pueblos jovenes*, "young towns." Velasco's regime couldn't stem the urban drift but made the best of the situation by granting titles to established squatters and getting them to organize street plans, communities, and eventually basic services. Here they have standpipes for water; the houses are well built of adobe and eucalyptus timber. But the hill is so steep that the roofs of one street are at the level of the doors above. How will they ever put in drains?

They are working on one house; a large jar of *chicha* (maize beer) receives frequent visits from tipsy but enthusiastic builders. Luís says this is a *minga*.

Minga has passed into Andean Spanish from Runasimi *mink'a*; it is what North Americans would call a "work bee." The beneficiary of the work invites friends and kin to raise a house or plant a field, and repays them, not in cash, but with ample food, drink, perhaps coca leaves, and the obligation to work in return when asked. In ancient times, mink'a was fundamental. It formed the basis of the moneyless economic system that Western writers have variously (and inaccurately) described as "socialist," "totalitarian," or "utopian." The best word is "reciprocal."

The Inca Empire drew its workers by a system of rotating levies called *mit'a*—an extension of the mink'a concept to the level of the state. In return for labor, the state fed the worker and his family on a generous diet, usually maize and llama meat—luxury foods of religious significance. The workers' home communities received security from crop failure and the benefits of imperial public works constructed by their own and others' mit'a: roads, terracing, and irrigation schemes. All this was in the enlightened self-interest of the Inca rulers—people were wealth; there was no profit in undermining the currency by abusing the populace, as the Spaniards later did.

Mink'a survives in rural areas today because it still has certain advantages: it cements the social fabric and, like barter, is immune to inflation, which is running at 80 percent.

═══

Beyond the shantytown are eucalyptus groves and small, steep fields of poor soil.

A cloud of dust is moving slowly across one of these fields. The cloud thins for a moment and I see there is a man inside it, and a pair of oxen dragging a primitive plough.

"Without rain soon there will be no crop this year," says Luís.

"Has the land reform been any help?"

"The land reform is a *fracaso*."

(Four years ago Velasco's land reform posters were everywhere, bright syntheses of psychedelia and socialist realism: *Peasant, no longer shall the landlord feast on your poverty! The land is for the people who work it: work the soil with your sweat and its fruits shall be yours!*)

"The landlords have gone, but they left the peasants with nothing: no seed, no equipment. So many cattle have been eaten that a pair of oxen like those now costs as much as a tractor."

"Luís, you are a pessimist. Land reforms are always like that at first. Give it time."

"There is no time. They say the bosses are coming back, now that Velasco is dead."

———

Cajamarca has disappeared below the swell of the hill. We top a rise and suddenly the land levels out. This is the *puna*, the flat country above twelve thousand feet between the mountain ridges. The soil is dark, rich, and moist, but it's one of Peru's ironies that little grows here because of the cold. Only small native potatoes can survive the hail and frosts, and they often need nine months to mature.

The only llamas in the region seem to be those in the plaza. A pity: everywhere there are spiky tufts of *ichu* grass, which only the native animals can eat; this is being burned to make way for tamer plants suited to the delicate tastes of Old World ruminants. The result is erosion—sheep nibble grass to the roots; cows' hoofs damage the sod. And all because llama meat is disdained by the urban classes as "Indian food."

I am beginning to feel soroche again, and the weather has turned cold. I have a windbreaker; Luís has nothing but his best clothes: shirt, polyester slacks, shiny black shoes—how like a Latin American—but he's stoic.

The landscape acquires a trancelike quality emphasized by stark lighting and drifts of mist. We pass below a strange rock formation, a vast mass of gray limestone eroded into spires and chimneys. It would be fun to enter this labyrinth and look for the ancient carving that I'm sure must be here—what a site for a wak'a.

Luís says no, there is a risk of getting lost and the Cumbe Mayo is still an hour away. He calls this outcrop Los Frailones, The Great Friars, and indeed it looks like a conclave of hooded figures.

The Andes abound with legends of people turned to stone, and vice versa.

———

The ridges have approached on both sides; we are hemmed in by a small valley with boulders and a torrent in the middle. The mist, the rocks, the dull military greens and tiny flowers, remind me of northern Scotland: here are all the colors of a Harris tweed.

Cumbe Mayo: a corruption of *kumpi mayu*, "finely wrought watercourse." (Kumpi was the fine vicuña cloth that the first Spaniards thought was silk. Figuratively, the word means anything fine.)

The aqueduct is hewn into the rock on the right-hand side of the valley at a higher level than the stream. It is cut clean and straight as if by a carpenter's grooving plane. Where necessary it turns in graceful radial curves. The channel is about thirty inches wide and up to six feet deep; the flat bottom maintains a uniformly descending grade, but the height of the walls varies through undulations in the bedrock.

Sometimes, inexplicably, the canal makes a sharp right-angled zigzag and then continues straight as before. Luís thinks these discontinuities are to slow down the water, but I am not convinced. Besides being an impressive irrigation work, the Kumpi Mayu was clearly of ritual significance. The zigzag, or step motif, is as deeply rooted in Peruvian iconography as the swastika in the East.

Nearer its source, the canal tunnels under boulders and cuts like a railway through spurs. On its banks there are more and more signs of virtuoso stone carving: a round altar like a huge wheel of cheese; steps and planes; the foundations of a megalithic building. It would be impossible to date such work were it not for the petroglyphs found in several places on the sides of the channel above the waterline. These are certainly not Inca; the crowded cursive designs with feline fangs, claws, and baleful eyes suggest a local variant of the Chavín art style.

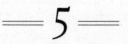

5

Next day, at the little museum. Professor Ravines, the curator (who remembers me from an earlier visit), is somewhat furtive: "Oh, it's you. Come in." There are three well-dressed young women in his office—students from Lima, I would guess. The professor is unlocking a solid wooden cabinet in the corner.

"I was just about to show the señoritas, ha ha, the forbidden things." (I can guess what these are.)

He straightens himself, sets a pot from the cabinet on his desk, assumes a slightly exaggerated didactic pose: "This is a ceremonial drinking vessel of the Mochica people, who flourished on the coast about a thousand years before the Spaniards came to our country." The pot resembles a toby jug—a squat human figure designed to hold liquid. But, though no more than eleven inches high, it has a monstrous tumescent penis, lifelike in every detail including size. The Mochica clasps his erection, an immodest smile on his highly mobile face. Across fifteen centuries the message is clear.

The curator picks up the pot by its appendage and taps the Mochica familiarly on the glans. "Observe how the vessel is made. The phallus is hollow, connected to the main part of the jug, and is pierced with a hole in the usual place at the top.

"Now, if you were to drink from this vessel, how would you do it?" He indicates a row of holes around the figure's headdress, just below the rim. "The normal way is impossible; the contents would spill. That leaves only the phallus. . . ."

Other treasures emerge from the cabinet, all in a similar vein: a couple making love; a man copulating with a llama; a man performing fellatio on another. The pieces are exquisite, modeled with the verve and attention to human detail that Mochica artists brought to every aspect of life.

How to judge what was erotic in another culture? This concerns Professor Ravines. The fellatio scene may in fact be nothing more prurient than a healing ritual. Sucking away illness (not necessarily from the sex organs) is a standard technique of South American shaman-curers. The llamaphilia? Perhaps to ensure a fertile herd. But the grin on the toby jug? Here the Mochica genius for modeling gives them away; it's just plain bawdy.

———

Elsewhere in the museum the exhibits are more decorous but no less fine. The young Limeñas, who remained tight-lipped before the indecent jug, now exclaim over the collection of textiles. These are from the desert, one of the few places in the world where such things survive. For that reason, there are far more weavings today from the Paracas culture of the fifth to third centuries B.C. than examples of the kumpi cloth of the Incas.

The Paracas people of the southern coast have left few monuments but their simple sandy graves. From these, however, have come textiles that hold world records for the fineness of the weave—hundreds of threads per inch, spun by hand from cotton or vicuña wool on a distaff, and woven on backstrap looms like those in use among the Indians of today. The designs are extraordinary: elongated, rather comical cats; centipedes, sinuous and menacing (Peru has many giant centipedes that are extremely venomous); sea creatures as fantastic as those on ancient maps; fey warriors dangling trophy heads. All in an exuberance of color: rich wine reds, yellow, Wedgwood and navy blues, orange, and grasshopper green, deployed by every cloth-making technique known to mankind and some used nowhere else in the world.

Were it not for the peculiarities of the Peruvian climate we would have nothing of the Paracans but the usual array of pottery and stone that one finds in any archaeological report.

———

There is something here from every major branch of Peruvian civilization: Paracas, Nazca, Mochica, Chimú, Wari-Tiawanaku, and, of course, imperial Inca. With some distaste the professor calls the latter Los Cuscos. He has no love of conquerors, native or European. He lingers over Chavín, the parent of Andean art—as fundamental to Peru as the Shang dynasty to China—and over exhibits of the Cajamarca culture, the local tradition influenced but never overcome by the three great *horizons*.

The cultural history of Peru is a three-thousand-year tension between regional autonomy and pan-Andean unification. "Horizon" is an apt term for periods when the multiplicity of Peruvian cultures falls under the influence of a single great style—a style generally rather short in duration but widely distributed in space. By adopting such a metaphorical definition archaeologists have avoided unsound assumptions about ancient political structures where evidence is scarce.

The Early Horizon, the first, is most often called Chavín, after the impressive ruins discovered by Julio César Tello at Chavín de Huantar in the central Andes. From there, influence seems to have spread over all of Peru (except the far south) between 1000 and 200 B.C. Because this influence is seen mostly in iconography, some argue that the Chavín Horizon denotes a religious cult, not a state.

The Middle Horizon had its focus farther south; it has the composite name Wari-Tiawanaku, from a ruined city near Ayacucho and another near the Bolivian shore of Lake Titicaca. There is growing evidence that the Wari portion, at least, was a true state. Between A.D. 500 and 800 it built roads and garrison towns over much of Peru. Wari's political relationship with Tiawanaku is unclear, but the two seem to share a common art style and religion.

The Late Horizon is the Inca Empire, Tawantinsuyu, "The Unity of Four Parts," or "The Four Quarters of the World." There is no doubt that this, as its name implies, was a highly centralized state ruled from Cusco, the capital, at 11,500 feet in the southern Peruvian Andes. Numerous accounts by Spaniards and the Incas themselves describe an exceptionally well-governed empire created by both conquest and diplomacy. The Incas devised a sophisticated nation-building strategy to counter the centrifugal tendencies of the regions, and created a state-run economy powerful enough to produce an astonishing body of roads, agricultural terraces, monuments, and public buildings in the hundred years between the empire's foundation and its fall.

For a remarkable discovery of modern research is that the Inca Horizon, which has left so deep an imprint on Peru, began only one century before the invasion by Pizarro.

The modern age, beginning with the Spanish occupation, is perhaps a fourth horizon, but it differs from the other three. It ended Peru's autonomy and imposed an unequal relationship with Spain and Spain's successors, notably Britain and the United States. The coming of the "fourth horizon" eclipsed the internal rivalries of Inca and pre-Inca times. Now there is just one tension: the semiconscious struggle of native Andean civilization against the incubus from outside its world. And this tension still strains the national fabrics of Ecuador, Bolivia, Peru—those countries that were once the Tawantinsuyu.

———

The Cajamarca culture appears after the first horizon and endures until just after the third. Five distinct phases have been recognized from the pottery. The last, Cajamarca V, is contemporary with the Inca Empire; a few late pieces of this ware are daubed with lead glaze of European origin. Cajamarca IV was a period of local autonomy, but III shows influence of the Wari-Tiawanaku Horizon. Cajamarca I and II are entirely local in style.

Despite changes over almost two thousand years, the beautiful Cajamarca ware maintains the integrity of an unbroken tradition. It is finely painted with cursive designs in black and red on a white or cream background. In the later phases use of a kaolin clay produced vessels that are wonderfully delicate and light. These are the joy of Professor Ravines.

Not much archaeological work has been done in the region since Henry and Paule Reichlen made a survey in the 1940s, when they dug some test pits on Santa Apolonia hill. The deposits were shallow and in a confused state, but there was little doubt that "Chavinoid" pottery was associated with the carved rock now called the Inca's Seat. Other test diggings enabled them to work out the five pottery phases of the Cajamarca culture.

But their most remarkable find was on the hill of Chondorco at Otusco.

=== 6 ===

OTUSCO
The drive out here is delightful. An ancient bus (I can see the drive shaft through holes in the floor) takes me across the rich farmlands of the Caja-

marca basin to the hills on the far side. As the hills close in, the bus advances up the tiny Otusco valley, passing beneath bald eminences of rock with hollowed eyes like the sockets in a death's head. The eyes become more numerous, until the hill is riddled; but there is a regularity to them that reveals the hand of man. Their outlines are more square than round, and often they run in rows like portholes in the superstructure of a ship. They are well named— Las Ventanillas de Otusco, The Otusco Windows.

Some of these "windows" are small cavities, just large enough to crouch inside. Others are doors to little passages that enter the rock for two or three yards; from these lead smaller chambers like the single ones. There is often a recessed rim to the entrance, designed to accept a stone lid or door, for these were sepulchers.

The Reichlens were lucky enough to find one burial that had not been disturbed. Its entrance lay sealed beneath several feet of nicely stratified deposit, and inside were two skeletons accompanied by the post-Chavín pottery of Cajamarca I. This proved that the tombs were much older than had been thought, although it was known that they preceded the pragmatic Incas, who cleaned them out and used them for storing grain.

The hill above the sepulchers is rocky and traversed by a hewn aqueduct of uncertain date. A few people live up here in rude huts no bigger than pigsties, made of stones and plastic. They tend stony fields and gaze enviously at the valley below: waving eucalyptus trees and lush irrigated pastures, with Cajamarca a spatter of whitewash on the far side. Such land is rare in Peru; it lies like a polished emerald in a setting of folded rock. (Of Peru's 500,000 square miles, total arable and pasture land covers only 2.2 percent. Population on this good land is 1,558 persons per square mile, while for the country as a whole the average is only 34 persons per square mile.)

The higher I climb, the more mountain ranges appear, one behind the other, until it seems that this valley is the only flat land in the world, the only spot of calm in a violent ocean of stone and ice. This is the real treasure of Cajamarca: the prize that has attracted conquerors throughout the ages since people learned to farm.

Up here the sun and wind vie to cause discomfort. In Peru it seems one is always too hot or too cold, often both at the same time; but the view is too grand to be abandoned in a hurry.

Ragged Indians approach with fragments of pottery to sell. It is genuine, but I have no wish to drag around a shard collection on my travels. When they see I won't buy, they tell me they are hungry; there has been no rain and it is long past seeding time. Dry ditches and fields confirm what they say. I give them a little money and we talk.

I ask if they speak Runasimi. They look ashamed and say no, but the way they speak Spanish gives the lie.

"*Imatam sutiyki?*"

"Pedro Alvarez."

"So you do understand!" I say.

"Only a little; my grandparents speak it."

Now that I have spoken Runasimi they are less reticent. They teach me a few phrases:

"*Rishaq Cajamarcatataq,*" says a boy. "That means 'I am going to Cajamarca.' " I write it down.

"Do you learn Runasimi in school?"

"No. They want us to speak only Spanish."

"But Runasimi is now an official language of the country."

"Yes," the boy says politely, with a look of *Who is this crazy gringo?*

Obviously, Velasco's language reforms have not reached the one-room school in Otusco.

———

Rishaq Cajamarcatataq. The return bus is even older than the one that brought me here; there is no glass in the windows and the seats are wooden planks. Miraculously, it is almost empty and I can see out.

Great gnarled eucalyptus with trunks thicker than oil drums shade the road. Younger ones with silvery leaves glint in the sunlight filtered by the giants. Above, the sky is blue, bluer than it ought to be—the kind of blue one sees from plane windows because of the altitude. It is now late afternoon; colors are deepening. Whitewashed walls are turning gold; ungainly Jerseys leave the shade of trees and amble toward the milking sheds.

It is hard to equate this pastoral scene with violence, yet violence has been here. There is an outworn phrase from the sixties: "the violence of the capitalist system." A piece of cant, perhaps. But here in Cajamarca it has some meaning for me. Land reform or no, the people who once owned this land are starving in the hills.

7

CAJAMARCA

There remains one thing I want to investigate here. In 1968, the University of California Press published a book that made the rare transition to a bestseller.

The book soon had a sequel, then another, until five or six volumes were published in numerous editions. Their author became a celebrity and appeared on the cover of *Time*. Before long he was one of only two anthropologists (so far as I know) ever to become millionaires from their work.

Each book was more readable—but less credible—than its predecessor. By the time the third volume appeared, few scholars still thought that genuine fieldwork was being described, or that the central character, a Yaqui Indian, really existed. The first book was called *The Teachings of Don Juan: A Yaqui Way of Knowledge*. The author calls himself Carlos Castaneda and describes his topic as "sorcery."

In 1976, Richard de Mille published a critique of the Don Juan books entitled *Castaneda's Journey: The Power and the Allegory*, in which Carlos and his fellow sorcerers are exposed to ridicule and confronted with serious internal inconsistencies. Most damning of all is the disclosure of suspiciously close parallels between earlier work published in obscure journals by other ethnologists and Castaneda's "fieldwork."

De Mille had considerable difficulty in clarifying the biographical details of Castaneda's life. The mysterious *brujo* had put out different tales of his age and origin, although he usually admitted to being from South America, most often Brazil or Argentina. By checking arcana such as United States immigration records, de Mille established that one Carlos Arana Castañeda was born in Cajamarca, Peru, in 1925.

This person entered the United States in 1951. He became known as Carlos Castaneda, taking his mother's maiden name, without the tilde, for a surname. In 1959 he enrolled at U.C.L.A., and received a Ph.D. in anthropology in 1973. By that time three of his books had been published, and he was already rich and famous.

Castaneda continues to write more books and so does de Mille. The latter's iconoclastic bloodlust unfortunately leads him into a gratuitous and academically unsound attack on the Incas (simply because they, like Castaneda, are associated with Cajamarca), but his analysis of the Don Juan books leaves Castaneda's factitious mystique in shreds. Anyone still seduced by Don Juan and the ingenuous apprentice should read *A Yaqui Life* by Moisés, Kelley, and Holden. In this book a real Yaqui talks to a real anthropologist; the difference is self-evident.

———

Luís has never heard of the Don Juan books, but he does know a Carlos Castañeda. I wonder for a moment if the notorious sorcerer has not perhaps flown home to roost: "What does he look like, Luís?"

"Tall, big, like a gringo." (No, it can't be the writer—according to de Mille he is five feet five and looks like a Cuban waiter.)

Carlos Castañeda is indeed a "gringo": handsome European face, muscular build, thirtyish, well over six feet—more like a Canadian footballer than a Peruvian. Beside him Luís looks tiny and very Indian—like Cipriano beside Ramón Carrasco in Lawrence's *Plumed Serpent.* I am pleased that these two can be friends in a society such as Peru.

Like all colonial mansions in the Andes, the Castañeda house presents nothing to the street but an expanse of whitewashed adobe wall with a few windows, well shuttered and barred. Above the upper story, ragged Spanish tile hangs three feet over the pavement. (The large overhang is needed to keep rain from the mud walls.)

We enter through an arched doorway to a patio full of washing lines and potted plants. Carlos takes us up some wooden stairs on the outside wall, and along a flimsy-looking wooden balcony that gives access to the upper rooms.

The reception room does not seem to be used much by the family: a formal space, large, spare, slightly neglected, where guests are received. The walls are washed a faded blue, their only decoration some old photographs and religious pictures. The lofty ceiling has exposed beams like those of English timber-frame houses of about the same period. But while an English house would be lit generously by mullioned windows, the life of the Spanish colonial residence turns in on itself, away from ruffianly streets and the fear of Indian attack. This place has the moist gloom of a castle, but it is peaceful, and how preferable to the "colonial" Hollywood bungalows of the coastal rich.

At the far end of the room are three chairs and a sofa in typical Latin taste: red vinyl with transparent plastic covers like those used to protect the upholstery of new cars. They are more comfortable than they look.

"Yes, I have heard of him. Actually, he's not closely related to me. He comes from another branch of the family. They live now in San Pedro de Lloc. You know where that is? I did hear that one of that family went to the United States and became a famous writer about witchcraft." San Pedro de Lloc is a small dusty town in the Jequetepeque valley—I passed through it on the way to Cajamarca. I wonder if it's worth going back there. But then I'm not really that interested in Castaneda's family life. What concerns me are the antecedents of his "anthropology."

"Of course, this part of the world is full of San Pedro shamans. Everybody knows them. I myself have seen inexplicable things."

"What kinds of things?"

"Objects flying around the room. Remarkable cures. That sort of thing.

And bad magic, of course, curses and so on; though luckily that's quite rare. Most of these shamans work for the good."

The north coast of Peru is the homeland of a shamanistic healing cult based on the psychotropic cactus called San Pedro or *gigantón* in Spanish; *wachuma* in Runasimi (botanical name *Trichocereus pachanoi*). I did not know until now that the cult is also active in highland valleys like Cajamarca. Whether Castaneda (the writer) had lived in Cajamarca or San Pedro de Lloc, he would have been in the heart of country populated with real-life sorcerers and users of hallucinogens. And he would not have been isolated from this cult by his family's social standing (middle-class artisans, according to de Mille), because knowledge and belief in its rituals have penetrated hispanic-mestizo society to a remarkable degree. Although the cult's grassroots following is the coastal peasantry and proletariat, who have scant access to modern medicine, the prestige of some San Pedro curers is such that members of the middle and upper classes—even, it is said, at least one president—consult them. And from what Carlos has told me, it is obvious that the whereabouts of shamans and details of their rites are common knowledge.

The anthropologist Douglas Sharon has worked for many years with one of these practitioners, a man named Eduardo, from the coastal city of Trujillo. In several books and scholarly articles, Sharon traces the origin of the cult to Chavín times: sculpture and pottery from that period show fantastic figures clasping large pieces of the cactus. The rite of Eduardo, as befits his coastal mestizo milieu, contains elements from Catholicism and European witchcraft; but the structure and basic mode of operation is undoubtedly native Amerindian.

Eduardo himself is an exceptional man, a skilled potter and fisherman who has also studied fine arts in Lima and taken correspondence courses in medicine. He does not hesitate to use modern remedies when he feels they are more appropriate. He is equally at home prescribing pharmaceuticals or battling sinister forces and supernatural animals from the "other world." Eduardo:

> San Pedro has great power . . . as it is "accounted" with the saints . . . with all the hills, ancient shrines, lakes, streams, and powers. . . . I salute the ancients, the powerful ones, men who lived in antiquity . . . for their intellectual force, their power, their magnificence. . . .

Eduardo's system of belief stresses the difference between "looking" (everyday perception) and "seeing"—the ability to perceive the inner nature of things with the aid of the cactus.

It took Don Juan years to teach Carlos Castaneda to "see," and in fact it is never quite clear if he succeeded. But I think I can see—in Eduardo and the shamans like him whom Carlos Arana Castañeda must have known—the inner nature of the world's most famous "Yaqui" sorcerer, mentor of the world's richest anthropologist.

═══ 8 ═══

Mary is here from Canada. She has a month's holiday; we plan to visit Celendín, Chachapoyas, and the jungle.

Luís has come to the bus station to see us off. Co-operativa de Omnibuses Atahuallpa: I wonder which the ghost of poor old Atau Wallpa dislikes more, the bus company or the radio station? In Mexico they named a brewery after Moctezuma. What do we do with our English monarchs? Of course: pubs. Mary says, "That reminds me of a shop that sells 'slightly imperfect merchandise.' It's called Henry the Second."

On either side of the entrance to the Atahuallpa bus company is painted the symbol of the co-ops that Velasco encouraged—two pine trees in a circle. The buses in the yard are sleek new Volvos; these must be for the Lima run. Any minute I expect to see the usual junk come rattling into the station to take us over the mountains to Celendín. I dread these contraptions with their tiny seats and broken windows—it's years since I thought them picturesque.

I am wrong: the boy on the roof of one of the Volvos is shouting for the luggage to Celendín.

Luís gives us both a warm *abrazo*. Inhibited Anglo-Saxon that I am, I find these Latin embraces rather awkward. I hope Luís does not mistake my bungled effort for lack of sincerity. He has been a good friend.

═══

The bus follows the asphalt road to the Baños del Inca. On the right we pass the buildings of the strike-bound university—abandoned concrete cubes with shattered windows. Every stripe and color of political graffiti are daubed on walls that look like Jackson Pollocks. Someone has painted a lot of signs for APRA (Alianza Popular Revolucionaria Americana); someone else has changed them all to CABRA, which means "nanny goat." It's a concise history of the party. In the 1930s APRA was a radical movement, soon banned for trying to help workers and Indians. The party was never communist, though it freely borrowed Marxist ideas, and at times there was an element of *lumpen* national socialism. After the Second World War, APRA purchased respectability by selling out its more progressive ideals. By the time it was allowed to share power in the early sixties, APRA was a bourgeois party of old men worn out by too many compromises. The last years of the leader, Victor Raúl Haya de la Torre, were spent opposing Velasco, who was implementing many of the programs that Haya himself had once championed.

Beyond the Inca Baths we climb back into the world of mountains. Gray cloud banks are scudding across a fickle sky; I hope the Indians will get the rain they need. Seen from this height, their fields lie among the rocks like wrinkled brown garments put out to dry.

As we reach the puna it does rain; then hails; then snows, all in the space of an hour. Then the sun bursts out as the clouds drop suddenly below, and the bus for a moment is a soaring glider. The land has disappeared, except for a few distant peaks, and its place has been taken by a rolling fleecy landscape like a child's idea of heaven.

We have almost reached Cumullca pass and will not see thirteen thousand feet again until half an hour down the far side. Mary is silent from the altitude; the air in the bus has become thin and intoxicating. As we re-enter the clouds I decide to read. There is plenty of light, as bright and diffuse as the glow from a fluorescent tube. Co-operativa Atahuallpa seems the right place to open *The Peruvian Experiment: Continuity and Change under Military Rule*, a good collection of essays on Velasco's reforms and his quest for a middle way between communism and capitalism.

While a Marxist administration in Chile was drawing the attention of the world—and the CIA—the Peruvian "Revolutionary Government of the Armed Forces" quietly followed its own program of reforms, reforms that ultimately proved more far-reaching and durable than those of the short-lived Allende regime.

When Peru's army took power in October 1968, most observers assumed that talk of revolution and reform was simply that: talk, as it had been so many times before. Surprise followed as foreign petroleum and sugar interests were nationalized. Within nine months a radical land reform was launched spectacularly by General Velasco in words ascribed to the last Inca leader, Tupaq Amaru: *Peasants, no longer shall the landlord feast on your poverty!* Tupaq Amaru became the symbol of a revolution in values that was intended to replace the old ghettos of race, culture, and class with a "new Peruvian man." And this was to be achieved, in the good Inca tradition of paternalism, by a long-overdue expansion of government into every area of national life. At that time the Peruvian state was one of the weakest in South

America, virtually unable even to collect its own taxes, let alone exert any control over the feudal oligarchy of a dozen white families who ran the country much as they had since the days of the conquistadors.

The cooperative ideal was central to the Velasco reforms. Expropriated sugar estates were turned into co-ops, and the same model, with modifications, was applied to the old *sierra* haciendas. It seemed the perfect solution: neither capitalist nor communist, and with a respectable Peruvian precedent in the mink'a system of the Indians.

In industry, Velasco envisioned a pluralist economy. Small-scale private enterprise would coexist with two other categories: reformed private firms, and worker-controlled "social properties." (It was hoped that the unreformed private sector would atrophy as the new Peruvian man evolved.)

In reformed private firms, a percentage of the company's profits was used to buy shares in the name of the workers. These shares were supposed to accrue until labor owned 50 percent of the stock. Companies formed under the "social property" law were to consist exclusively of workers. They were to borrow the capital they needed from state agencies and, with some guidance, participate fully in all functions of their firm, including management. All very fine on paper. But the social property sector, intended to predominate within fifteen years, was to be almost wholly composed of new firms. This would have required massive amounts of capital and expertise, neither of which was notably abundant in Peru.

Before these inherent problems had time to show themselves, the Peruvian economy was already in serious trouble, for reasons not all of its own making, and Velasco, the force behind the more ambitious programs, was a sick man.

In August 1975 Velasco was forced to resign and was replaced as president by Morales Bermúdez, one of the architects of the land reform. Morales Bermúdez, however, was a fiscal conservative. Before long, the wreckage of the Peruvian revolution was in the unsympathetic hands of the International Monetary Fund.

———

Reading on the mountain road has given me a headache, or perhaps it's the music blazing from a loudspeaker above my head. Sometimes I curse the arrival of cassette players in Peru. When I first traveled here, bus drivers used to tune their radios to the little mountain stations. In the heyday of the cultural reforms these played the beautiful indigenous music of the Andes: tinkling *waynos* with the Oriental sound of a young girl's high-pitched voice, or more rarely the *harawi*, a lament derived from the court music of the Incas. But professional drivers everywhere are inclined toward the meretricious; in Peru this means a predilection for the baser trappings of mestizo culture. The last thing a mestizo will listen to is Indian music.

I think I can blame my headache on the preceding half hour of *música tropical*, fatuous Afro-Latin ditties from the Brazilian brothel school of music, as welcome in the sierra as tangos at an eisteddfod. And this is now being followed by a tape of *canción criolla*, romantic harmonized singing in the Spanish style of the coast with words that make country-and-western ballads seem deep by comparison.

Now the driver switches to Mexican mariachi songs; at least they have a raucous honesty lacking in the other pap.

=== 9 ===

CELENDÍN, 4:00 P.M.
A gray tide of uniformed schoolchildren swirls around the bus and runs behind it shouting. A demonstration?

No, it is simply that school is out and the arrival of the bus is one of the day's events. Mary and I get out and wait for our things to be handed down from the roof. We are surrounded by precocious boys wanting to show us a hotel and their English:

"Mister! You go to Chachapoyas? I know a truck."

"*Quiere hotel?* I chow you!"

"I carry you bag, OK, mister?"

Celendín is a children's town; they seem to outnumber adults ten to one. Those I ask all have eight or ten siblings. At seventeen million, the Peruvian population is not so large, but the growth rate of 3 percent is far too high for a country with so little arable land. The basic education that these young Celendinos seem to be getting will do little more than equip them for the drift to the top-heavy metropolis, where they will join the other six million in the Lima-Callao conurbation. There, the lucky ones will work long hours for low pay in Dickensian conditions; the rest will have to live by selling lottery tickets, newspapers, roadside snacks, or cheap toys. Some will be forced into crime: like old London, Lima is alive with pickpockets, prostitutes, and confidence tricksters.

There are only two hotels in Celendín, neither of them good. A boy shows us a dark, musty room with sagging beds. In one corner, behind a partition, is a foul-smelling bathroom. I glance at the lavatory; three large fresh turds insolently return my gaze.

"How about cleaning the bathroom?" I ask the boy

"But it has been cleaned, *señor*."

"Well, it needs cleaning again."

The boy returns with a filthy cloth, flushes the lavatory, wipes the top of the bowl (there is no seat), and then wipes the washbasin with the same cloth.

———

Before I left Cajamarca, Professor Ravines showed me some photographs of archaeological sites. I told him I was leaving soon for Chachapoyas via Celendín.

"Then you must visit the *ch'ullpas* of La Chocta near Oxamarca. No one ever goes there. It is ten years since I was there myself." He held out a picture. On a hilltop fogged with cloud stood a cluster of stone towers. "Chavín period," he breathed, "a thousand years before Christ." (Chavín haunts him the way the Incas do me. Luís said that the archaeological topiary in the plaza is the work of Professor Ravines.)

"From Celendín you can catch a bus to Sucre. There you will have to rent horses and ride for half a day to Oxamarca: there is no road; just a trail."

Mary is keen to go to Oxamarca but I don't like Celendín and am afraid of being stuck here. I go to the plaza to ask about transport to Chachapoyas, where the ruins of Kuélap await us. Somebody called Díaz Díaz is leaving tomorrow, I am told.

———

Díaz Díaz is a pompous man in a wrinkled suit. His dictator-style moustache is gray, and he talks with a peculiar singsong inflection that may be an accent, but I've never heard anyone else speak this way. Like his name, he repeats himself a lot: "My truck has not arrived from Cajamarca yet. Should have been here today. Very worrying. Very worrying."

"Can you keep us two seats in the cab?"

"Most certainly, *señores*, most certainly. Rómulo Díaz Díaz at your service." We shake hands elaborately. "But I will not be leaving until the day after tomorrow."

"That leaves us time for Oxamarca," Mary says in Spanish.

"To Oxamarca! Why?" asks Díaz Díaz.

"To see the ch'ullpas."

"Ah . . . the ruins of La Chocta. It is far. Very far. But you gringos are so strong"—feeling my arm like a buyer at a slave market—"you will succeed where we Peruvians fail. You gringos are so strong; that is why you rule the world!"

=== *10* ===

This morning we took the packs and camping gear, but left the rest of our things in the car of Señor Topa, the hotel factotum. His name is a form of *Tupaq*, an Inca title meaning "royal" (Tupaq Amaru, Royal Serpent). Perhaps his ancestors once ruled this land, but poor Topa's work is never done: he lives and sleeps behind the hotel desk. His explanation for the success of gringos: "We Peruvians have too many children."

The small bus to Sucre makes a run every day at "half past eight."

At half past nine the driver appears. Then—and this is typical—another half hour is spent driving up and down streets with the conductor leaning from the door shouting "Sucre! Sucre!" There is no need for this. Everyone in Celendín knows the bus and its schedule, but this piece of theater satisfies (as a psychiatrist would say) the driver's ego needs.

At last we grind up the hill out of town; then, infuriatingly, stop at some outlying huts ten minutes later.

"Is there gasoline?" the driver shouts.

Mary laughs: "What if there isn't any?"

"*Sí!*" comes the reply. The conductor fuels the vehicle with a funnel and a battered tin. We are off.

It can only be twelve miles to Sucre, but it takes an hour and a half. The bus's main function is that of a milk truck. Before long the aisle between the seats is filled with slopping churns. A dozen white trickles run along the floor and out through rusty holes in the steel.

SUCRE

It is still the nineteenth century here. The town reminds me of E. George Squier's engravings. He never came here, but he drew many places like it when he toured Peru in the 1860s.

The houses are whitewashed, their walls splashed red at the bottom from the muddy sidewalks. There are patches of cobbled paving on some streets, and drains down the middle as in Inca times. Dogs nap on doorsteps, pigs in the drains. Here and there a tethered donkey is dozing on its feet.

It has rained during the night and the air is fresh; but a hard sun now burns from a deep blue sky and draws vapor from the earth.

Nobody wants to rent horses. Mary asks me: "Would you rent your car to foreigners who appeared from nowhere and wanted to drive it over mountain roads?"

NOON
Lunch in a tiny "restaurant." The woman apologizes for not serving rice. Potatoes are considered infra dig by whites and mestizos. She thinks we are being polite when we say we prefer potatoes. (Peruvian rice is terrible.)

1:00 P.M.
We are directed to Señor Avila, a prominent local citizen. His horses, he says, are up on the *jalca*, another name for the puna. But he's anxious to help and takes us to see a friend who has "beasts."

Twenty minutes of entreaties from Señor Avila and the beasts are ours.

2:00 P.M.
The tiny animals—no more than ponies, really—are finally saddled. Several nails protrude from my saddle, a Spartan affair of wood and leather with no padding.

The road becomes a track, then a path, and turns into a rocky cleft as it drops out of sight downhill. Just when we are sure we are lost, an Indian comes briskly along behind a loaded donkey: "Yes, to Oxamarca. But you must hurry or night will fall before you arrive. Use the whip on those brutes."

"Just where is Oxamarca?"

"From here you can't see it. It's about half an hour beyond that ridge." He points up at a sugarloaf looming above a chasm. The ridge is perhaps only three miles away as the condor flies; but to get there we must drop two thousand feet into a ravine, cross a river, and then regain the lost altitude plus half as much again.

The trail has become steep as a flight of stairs, but instead of steps there are only loose pebbles and rocks. Sensing our inexperience, the horses often refuse to move; I have visions of my brain splattered like a dropped egg on the rocks. It amuses passing riders to see us dismount and drag our beasts along. The locals bounce by at a trot, with frequent applications of the whip at the most dangerous places. No European horse could tackle this, I am sure. Centuries of breeding in the Andes have produced a creature that is at least half goat.

3:00 P.M.

We are little more than halfway down. The horses are slowing us: we would have been better off hiking.

4:00 P.M.

We have reached the river. Down here the climate is tropical. A few banana trees grow wherever the lie of the land allows. We cross on a stone bridge that looks absurdly well made for the trail is serves. A fallen log was what I expected.

On the other side my spirits rise with the ascent. The road seems better, the fear of falling headlong has gone, and the saddle has shifted its sadistic attentions to different areas of flesh.

As the animals pant gamely up the hill the views are ever more magnificent.

6:30 P.M.

Darkness has come suddenly. Before it left us, the sun illuminated the winding gorge below with horizontal shafts of golden light. In this terrain, so near the equator, you can see the world revolve: in minutes the planet rolled away and the abyss filled with gloom.

We reach the ridge in the last of the visibility and are challenged by a youth. He points to a scattering of feeble lights in the distance: Oxamarca.

We are on foot now, leading the horses, I in front with a pocket flashlight. Nowhere is there a scrap of flat ground big enough for the tent. Señor Avila mentioned a name in Oxamarca; we can only press on and beg for hospitality.

I walk off the edge of the trail, but am saved by the reins in my hand. Now Mary is regretting the trip.

We are wondering if we have passed the village, when I see a woman ahead. The glow from the flashlight reveals a squat outline with a long braid down her back.

"Good evening," I say. No reply.

"Good evening. Can you direct me to the house of Señor Pérez?" Silence. The woman keeps the same distance ahead.

"Good evening" the third time, and I realize I am talking to a cow. What I took for a braid is its tail.

Five minutes later we notice we are in Oxamarca. The trail has become a street with houses on one side. The lights seen from the ridge must have been extinguished. Mary asks directions at the door of a dark house.

Señor Pérez is not at home, but his wife and daughter question us for several minutes. They are suspicious of archaeologists, and become more so when I mention Julio Tello, discoverer of the ch'ullpas. They say he took gold and mummies to Lima. I assure them we have come only for photographs.

Once satisfied, they invite us indoors and bring thin coffee and soft-boiled eggs. A single candle lights the one-room dwelling. It is built entirely of stone, against a rock cliff, which forms the back wall. There are no windows and only one door. Most of the floor is occupied by three metal beds. A baby is asleep in a hammock slung diagonally across the room. Except for the furniture, the house is identical with those of ancient times. One of the beds is offered for our use, and we roll out our sleeping bags on it.

Like many Peruvians, they are curious as to why we have no children. (To avoid embarrassment we have been telling people we are married.) Mary tries to explain about birth control; but I am sure they are left with the idea that sleeping in separate bags is the secret of our low fertility.

Our pretense of matrimony is an unnecessary fiction among these people. Isabel, Señor Pérez's daughter and mother of the baby, has told us that she and her "husband" are not really married. Perhaps some day. A legal wedding is not considered very important by Peruvian Indians, who still abide by the old tradition of trial marriage known as *sirvinakuy*, "mutual service." As the name implies, reciprocal obligations between the couple and their "in-laws" are the true measure of the match. If for any reason the arrangement does not work it can be dissolved after a year or so with no stigma attaching to either spouse. There is room for love in this sensible system: sirvinakuy usually begins with trysts in the fields, and a romantic elopement, at which both sets of "in-laws" (who most likely did the same) pretend to be outraged.

Isabel's husband offers to take us to the ruins tomorrow, and will wake us at 4:30 A.M.. Curious, how these people use precise units of time, though they have no watches or clocks.

———

Last night we slept little. It did not take long for the fleas to work their way up from the mattress. Fleas are a fact of life in the Andes; but their presence is more than compensated for by the lack of bedbugs and cockroaches.

In the early morning darkness, Wilder (as he is inexplicably called) takes us to the upper story by an outside flight of stone steps. This upper room with a steeply pitched thatch doubles as kitchen and granary. Sacks of grain lean against the low stone walls; the roof is festooned with bunches of multicolored corncobs. There is a wheaty smell of home and plenty.

We make porridge on our camping stove. Isabel makes breakfast in the Indian way—by blowing through a long tube into a tiny fire of twigs beneath an earthenware pot. We offer them some porridge.

"No, thank you"—big smiles—"we only feed oats to horses."

Their morning snack is sweet coffee into which they dunk spoonfuls of barley flour.

———

It is time to dispose of the word "Indian." In Latin America the word is about as polite as "nigger." *Indígena*, "native," is more acceptable, and so is *campesino*, "peasant" or (to avoid a negative connotation in English) "country person." Indians who speak Runasimi I shall henceforth call Runa, which is the term they use for themselves (Runa means "The People" or "people" in general; Runasimi, "Language of the People").

The class structure of Peru is extremely complex; I would find it utterly baffling had I not grown up in the equally subtle hierarchy of England. To a superficial glance, Peru is a racist nation: people are known as whites (criollos), mestizos, or Indians, in that order of prestige. There are esoteric subgroups such as *zambos* (Indian-black mixtures) and *cholos*, between Indian and mestizo.

But the criteria for defining these groups are predominantly ethnic and cultural. Most mestizos are in fact of almost pure Indian descent; taken as a whole, Peru's population must be at least 80 percent native in its genetic makeup. Most "whites" (except for recent arrivals from Europe) are of mixed ancestry. Some great criollo families can trace their origins to unions between conquistadors and Inca noblewomen—yet they would be outraged if called mestizo. Money whitens; but it bears repeating that the chief criteria are outward, visible manifestations of cultural allegiance. Acquisition of Western dress, Spanish language, and Latin values (for example, criollo pop music, a macho attitude toward women, and shiny shoes) will convert an Indian into a mestizo.

This "ethnicism" is a far more effective strategy for domination than the crude racism of Anglo-Saxon countries. In South Africa or Canada, a native person can learn English, go to university, and become an effective spokesman for his group. A Canadian Indian is always an Indian. But in Peru there is no such thing as an educated Runa. Since the destruction of the native aristocracy at the end of the eighteenth century, there has been no model of the

Indian as anything other than a backward peasant. The very process of education (in Spanish, of course) converts the successful Runa into a mestizo: advancement costs him his *ethnos*. He is co-opted and isolated as surely as the Oxford graduate with working-class origins.

The Oxamarca people are hard to define. Their way of life is Indian, little changed from Inca times, but like much of northern Peru they have lost Runasimi and replaced it with rustic Spanish. Apart from their ponchos, the dress of the men is Western; that of the women—long skirts, blouses, and shawls—a mixture. The best term must be "campesino," as this is probably how they define themselves (one can never ask).

There's nothing much Spanish about Wilder: his last name, Chupaca, comes from Runasimi, and his first is English. I would love to know how he came to be christened Wilder.

We leave for the ruins on foot, to give the horses and our rumps a rest. Along the way Wilder points out his fields. It is much wetter here than in Cajamarca; young potatoes are already thrusting through soil very black and moist in the early light. I ask if the land is owned in common or by individuals.

"By individuals. Once there was a *hacendado*, but he left years ago."

"Before the land reform?"

"Yes, before that. Then the government sent some people here to organize a co-op, but we got rid of them, too."

———

We have reached a mountain saddle between two peaks. The sun has not yet burned away the cloud that spreads below us on both sides a diaphanous garment gone to holes. The land, half hidden, falls in faint green canyons to the Río Marañon.

Rounding a bluff, we pass some shepherds' huts, and in the distance can see the mushroom forms of towers. They stand on a peninsula rising from a sea of cloud. From time to time, mist blows across like spray driven on a Scottish coast.

In the 1930s, Tello counted forty ch'ullpas here. Now only a dozen or so are left. Regular stones in nearby shepherds' dwellings tell where the rest have gone.

Wilder says no one lived here until recently. For more than two thousand years La Chocta was a city of the dead, which the living were loath to visit. But now land hunger has brought settlers who do not have many qualms about destroying the monuments. The buildings, they say almost with a shudder, are the work of "gentiles." The people have lost their language and a sense of kinship with the past.

Only the towers farthest from the settlement are standing. The best one rises more than twenty feet. Its walls are vertical and only ten inches thick, well made from slabs of cut stone joined with lesser stones and mortar. Two simple cornices divide the square shaft into thirds, at the levels of the floors inside. Each story consists of a single chamber about eight feet square and six feet high. There is no access from one chamber to the next; instead, each has a small door to the outside.

The roof is the most distinctive feature: a gently pitched gable of cut stone slabs which overhang the walls in a heavy cornice. The triangular pediments thus created on two sides remind me of Classical Greek architecture. But in place of sculpture, the apex of each pediment is decorated with a single small round stone—most likely a ridgepole lingering in skeuomorph. Traces of red stucco can still be seen in these protected spots, and it is quite possible that the whole building was once painted bright red.

These ch'ullpas have a lightness and delicacy rare in Peruvian architecture. Such a high proportion of interior space to masonry was seldom attempted in this land of earthquakes. Somehow they have survived millennia of natural assaults; but now their chief enemy is man. The doors, once sealed, have all been rudely opened. Scattered pottery and human bones testify to the "mummies" who resided here.

Near the ch'ullpas are the remains of a much larger building, which Wilder calls the Fortress. It is in ruins, but a series of rooms and courtyards can be made out. On one side, the solid masonry platform is pierced by a long tunnel. This suggests a relationship with Chavín de Huantar, where the temples are riddled with subterranean labyrinths.

On the way back to Oxamarca, the clouds part briefly to reveal a strange sight half a mile below us on a terrace. A team of horses is rushing round and round in a tight, fast circle; in the middle stands a man cracking a whip and shouting like a circus ringmaster.

"Threshing barley," Wilder explains.

Our rested horses need no encouragement to return home. At places along the road I see the remains of stone steps, enough to show that this was once a step-road of the Incas or an earlier people. After the Conquest much of the paving was torn from the old roads because the Spaniards found that the hard surface wore out their horseshoes too quickly. Maybe this happened here, or perhaps time accomplished the same end: in places the track has worn so far into the softer rock below that we squeeze through miniature ravines and pass traces of old paving at eye level.

Near Sucre the horses break into a trot, led by the mare, who has left her foal behind. I haul desperately on the reins to try to save what's left of my rump.

The foal comes rushing out to greet his mother. There is a touching scene as the two rub necks and whinny. But then he gets too greedy at her nipples, and she kicks him smartly in the side.

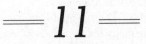

CELENDIN

In the courtyard of the hotel two gringos are sitting in the lotus posture, one behind the other.

"Hi," says Frank. He is smoking an Inca brand cigarette (which smells like burned feathers) while Greg combs his (Frank's) hair.

"You going to Chachapoyas?" Frank asks.

"Yes."

"Don Rómulo was just here."

"Díaz Díaz?"

"The same. His truck hasn't come yet. He *says* he's leaving Friday."

Frank is big, thirty-five, and hyperthyroid. It shows in his red face and enlarged fingertips like those of a tarsier. He talks a lot: about India; Nixon; his radical days in the SDS (Students for a Democratic Society).

Greg is eleven years younger, Australian, mild-mannered, with eyes the color of crushed bluestone. He wears a jaunty peaked cap, like a cabbie's, which he "found in the road in Ecuador." Beneath it, a thick blond braid shows briefly and disappears inside his collar.

TWO DAYS LATER

Of course, we have not left. Mary has gone to draw an adobe church.

I spend the day wandering around town, buying a few books, including a new Runasimi grammar, and talking—or, rather, listening—to Greg and Frank. They have been on the road a long time: three years in India (six months of that in jail for traveling on expired visas) and now a year in South America. Each wears a single earring, and people often call them *maricones*. Despite this some Ecuadorian girls tried to hire their services as studs. It was

Greg's eyes that did it, I think: *ojos de gato* they call them here, "cat's eyes," which in South America is meant as a compliment.

———

The truck has arrived. It is a two-ton Dodge with its name, El Amigo del Oriente, painted across the box above the cab. (*Oriente* means the *selva*, or jungle.) The motor needed a complete overhaul in Cajamarca—hence the delay. A quick inspection of the vehicle does not bode well for the trip: leaking radiator, two bald tires, the spare flat.

Díaz Díaz is effusive: "Doña María! Don Ronald! *Qué tal?*" (He calls everyone "Don"; we are doing the same.) "You went to La Chocta?"

We tell him about the state of the ruins.

"I will write personally to my very good friend, the Mayor of Celendín. Something must be done!" He clutches my arm and gazes at us in admiration: "But you are the only gringos ever to go there. *Qué valientes!*"

Don Rómulo is proud of his new engine ("*Qué motorazo!*"), but broke. Frank refuses to pay the fare in advance: "I don't like this guy. He's trying to cheat us. We always pay at the end." His face is twice as red as usual, and so is Don Rómulo's. Eventually they agree on half now, half later.

Mary and I ride in the cab with the driver, a shy, likable man called Don Segundo. Díaz Díaz, three other Peruvians, Frank, Greg, some freight, and a live turkey all ride in the back.

The road from Celendín climbs over some hills and then makes a long descent through extremely dry country to Balsas at only four thousand feet, where there is a bridge across the Marañon, parent of the Amazon. This watershed is the setting for one of Peru's great novels, *La Serpiente de Oro* by Ciro Alegría. Northern Peru is rich in writers. Besides the dubious honor of producing Castaneda, the department of Cajamarca is the birthplace of Alegría (from Cajabamba) and the poet César Vallejo (from Santiago de Chuco). The other major literary figure, José María Arguedas, was born at Andahuaylas in the southern Andes. I am sure it is no mere coincidence that Peru's great modern writers are from the sierra: the tension between native and hispanic culture has stimulated all her best fiction.

Balsas lies at the bottom of a rainless rocky gorge as if thrown there. The heat is stifling; dusty phallic cacti and purple-flowering acacias the only vegetation.

Lunch is unspeakable: a thin dirty soup containing what we have come to know as UFOs, unidentified floating organs. Díaz Díaz is busy drinking beer and embracing people who look as though they scarcely know him.

It is a ten-thousand-foot climb from here to the next pass.

Our reward for patience is a succession of magnificent views enhanced by the chiaroscuro lighting of late afternoon. With altitude, the valleys have grown lush again; the merest haze fills them and catches the last of the sun in a series of transparent cataracts.

It is almost dark when we reach Calla Calla pass, but there is enough light to show the character of the place. Sleet is blowing across a tundralike landscape in which a few optimists have planted small potato plots.

The name can be translated as "a beginning place, where water is driven before the wind."

LEIMEBAMBA

The journey has not been pleasant for those in the back. It was bitterly cold, and a fuel drum fell down and severed the turkey's foot. "Blood and shit all over the place," according to Greg.

Díaz Díaz decides we must go to the *control.* These are checkpoints manned by the Guardia Civil on all the highways of Peru. Travelers are routinely entered in a log.

The control here is down a muddy side street for some reason, and could easily be avoided. But Don Rómulo insists—wanting to show off his gringos, I suspect.

Two junior constables are playing cards and drinking pisco. Obviously they do not expect visitors at this time of night and do not enjoy the interruption. Nor do they have the faintest idea what to do with our passports. Seeing the stamps on the inside pages, the policeman lays them out open on his desk and produces an enormous rubber stamp.

I have to stop this: "Just a minute. They are only supposed to be stamped at international frontiers."

"Oh. Then what's this one here: Aguas Verdes, Peru?"

"That's the border town with Ecuador. If we got stamped at every control in Peru, we'd need new passports every fortnight."

Luckily he believes me; we leave quickly (practically dragging Díaz Díaz) before he can change his mind.

An hour later, the truck stops for the night in a small unlit town. Don Rómulo finds us a place to stay—a small storeroom with rusty cans piled on shelves and several posters for Inca cigarettes on the walls.

Greg eyes the concrete floor: "A bit 'ard, innit?"

"It'll just have to do," Frank says. "I'm going for a stroll while you make the bed."

Greg does his best, neatly unrolling the blankets they bought in Asia, and making a double bed with them. Their jackets serve as pillows. Mary and I are glad of our sleeping bags and small foam-rubber pads.

In the middle of the night I hear a splash and a petulant Frank: "Greg! Where's this water coming from?"

"It smells soapy."

"Goddammit, someone upstairs must have tipped over a basin."

"Good thing it wasn't a piss-pot."

===

Next morning we make rapid progress downhill, following the Utcubamba (Cottonfield) River in spate: a brown fury sometimes no more than a foot below the truck's wheels. In places there is room only for the river and the road between perpendicular rock walls.

The Kuélap ruins are above the village of Tingo, a few miles before Chachapoyas. (There are many Tingos in Peru; the word means "where rivers meet.")

=== *12* ===

TINGO

There is a small hostel here, so we have been able to escape from El Amigo del Oriente and Díaz Díaz, but not from Frank and Greg.

The proprietor is a theatrical man from Lima. He has decorated the place with posters of Machu Piqchu and buxom girls in wet T-shirts. Otherwise it is tasteful: whitewashed adobe walls, rustic furniture made of rushes and rough-sawn planks.

Greg and the owner are kindred souls in parsimony. I hear the following antiphon, one side in a lispy Lima accent and the other in a Spanish that has not strayed far from Sydney:

"*Cuánto vale una cama?*" ("How much is a bed?")

"*Barato.*" ("Cheap.") The word is drawn out with an eloquent toss of the hand.

"*Cuánto es 'barato'?*" ("How much is cheap?")

"*Barato . . . baraaato.*"

This does not amuse the owner's mother. She seems to do all the hard work and looks as if she has chronic hepatitis. Her face is a yellowed mask of old newsprint; her eyes two small pieces of raw meat. If she sits for a moment she's asleep.

===

A policeman has come to accompany us. Apparently nobody has been allowed to visit the ruins without a guard since some French were found digging there illegally. He orders pisco while we get ready for the hike.

A sign in the village says it is eleven kilometers to Kuélap. The path is a cow trail up a precipitous hillside covered in cactus and thorny scrub. Soon, Greg and Frank are a long way behind. Their shoes are remarkable: heels flapping, bare toes visible beneath visors of wrinkled leather. I wonder how they can use such footwear without finishing it off in a day.

The answer is, they never walk faster than a geriatric stroll.

The policeman walks at the brisk trot used by mountain Peruvians to dispose of long distances in a surprisingly short time. He has a leather satchel, which I presume contains his lunch. Mary and I struggle to keep up and make conversation between gulps of air.

"They are father and son?" he asks.

"No, amigos."

"They walk like old women." From the satchel comes its only occupant, a large bottle of pisco. "Very good for energy."

The trail makes several steep ascents punctuated by relatively flat "pampas" where there are a few huts and fields. We climb about three thousand feet from Tingo before the ruins can be seen: a jagged crown of stone walls circling a hilltop. Above the crown, exotic greenery sprouts like an unruly shock of hair. Although we are now over ten thousand feet, tropical vegetation is supported here by the moisture of clouds. Peruvians call the cloud forest *ceja de la selva*, "the jungle's eyebrow."

From a distance the walls seem low, but that is only in relation to their length. As one draws near, the city's true size becomes apparent. The best-preserved parts of the outer rampart (more accurately a terrace rather than a free-standing wall) are sixty feet high; nowhere is it less than twenty-five.

We enter by the south gate, a dark cuneiform slit with the same proportions and construction as the sharp corbel vaults in the facade of the Governor's Palace at Uxmal in Yucatan, but far higher. The lofty tunnel, partly collapsed, opens into a long corridor running between thirty-foot walls and watchtowers. The corridor winds slightly, with the sinuosity of a medieval street; I have seen few pre-Columbian sites so obviously built for defense. The curving lines, the roundness, and the coursed granite masonry remind me of the great *kraal* at Zimbabwe.

Inside, a riot of gangling trees and undergrowth confines us to the paths worn by cattle sometimes driven here to browse. The jungle is cool, moist, silent.

Near the north gate, which overlooks a precipice and an opulent view, we disturb some wild turkeys. The policeman praises their flesh as if it were a woman's, and stalks them with a child's catapult. But they are much too wary.

Turkeys abandoned, our guard gives us a tour of the ruins. His pride in the place is stimulated by our interest, and he conscientiously shows us everything significant. There are about three hundred round stone houses arranged on broad terraces. Their interiors are relieved by niches; the finest dwellings have chevrons and other geometrical designs in friezes around the outside. Near the main entrance is an odd-shaped tower. It, too, is round but flares outward as it rises, like the inverted stem of a champagne cork. One side is damaged and gives us access to the top. In the center of the flat roof (or what remains of it) is a hole leading to a beehive-shaped cavity occupying most of the tower's interior. It is hard to imagine what the chamber might have contained since it has no outlet at the bottom. Most likely it was a tomb or dungeon.

Someone has put a long thin tree trunk down the hole, at an angle like a straw in a bottle. But the idea of scrambling down it appeals to none of us.

The roundness of Kuélap is enchanting: a very different vision of architecture from the formal squares and parallelograms of most other Peruvian cultures. Kuélap grows from its hilltop in a great ellipse, about two hundred by eight hundred yards on its axes. The impression is something like the lines of a ship with a rounded bow. At the eastern end rises an acropolis, like a superstructure on the stern of a tanker. Its walls are as massive as the outside rampart, built of granite blocks about a foot thick by a yard long. I counted forty courses. The acropolis has more round buildings, and a lookout atop three terraces. From here the view is commanding in every direction: the countryside is focused and controlled as by the keep of a medieval castle. But the wildness and amplitude of this landscape are on a scale never seen in Europe.

The first outside visitors reached Kuélap in 1843, but no archaeological work of consequence was carried out until more than a century later, when the Reichlens, having finished at Cajamarca, dug some test pits near the south entrance. Their work was hampered by lack of time and difficulty in hiring labor, but they managed to discern two epochs in the pottery. The builders of the city made an unpainted ware of "somber color," decorated by incision and application. Fortunately, a few shards of Cajamarca III were associated with this, giving a date of A.D. 1000 or earlier. The second period produced painted ware of the Chipurik culture, which flourished here until the Inca occupation under Tupaq Yupanki (Atau Wallpa's grandfather) in the fifteenth century. The Chipurik people are best known for their anthropomorphic clay mummy cases. Many of these still gaze eerily from inaccessible cliff ledges throughout the region.

At the modern village of Wanka there are also remains of round houses on terraces, and the villagers make a painted pottery much like that of the first period of Kuélap. They are thought to be descendants of the Chachapuya, builders of the ancient city and namesakes of the modern.

———

The guard takes us back to Tingo by a different path. Descending, we leave the cloud forest for the dry country of the valley, but in the acacias are small green parrots, and on the ground we startle tawny *puku* doves. When he is far ahead the policeman plucks a leaf and plays waynos to himself by cupping it between the hands. The sound carries well in the thin air, but we make the mistake of complimenting him; he becomes self-conscious and does not play again.

At Tingo we offer him a tip, for being not a guard but a guide. He refuses, saying, "This is just my job."

Mary, who grew up in Argentina, is impressed.

TINGO, THREE DAYS LATER

We are stuck here because of progress. A road is being built to Kuélap, and there are plans to clear the jungle from the ruins. Local entrepreneurs hope to create a Machu Piqchu of the north. The trouble is, the new road passes above the main route to Chachapoyas, and blasting has caused landslides below. They say they will have it clear tomorrow.

Yesterday, the Ministry of Health was active in town. Two men went from house to house with sprayers and tanks on their backs. Killing bugs with DDT, I was told. Later I saw them cleaning their tanks in the smaller of the two rivers. A hundred yards downstream a woman was washing lettuce.

=== 13 ===

There is no need to go into Chachapoyas itself; we can catch a short ride in a pickup truck to the crossroads where several routes converge like rivers and run down to the jungle: Moyobamba, Tarapoto, and Yurimaguas. From Yurimaguas there are boats to Iquitos on the Amazon.

Parsimony separates us from Frank and Greg. After two hours of waiting at the crossroads, a large luxurious bus appears. Incredibly, it is almost empty:

the first run of a new service, explains the driver. He offers us tickets to Moyobamba (a ten-hour trip) for the equivalent of two dollars, but this is too much for the others; they think they can do it for half the price if they wait for a truck. It's a relief to be by ourselves again. We are no longer inevitably taken for hippies by association.

The road is blasted from the gorge in a daring way to form a three-sided tunnel: there is rock below us, rock above, and rock on the right; but where the other side should be it is open to the river. The effect is like those tunnels against glass made by the earthworms in a terrarium I kept as a child.

As we leave the Utcubamba canyon, the landscape opens into a panorama of wild hills. The semidesert has been replaced by a dark green fleece that is almost oppressive. But the excess is relieved by a few bright plantings of young maize, by waterfalls and limestone cliffs garlanded with vines.

After dark, the bus descends a flight of corkscrew bends so rapidly that sharp pains stab my ears; then we level out on the warm clammy plains of the selva, and I can hear the orchestral buzz of frogs and insects when the driver stops to check his tires. Two hours later we are in Moyobamba.

MOYOBAMBA

The hotel here has separate cabins like a North American motel. It is good, and cheap thanks to the feeble sol.

Daylight reveals a quiet, pleasant place. The whitewashed buildings and shaded plaza with surrounding colonnades belong to a sierra town: Moyobamba must date from the early wave of jungle colonization between the world wars.

As a substitute for land reform, mountain peasants were urged to settle in the lowlands. Many found the physical and cultural adaptations too difficult and returned to their crowded Andean villages. But some stayed, living in settlements with names like New Cajamarca, gradually becoming acclimatized to the heat and the hispanic way of life.

The mestizo character of Moyobamba shows in its large Coliseo, the cockfight arena. I have always found this sport offensive, not just because of the senseless cruelty, but because it seems to typify the ignoble obsession with machismo that is one of the more distasteful attributes of Latin culture. However, the Peruvians are guilelessly practical: attached to the Coliseo is a chicken restaurant, where the losers make their last appearance.

1:00 P.M.

About halfway between Moyobamba and Tarapoto we are stranded by a breakdown. There is nothing to do but drink warm cola and play a local game that involves flicking bottle caps into the gaping mouth of a large bronze frog.

We got this far in a more typical bus: crowded and decrepit. It needed frequent substitutions of one ignition coil for another, also defective. As soon as one coil became hot it would begin to fail, but the cold one would allow the bus to run for a further half hour or so. As the heat rose toward midday the rejections became more frequent, until the bus finally expired like the unsuccessful recipient of an organ transplant.

At the hottest time of afternoon we transfer to a passing truck (after a squabble with the bus driver concerning a refund for the uncompleted part of the journey). There is no shade at all; by the time we reach Tarapoto Mary is collapsing from thirst.

TARAPOTO

While Moyobamba is sleepy and understated, Tarapoto has the brash hustle of any boom town. Oil money has produced a settlement whose architecture shows all the color, taste, and permanence of fairground scenery. Air conditioners and scratchy jukeboxes blaring the syncopated monotony of musica tropical have banished the vociferous jungle creatures.

There are refrigerators in the shops here for a thousand dollars each. Listless young girls in sweat-stained cotton shifts are also for sale.

People walk only on the shaded side of streets that smell of rotting mangoes, alcohol, and urine.

========

The usually reliable *South American Handbook* recommends a *chifa* (Chinese restaurant) here. I salivate at the thought of Chinese food after the congealed potages of the sierra.

In Chifa Chang a moronic boy emerges from the "kitchen"—a cooking area behind a greasy sheet.

"What's on the menu today?"

"There's *sopa.* There's *segundo.*" Soup and "second course": this is what I've been hearing for weeks. (If you ask what the meal consists of it is taken as a stupid question: there is what there is. Peruvians have much the same attitude to food as the English—food is fuel for the body; flavor, temperature, and preparation are of minor importance.)

"Haven't you got anything Chinese?" I persist.

The youth leaves with a blank stare and returns with the owner. "I can make you chicken with vegetables if you like."

"Terrific. I'll have that."

Mary more wisely opts for the set meal of sopa and segundo. When my "chap suey" (as the local spelling has it) arrives there is a distinct whiff of rancid fat; but I am too hungry to be deterred.

===

For three days I have food poisoning, courtesy of Chifa Chang. Anything I consume takes only fifteen minutes to speed through my innards and emerge in liquid form. Mary is keeping me from dehydration—the main danger—by plying me with bottled mineral water. There are two kinds: Selva Alegre (Happy Jungle) and Agua Jesus. Jesus is better, but hard to find.

We have decided to forgo Iquitos. Mary hates the heat, and I am feeling too weak to face a river trip. Instead we shall fly to Tingo María, where there is supposed to be a pleasant hotel.

=== *14* ===

TINGO MARIA

It is still tropical here, but cooler because of a two-thousand-foot gain in height from Tarapoto. The mountains are reassuringly close—Huánuco, in the sierra, is only a few hours away by good road.

The State Tourist Hotel is a collection of wooden buildings raised on piles amid mature gardens of exotic plants (exotic, that is, to us, not the area). Thanks to the sol, we can afford to stay here. From the dining room there is a fine view of the Huallaga. Sheer hills on the far bank of the river are a rich bottle green, but the water is carrying so much lateritic silt that it is almost orange.

The Canadian writer George Woodcock stayed here with his ailing wife in 1956. (She, also, was suffering from a bad stomach.) He described the place then as already run-down. In those days, gringo mining engineers from the Cerro de Pasco Corporation would come down from the mountains to escape the terrible bleakness of the puna their company was poisoning. The gringos are gone now because of nationalization, but twenty years have not invalidated Woodcock's impressions. The place is still run-down, but not abandoned: there is a genteel state of what my first dentist called "arrested decay." It is as if a truce exists between the termites and the management, who have concealed the former's activities beneath many layers of dark brown varnish and green paint.

===

A political convention has arrived from Huánuco. The delegates drink beer all day beside the swimming pool and occasionally push each other in. One of them is making a point of talking to us.

"You are Americans?"

"No."

"You speak English?"

"Yes."

"I speak English!"

"Where did you learn it?"

"I study medicine four jears in California. I lov United Stays!"

"But you have come back here."

"Yes, I come back because I see what things I want to do for my Peru."

"What kind of things?"

"We must build roads to the ruins. Good roads. With roads come tourists, and tourists bring money."

"Tourists create a nation of bellboys. Look at Cusco—swarms of tourists but only a handful of Peruvians get rich."

"In Huánuco nobody is getting rich!"

"Nobody is rich?" I glance at the hairy potbellies, now mostly supine, around the pool.

The aspiring politician changes the subject: "We celebrate today because I am chosen candidate by my party. I think I will win because the people love me!"

"Which party is that?"

"PPC."

In the Constituent Assembly called this year to draw up a new constitution as a prelude to elections, the PPC (Popular Christian Party) has been campaigning hotly against universal suffrage.

Under the old constitution, a literacy requirement prevented half the population—the poor half—from voting. "Literacy" of course meant literacy in Spanish, so the voting rules were yet another case of cultural discrimination against Runa. The PPC want things to stay that way: they are afraid of the Runa vote going to Hugo Blanco, a former guerrilla leader from Cusco. In recent Lima municipal elections, Blanco's FOCEP (Front of Peruvian Workers, Students, and Peasants) was supported by a third of the electorate.

We have heard no politics around the pool; but that is not to say that there hasn't been heated debate. The delegates are exercising themselves over the possible outcome tonight at the cockfight arena. Those with "candidates" of their own have been solicitously feeding and grooming the birds tethered outside their rooms.

= *15* =

HUANUCO

The road has brought us up from Tingo at twenty-five hundred feet, over the ten-thousand-foot heights of Carpish and down to New Huánuco at six thousand. There is an Old Huánuco on a great puna more than twice as high, but the Spaniards moved the city down here to escape the icy winds and, more important, to dominate the coca plantations of the lowlands. Cocaine still makes a lot of Huanuqueños rich today, besides more legitimate products such as sugar and rum.

In contrast to the nearby selva, this valley is uncommonly dry—one of the stark climatic anomalies that continually surprise the traveler in Peru. Candelabra cactus and acacias dot copper hills more Mexican than Andean; haze and reflected light make for an impure sky, bronze above the hills, fading to platinum at the zenith. Huánuco is a windy city: dust stings the eyes along the narrow streets, and unsilenced vehicles are answered from above by tin roofs flapping on half-completed buildings.

The few colonial monuments have been clumsily restored; there is an air of cheap modernity, like that of a coastal town. But an hour's walk up the valley of the Higueras (Figtree) River brings one to the Temple of the Crossed Hands, whose cult flourished more than thirty centuries before the first Inca received his mandate from the Sun.

A Japanese archaeological team that dug here in the late 1950s left a steel-cable suspension bridge (like many in Peru, of Inca design but modern materials) to give access to their site on the far bank of the river. Unfortunately, a change in the river's course now means that anyone using the bridge will simply walk the plank to a watery destination: the far pier now stands in the deepest part of the flow. Mary and I cross on a fallen log leading to some huts near the ruins.

The mound reveals a series of occupation levels in much the same way as a Near Eastern tell. By 1960 the excavators had removed more than ten tons of potsherds and were well into levels older than the Chavín Horizon. The real excitement came when they stopped finding pottery and began to uncover a sophisticated building—a structure dating from the preceramic age.

The archaeology of the Old World has been classified by members of our technological culture into periods defined by technology: Stone Age, Bronze Age, Iron Age, and so on. In the Americas this scheme has very little usefulness because American man progressed culturally and intellectually without much interest in metals and gadgetry. The Classic Maya, for instance, developed an arithmetic that puts the Greeks to shame, and an astronomy unrivaled in many respects until the European Renaissance; but technologically they were a "Stone Age" people. The Aztecs had wheeled toys but never built a cart; and the Incas ran one of the world's most efficient administrations without writing (though they had a substitute in the *khipu*, a complex system of knots and cords which is not well understood).

Here at Kótosh, a people who had not invented pottery built a temple with a grasp of aesthetic design that impressed the exacting Japanese as achieving "harmony." And it is, I think, appropriate that Peruvian civilization should have been precocious in architecture—its genius for the handling of stone and space is consistently the great material achievement of Andean man.

The temple is a square room built of stones set in mortar. Originally the walls were smoothly plastered and painted gray. At the midpoint of each wall a tall trapezoidal niche extends up from the floor. These large recesses are flanked on either side by two smaller ones of the same shape above a cornice at half the height of the wall. The effect is elegant, and curiously foreshadows the Incas' use of very similar motifs more than three thousand years later.

The central part of the floor and the temple's entrance are also recessed in something like a modern split-level arrangement. In the middle of the sunken area is a hearth supplied with air from subterranean flues. Perhaps a holy flame was tended here—an idea supported by the charred remains of sacrificial llamas and guinea pigs. (Burnt offerings were also common in Inca worship, and are still practiced on a small scale by Runa of today.)

But the most remarkable feature of Kótosh is the pairs of human hands modeled in high relief below the smaller niches. These are in fact complete forearms, somewhat more than life-size, crossed at right angles at the wrists. Two carvings were found in good condition and wisely removed. Their meaning is a mystery. Nothing comparable has been found at any other site—unusual in Peru, where religious symbols recur again and again in the long parade of cultures.

Radiocarbon dates put the first Kótosh period between 2000 and 1500 B.C. The temple now revealed was built around 1800 B.C., and there may be an even earlier structure beneath it.

The remarkable preservation was owed to later Kótosh builders: it was their custom carefully to "bury" or fill in an old temple before building a new one above. Unhappily, the Temple of the Crossed Hands has not fared so well since its exposure. The excavators left the ruins under cover of a metal roof supported on concrete posts; but it seems they underestimated the local weather, and were equally mistaken in the belief that the Huánuco citizenry would lift a finger to care for this New World Çatal Huyuk.

The shelter has collapsed completely; drunken concrete beams lean heavily against the ancient walls they are supposed to protect, like palace guards after a night of carousing. Among the remains, a few mutilated sheets of corrugated iron flap mournfully in the wind. The rest have flown to a nearby peasant's roof.

=== *16* ===

I have been under the delusion that the ruins of Old Huánuco are somewhere near the modern. Today I learn that they are more than eighty miles away, near the town of La Unión—a journey variously described as six to ten hours by bus.

At the market there is a row of juice stalls where chola matrons produce an extraordinary range of substances from battered blenders. The carrot juice is excellent—much sweeter than one might imagine—but we are not brave enough to try the *extracto de alfalfa*.

Outside is the bus to La Unión. It has a fallen look, as if partly melted over its chassis like a Dali watch, and I am not too disappointed that there are no seats available for several days.

Alternative transport exists in the form of a *mixto*, which, as its name implies, is the misbegotten progeny of truck and bus. This contraption deserves description. An over-width homemade cab has been built onto a three-ton Ford chassis. Six people are sitting on the front "seat" (an unpadded plank): one passenger outside the driver and four to his right. There are three more benches behind, sagging like thwarts in a Roman galley from a full load of Runa ladies who are as well upholstered as the seats are not. The vehicle's coachwork is made of planks and staves bolted together with crude but massive iron brackets to support the excessive weight always carried on the roof. Behind the seating area, which occupies about a third of its length, the mixto metamorphoses into a high-sided truck box by omitting the roof.

A hernia of inner tube is bulging through a cut in the sidewall of a rear tire, and there is an ominous steady hiss of escaping air from one of the front brakes.

It is called El Andino, The Andean.

After the usual procedure of looking for passengers and fuel, we stagger out of town by the road past Kótosh. The truck body flexes and creaks like an old barge. Every half mile or so we stop to pick up people, freight, or livestock. By noon we have covered thirty miles. Our lack of progress is made all the clearer by kilometer stones along the road. The back, where we sit, is already crowded and the sun is fierce.

2:00 P.M.

The open part alone now has forty-two passengers, a sheep, a bag of piglets, some wilting guinea pigs in a box, and a man with leprosy. The flesh of his face and hands has receded from the surface like melting snow and left a red tangle of veins in relief. Parts of his nose and upper lip have gone, and there is a hole through one cheek and a nostril. He is standing next to me and I am terrified of contagion; but the truck is too crowded for me to move away discreetly and his hand on the center pole of the tarpaulin sometimes brushes mine. His wife and young daughter cling to him only with love, and they do not seem to be infected. Actually, the disease is probably *uta* (from Runasimi for "rot")—a kind of leishmaniasis spread by the bite of a fly and otherwise hard to catch. The Mochica show its victims, in their usual graphic way, on their pots.

3:00

Everyone is subdued by the heat and crowding; there is little talk. Two Runa have the right idea—they chew coca steadily, from time to time dabbing their molars with the lime paste that is needed as a catalyst with the leaves. Their eyes have a glaze of vacant contentment. We are again in a part of Peru where Runasimi is spoken and old ways observed.

5:00

The sheep has become more and more agitated as the mixto fills. She is constantly being crushed by sections of a hideous steel bed with tin cupboards in the headboard and an arrogant owner. At last, at a crossroads, the sheep flees. With a fine leap she clears the tailgate and alights nimbly seven feet below. The owner jumps down less nimbly and gives chase up a dry stream bed. By now the somnolent passengers are cheering like soccer fans, but it's not clear which side they support. Two legs cannot compete with four, but eventually a knot in the beast's trailing halter catches between two rocks and sends her sprawling.

7:00
It is dark and already cold.

8:00
We have reached the La Unión control. One hundred thirty-six kilometers in twelve hours. Average speed: about seven miles per hour.

LA UNION
A dismal place, scattered along both banks of a tributary of the Marañon, confined by high canyon walls to precious bottomland that the Incas knew better than to use for building.

We are staying at the house of a big man in town; he has a lorry and is away somewhere selling cattle. His wife, like all the rich, complains of hard times: "We're up to our necks in it here in Peru. Up to the neck. I don't know how the economic crisis will end. Two soles for a piece of bread. Imagine! A few years ago it was twenty centavos. Here, help yourselves. . . ." Some stale buns are pushed across a filthy table. "And the land reform! Now you can't get any milk or meat at a decent price. The indios have eaten all the cattle. Without a landlord to whip their flea-bitten arses they do nothing. They are animals!"

"Have you been to Old Huánuco?" I ask.

"Yes . . ."

"Then surely you must admit that the 'indios' managed their affairs quite well before the Europeans came here?"

"Ah, but then the Inca made them work. The Inca had three laws: *Ama suwa; ama llulla; ama qella*—do not steal; do not lie; do not be *lazy!* Ha! If they wouldn't work . . ." She draws her thumb across a flabby throat.

I do not bother pointing out that the Inca was also an "indio," and that he seldom compelled his subjects by Draconian laws. The concept of reciprocity worked to mutual advantage, and the construction of the temples made sense in a religious system understood by all: it was sacred work, like the building of the great cathedrals of the Middle Ages. Labor for Spaniards was never returned to the populace, either in symbol or in kind. It was Europeans who made the mit'a into slavery.

Our hostess's children are in the room; they are all fat. A doughy figure is cultivated by the Latin American bourgeoisie to show disdain for manual work—like a Mandarin's fingernails, but not so elegant.

= *17* =

We start early for the ruins. On the bridge across the river (which serves as the town dump and lavatory) a dog is chasing a pig. The pig, ears flapping like an enraged elephant's, suddenly turns on its pursuer, and the dog shits in fright. Dog runs off yelping; pig stops to eat. Mary says: "That's why I never touch pork in Peru."

Perhaps there is wisdom in Leviticus.

———

A road cut deep into the canyon walls snakes upward between hanging fields and groves of eucalyptus. This tree, which Australians find little use for, has given sierra Peruvians both fuel and timber for their houses. Before its introduction in the last century, wood was so scarce that lintels were made of bundles of twigs, and animal dung was dried and burned for fuel.

The charm of the climb is spoiled by the sight of a pitiful horse tethered outside a well-to-do house. Its back has been rubbed so raw by the saddle that the flesh and protruding rack of the spine seem to belong to a slaughtered carcass rather than to a living creature. Both horse and owner should be shot.

The cliffs are an aggregate of compacted gravels; here and there small springs ooze from the strata. Above us, the horizon is flat-topped but folded by erosion into a fussy pelmet against the sky. On the plateau I think I can see the silhouettes of walls. The ruins?

As our heads reach the height of the plateau, the world changes abruptly from a precipitous valley to an immense plain. This puna continues at exactly the same level on the far side of the canyon from which we are emerging, as if interrupted by a trivial crack. Beyond, on the horizon, the teeth of the Andes make the cliffs we have climbed for the past hour and a half seem like scale models of the real thing.

There is no sign of Old Huánuco; the walls I saw belong to the sod *kanchas* (farmstead enclosures) of local Runa.

An old woman sits in the sun near a tumbledown hut. She is black with filth, and the urchins at her feet are playing in a rubbish pile of bones, dung, and scraps of plastic.

I try my Runasimi, but evidently the dialect here is very different from that of Cusco.

"*Allillanchu, Mamáy?*" ("Are you well, madam?")

"Eh?"

"*Maypim Inka llaqta, Machu Wánuku?*" ("Where is the Inca city of Old Huánuco?") My grammar is shaky, but I think she'll understand.

She replies in thickly accented Spanish: "I'm sorry, gringo, I do not speak English."

While Mary is laughing, the old crone goes on to demand money, aspirin, and sweets, in that order. Some toffees elicit a surly wave in what I hope is the direction to the ruins.

This is the bad old Peru seen by early travelers like Squier and Harry Franck. (Franck, an American, walked the length of the Andes circa 1914, carrying little besides a revolver and a Kodak.) The "whites" are callous and tyrannical; the Runa abject, filthy, and demoralized. Landlords may have gone but there is no evidence of the new Peruvian here.

The condition of Huánuco Pampa gives the lie to assertions that the peasants have devoured the livestock: in an hour's walking we have seen no grass longer than a G.I.'s haircut. There are patches where overgrazing (mainly by sheep) has exposed the red earth in wounds like those on the wretched horse. A stream meanders across the pampa from the direction of the ruins; it has been dammed in places for irrigation, and floods the pasture in great puddles not more than two inches deep. Some gulls are wading; and crowlike black caracaras are dotted about, as conspicuous in the empty landscape as blowflies on a billiard table.

I presume the pampa was less barren in ancient times; even here the Incas followed their policy of building on the poorest ground. The ruins lie on a barely perceptible rocky rise below a hill. We scramble through the outlying wards, which are little more than scattered rubble. Fragments of upright wall bear the Inca hallmark of trapezoidal niches, but the remains are confused by unsteady recent barriers thrown up to contain flocks.

We emerge suddenly from this maze and enter an enormous plaza—the largest I have seen, ancient or modern—a quarter mile wide by a third of a mile long. And in the very center sits the squat but imposing mass of the building I have come to see: the Inca *usnu*. With characteristic lack of imagination, the Spaniards called it El Castillo, a name they gave to any large and unfamiliar structure, from this to the soaring pyramids of Tenochtitlan.

As one approaches, the usnu sheds its forbidding aspect and acquires the austere charm that is the essence of Inca taste. The rectangular building repeats the proportions of the plaza at one-tenth its scale. The walls are featureless except for the finely fitted, slightly convex blocks, which ask no further decoration; they rise fifteen feet with the usual inward slope, and then turn outward in a cornice shaped like a lower lip.

One guesses from its solidity that the usnu is no hollow structure, but a platform. On the far side a broad ramp, once surfaced with stone steps, rises to the level of the inside floor—about three feet below the cornice. Two doors pierce the parapet, flanked by rare examples of Inca sculpture: weathered pumas with spiral tails. Inca sculpture has a naive, furtive quality, like doodling on a blank page. (It is curious how Andean cultures became progressively less interested in adornment as their masonry technique improved. Chavín stonework is competent, regular, like that of the Romans, and ornamented with exquisite bas reliefs. At Tiawanaku the masonry excels while the few reliefs that exist—including those of the famous Sun Gate—are stiff and repetitive. And with the Incas, decoration is virtually abandoned but the stonework itself becomes a form of abstract art explored more deeply than by any other people in the world.)

From the top of the usnu one commands the plaza and, turning east, looks straight through a series of six monumental doors perfectly aligned on the platform's center. These are entrances to successive courtyards of the Inka Wasi, or Inca's Palace, which extends from the eastern edge of the plaza to a temple group and reservoir system half a mile away.

The usnu and square of Huánuco are incontestably imperial, still proclaiming the vanished Inca raj. Gasparini and Margolies, in their excellent *Inca Architecture*, note how "the magnificent spatial generosity of Inca urbanism" is stressed more at the outposts of empire than at the center. Not even Cusco had a plaza and usnu as large as Huánuco's; similar generosity can be seen at the other great provincial cities such as Pumpu and Willkaswaman. Obviously, the capital, because it had developed before the empire, had inherent constraints on its scale—just as London lacks the grandiosity of Lutyens's imperial vistas at New Delhi. (The Spaniards considered Huánuco's plaza far too big and began to fill it in with house lots arranged in their usual hundred-yard blocks. Fortunately, they moved to New Huánuco before they had time to destroy the native city, and their crude houses have crumbled to nothing but faint outlines.)

All Inca cities, though they differ considerably in plan and scale, expressed certain fundamental concepts of symbolic order. They were conceived as "models" of society, and Cusco was thought of as a microcosm of the whole empire. The name of the empire, *Tawa-ntin-suyu*, expresses the division of horizontal space into four quarters or directions that are united by a fifth organizing principle. *Suyu* is the Runasimi word for "region" or "direction," *tawa* is the number four, and the suffix *-ntin* implies a unit of things that are inherently complementary or indivisible. This suffix, because it indicates axiomatic unity, is really the linguistic analog of the human organizer, the Inca emperor. *The* Inca (sometimes entitled Sapa Inka, Unique Inca) was the principle from which order flowed, and the mediator between man, god, and other structures of Andean space-time. In geographical terms, the city of Cusco at the hub of the four suyus was the pivot of the world; and in any town or city, the usnu at the center of the four-sided plaza fulfilled the same role at the local level.

The chroniclers had trouble translating the word "usnu" into Spanish, rendering it variously as "throne," "shrine," "judgment seat," "castle." They were not helped by the fact that no two usnus were alike. Some were as small as the pedestal of a modern South American statue; at least one was shaped like a Mesoamerican pyramid (at Willkaswaman); and that of Huánuco is large enough to be a plaza in itself. It is clear from the native chronicle of Waman Puma (who claimed kinship with the rulers of Huánuco) that the Inca sat "on his throne, the usnu" to perform religious rites and political functions. Modern studies have shown also that the Cusco usnu (whose site is known, though nothing of it remains) was a reference point for astronomical observations. I think it is fair to think of these buildings as shrines to the god of order. When the Inca sat on the usnu of Cusco, all was right with the world: human and cosmic structures were in harmony.

$$=18=$$

I have to admit that we, secular gringos that we are, use the usnu for a different purpose. We sit here under the vastest sky we have seen since Alberta, and eat our lunch: a tin of pilchards in tomato sauce and a round, dry loaf like a discus.

After lunch we climb up the bald rock hill above the city. Here are examples of the storehouses by which the Incas regulated their moneyless economy. These *qollqa* are mostly round and quite small—deliberately kept separate from each other to guard against the spread of fire or vermin. Five hundred of them stand like ragged ninepins in rows along the hill; their total capacity has been calculated at 1.34 million cubic feet. Here was gathered the surplus wealth of the provinces under Huánuco's administration: military equipment, quantities of cloth in all grades, maize, *ch'uñu* (dehydrated potato), coca, dried fruit, meat, and vegetables. Much of these supplies of course accrued to Cusco and the purposes of the state, but food was issued to any area suffering famine (common in the Andes, where one crop in three is prone to fail), and a complicated system of exchange between different climatic zones ensured a balanced diet.

These systems of labor and exchange involved large movements of people on a seasonal and sometimes permanent basis. It seems that Inca Huánuco was a "new town," an artificial city of migrant workers, artisans, and administrators.

Recent studies of the sixteenth century show that the Conquest fell unevenly on the populace. In some areas power vacuums developed; people found themselves free, for a while, from both Inca and Spanish control. The ideal state of affairs from the Andean peasant's point of view has often been freedom from any government larger than his *ayllu*, his landholding community of extended kin. Certainly many ayllu members resented the demands of the Tawantinsuyu and were glad at first to see it fall, not realizing that the disintegration of the frying pan would drop them into the fire.

Much is known about conditions in Huánuco because the Spanish Crown commissioned Ortiz de Zúñiga to carry out an inquiry, or "visit," in the region a generation after the Conquest. (These "visits" were intended to rationalize tribute collection, facilitate conversion of the "heathen," and generally promote the interests of the Spanish Empire by gathering information. Runa were asked long lists of questions about how things had been in the time of the Incas, and how they were now. There were still people who kept and could read the khipus, so the information on the old order was probably quite accurate.)

Zúñiga's inquiry centered on the Chupacho ayllus, a community rooted in the area near the Spaniards' new city. His papers show a disaster of apocalyptic dimensions. The most shocking statistic is the population decline: 85 percent of the Chupachos had died in forty years. The predictable and relatively light demands of the Incas had been replaced by a tribute system in which flagrant extortion beyond already high quotas was the rule. The Chupacho leader, Shullka Kuntur (Young Condor), had many grievances: all the community's best bottomland had been taken when the Spaniards founded their city; his people were forced to work incessantly in the hot coca plantations (the local *encomendero*, a conquistador entrusted with the region, was taking four times the quantity of coca stipulated by Spanish law); the tribute was further unbearable because Spanish products were demanded and the Runa were no longer supplied (as they were under the Incas) with the land and raw materials to produce things; and "the Indians were many then and now are few." They had no time to tend to their own fields and "they are more tired than ever, because they all work . . . old and young . . . boys and girls, so that no one escapes this duty; and that is why they have gone to

Lima, to plead for justice . . . that the burden of tribute might be lightened."

The appalling death rate (two and a half times that during the European Black Death) was the result of several factors. Diseases such as smallpox, measles, and influenza, unknown in the New World before 1492, struck down the natives with the virulence of products escaped from a germ-warfare arsenal. The economy, already damaged, ceased to function because of the plagues, and many healthy people died of starvation. Others were killed in wars against and between the conquistadors; many simply committed suicide in despair. Women killed their babies "to free them from the torments."

The southern Andean peoples suffered less than the northern: only 50 percent died over the same period in the cold Lake Titicaca region. But on the coast it was worse. Whole irrigated valleys had become almost completely depopulated when the Spanish soldier Cieza de León saw them in 1547:

> There used to be many thousands of the natives but now there are
> not more than four hundred, a sad thing to consider . . . [also] the
> multitude of graves . . . all covered with bones. . . . Now there are
> so few Indians [that] most of the fields are untended and grown up
> to thickets and brush.

Peru has never recovered: the degradation of the modern Runa (where they survive) is worst in those areas where the destruction and exploitation of the sixteenth century was most severe.

=== *19* ===

We return to New Huánuco by the same route, in the bus we saw at the market. Its only advantage over the mixto is protection from the sun, but this is a doubtful blessing because most of the windows are jammed shut. Smells of gasoline, exhaust, unwashed bodies, and incontinent babies are struggling for dominance in the stifling air.

We have a comedian aboard: a wizened but mischievous little man who claims to be eighty-eight. He sits on a bundle in the aisle and makes suggestive remarks in a mixture of Runasimi and Spanish whenever voluminous ladies clamber over him.

At the first stop, when a woman with a sack of potatoes struggled by, he said: "Careful, *señora,* or I'll give your arse a bite." This earned him hoots of applause and the nickname Abuelito, Little Granddad.

HUANUCO

Only ten hours this time, but the seats were so close that I feel mummified in the fetal posture.

We both agree we have earned a night in the best hotel: the Hotel Cusco. It is almost new and still somewhat unfinished; a large double room with telephone (which we don't need) and shower (which we do) costs three dollars. Such prices are a measure of the floating devaluation decreed by the IMF. In two years, the sol has fallen from 43 per dollar to 185. This insulates us from inflation; but the Peruvians' real wages are half what they were four years ago. The current epidemic of thieving is no surprise in a country with 50 percent unemployment and no effective welfare system.

The hotel is a slender concrete pile of six floors with generous twelve-foot ceilings. At the top of the stairs (much quicker than the lift) is a flat, open roof, where the handwashed sheets and towels are dried in the sun. Only a low parapet guards the edge; sprigs of iron reinforcing rod sprout at intervals, perhaps with the intention of growing into further stories in more prosperous times. Being one of the taller buildings, it offers a fine view of Huánuco's ramshackle skyline: Spanish tile and corrugated iron, rusty as the distant hills.

Tonight there is a power failure, and the stars are splendid.

━━━━

The ground floor has a small lobby with a mahogany desk and a red plastic sofa; on the wall behind the desk, some wooden pigeonholes containing idle keys. Next to the lobby there's a tiny snack bar with its own entrance to the street; it sells cola, ice cream, and tired-looking sandwiches. But the kitchen proper makes the best food we have yet eaten in Peru—at least, it seems so after three days of bread and pilchards.

One wall of the dining room is entirely glass, looking onto a patio in which there are flower beds and a large turkey gobbler. Over lunch we watch him strut and fan at his reflection in the window. The time will come, I suppose, when he must cross over to the other side.

The rest of the room is enclosed by the Cyclopean ramparts of Cusco's Inca fortress in a frieze of giant photographs. These are a source of great pride for the owner, who is, of course, a Cusqueño.

Just as we are finishing breaded veal cutlets with mashed potatoes and enjoying the luxury of drinkable coffee, an uproar breaks out in the hall.

The door is flung open and a beaming black face intrudes: "Hi, gringos! What's happening? What's the food like here?" A dozen others follow the speaker, all black, tall; all dressed like Jamaican "rude boys'" come up to town. Only a frantic, lispy Spanish declares them Peruvians from the coast. Uniformed waiters watch, paralyzed, as the invaders drag two tables together, seize some chairs, and flop into them with casual grace.

"Listen, *comandante*"—the head waiter is addressed—"let's have some beer over here!"

"Footballers," the "comandante" explains to us on his way to the fridge, "here for the big match against the Huánuco Lions this afternoon."

7:00 P.M.

There were no tickets left for the game, but we have not seen the last of the Callao United. They are occupying the seats behind us on this bus to Lima (where Mary has a plane to catch).

Another new Volvo, assembled in Peru: reclining seats, tinted windows, and, alas, cancion criolla emanating from speakers along the luggage racks. The footballers don't like cancion criolla either, and they soon start singing parodies of the vacuous romantic songs. *Tus lindos ojos, tus labios rojos* (Your beautiful eyes, your ruby lips) has become *Tus ojos rojos, tus labios rabios* (Your red eyes, your rabid lips).

Demands for reggae and salsa are huffily ignored by driver and conductor.

The statistics of altitude on this route are like a market graph of boom and bust. Leaving Huánuco (six thousand feet), we have before us a steady climb to the Pampa of Junín at fourteen. Then a period of stability through the heartland of Peruvian mining. This will be followed by a final surge to the pass over the continental divide at almost sixteen thousand feet. And then the headlong crash to sea level, most of it in less than fifty miles.

The bus slowly quiets as we rise. Dust filters in; the air seeps out. Talk becomes an effort, but the mind, half intoxicated, remains active.

The black Peruvians: a small group, but they have kept an identity separate from the Indian/Spanish dichotomy. Though brought as slaves, they were often used to oversee the theoretically free Runa; and the blacks were generally better treated simply because they were valuable property. (Runa, though "free," were defined as legal minors. In colonial law, the testimony of three Indians was deemed equivalent to the word of one Spaniard.)

Despite the resentment felt by Runa for the blacks, Tupaq Amaru II proclaimed the Negro slaves free early in his revolt: there would be no slavery in the new Tawantinsuyu. This must have been one of the first political actions of its kind—there had been no such magnanimity in the North American rebellion four years before.

Slavery contradicted the Christian values of the Spaniards, but the Vatican concocted a loophole. After much debate following the discovery of the New World, it was decided that Indians were human and therefore not legally enslavable. But a Negro was *una cosa que habla:* not a person, but "a thing that speaks."

In this century blacks have found a niche in popular team sports, especially soccer. Black faces represent Peru at the Olympics and World Cup; white faces in the "genteel" pursuits of tennis, horsemanship, and golf. The Runa masses are as unrepresented in sport as in most other areas of national life. (Of course, any Runa athlete who did succeed would, by definition, no longer be a Runa.)

20

It is utterly dark when we reach the high puna; nothing can be seen outside but the stars. Even through bus windows, they shine with an opulence witnessed only at these heights.

But soon the black country of the Cerro de Pasco copper mine is shamelessly lit up by sodium lamps: great wheels and conveyors, dark sump holes, heaps of tailings. The ranks of company-owned one-room dwellings are more wretched by far than anything in South Wales; and the huge factory facades checkered with opaque windows, bleaker than those in L.S. Lowry's industrial cityscapes.

Must the Third World's industrial revolution, like ours, be a reign of terror?

Pasco was a silver town in the sixteenth and seventeenth centuries. Indians worked the mines with picks and candles, choking in the thin, dead air of galleries often poisoned by antimony and arsenic. They carried the lode to the surface in hundred-pound baskets. Failure to emerge with the daily quota of twenty-five baskets *per man* was rewarded with unpaid overtime and flogging. Women sorted the ore with raw hands, out in the open.

Such methods are still used in some of the small private mines of Peru and Bolivia, but in the twentieth century progress came to Junín with the rise of a new metal: copper. With it came the worst pollution disaster in Peruvian history.

Oroya, the scene of the disaster, is several hours beyond Pasco. All this time we have been traveling through the vast former domain of the American-owned Cerro de Pasco Corporation.

In 1922 the corporation opened a smelter in a ravine crossing pasture land that belonged to several ayllus and haciendas. Massive discharges of arsenic, lead, zinc, and sulphur fell out over the surrounding area. Within two years, nearly 1.75 million acres of fine sheep and cattle country had been severely damaged. Mortality in stock was appalling. In 1925, the government decreed that a scrubbing plant be installed immediately. Installation began that year but was not completed until 1942.

Meanwhile, the company was buying up the ravaged lands at bargain prices. As the pollution controls gradually took effect, the corporation went into the hacienda business itself. Eventually it became self-sufficient in foodstuffs, while the dispossessed peasantry proved to be a convenient source of cheap labor for the mines.

Under the Velasco government most of Cerro's landholdings were converted into the SAIS Tupac Amaru—a cooperative estate established by the land reform. The mining operations became part of the government monopoly Centromín. But neither workers nor peasants seem content: strikers' graffiti lend the only color to Oroya, and the SAIS, an unwieldy conglomeration of former hacienda serfs and ayllu Runa, has been plagued by disputes among its members.

= 21 =

We cross the divide beyond Oroya. The sixteen-thousand-foot Ticlio Pass is one of the highest in Peru; the railway, which parallels the road, is the highest in the world. All sorts of masochistic train buffs (including a morose Paul Theroux) flock here to experience vertigo and whiffs of oxygen courtesy of the Central Railway. Actually, "parallels" is hardly the word to describe the relationship of rail and road as they rush down the Rimac gorge, crossing and recrossing like two snakes engaged in ornate copulation.

At home I have a record with a wayno about this route; though really it is more about love (Huancayo is a major city south of Oroya, with a large Runa population):

Carrito pasajerito a Lima de Huancayo;	Little bus to Lima from Huancayo;
Chofer, donde llevas a mi paisanito?	Driver, where are you taking my man?
Camino carreterapi	In the road, on the highway
Suyawankiman karqa,	You would have waited for me,
Munaspa mana munaspa	Willingly or not
Pusawankiman karqa.	You would have taken me with you.
Iglisia punkuchallapi	In the doorway of the church
Suyakuykiman karqa,	I would have waited for you,
Munaspa mana munaspa	Whether you loved me or not
Casaraykiman karqa!	I would have married you!

The indefatigable and unscrupulous Henry Meiggs built the railway in the last century. Seven thousand Runa and Chinese coolies died in the work. Most of the altitude is lost in the first 50 miles from Ticlio, with the aid of 66 tunnels, 59 bridges, and 22 switchbacks; many of Meiggs's original trestles were built on brackets against the chasm walls, like bookshelves. These have since been replaced by steel viaducts.

Above us, in the cheerless dawn, I can see a derailed engine balancing on the edge of an embankment, its bogeys in midair.

Mining towns spill down the Pacific side of the mountains and pollute the upper reaches of the Rimac. The river gives Lima its name, its water, and its agriculture; but here the water runs green and red with mining slurry.

I never eat many vegetables in Lima.

The mountains give way to desert before we reach the coastal plain. Above, the green zone retreats until only the highest hills are crowned with a little cloud-fed vegetation. Occasionally one sees abandoned ancient terracing up there.

The resort town of Chosica looks uninviting to anyone but a desert dweller: a few dusty wooded parks, and beyond, a succession of small towns, each uglier and more industrial than the last.

I have been to Lima before and know what to expect, but for Mary the first impression (her last of Peru) is dismal. Land is cheap in the desert; Lima sprawls like a ragged mockery of a North American conurbation. The sleek factories of the big foreign companies along the road remind one of embattled diplomatic compounds: familiar names, high fences, guards, and watered lawns. Behind them, on bald hills without a scrap of green, the pueblos jovenes—the slums, short of everything but people.

22

LIMA

Lima is not a place where a man can console himself with much dignity. Perhaps I'm too fussy about drinking environments, but I don't enjoy the shiny airport-lounge atmosphere of the expensive bars, and even less the verminous dives strewn with paper, sawdust, and puke where the poor and thrifty go.

This morning Mary caught her plane to Canada, and I haven't yet gone back to the empty hotel room. Returning from the airport by taxi one passes miles of slums coyly hidden behind adobe curtain walls that frame the highway. And then the miscellany of spurious architecture that announces the domain of the rich: California bungalows, turreted castles, "colonial" posadas, and mock-Tudor mansions as repulsive as any in Totteridge or Shaker Heights.

In the city center, at a corner of the Plaza San Martín, a long, unruly queue is jostling to see *Grease, con John Travolta.* Above the shops in neon English: MACHU PICCHU SOUVENIRS . . . GENUINE INCA GOLD & SILVER . . . INDIAN HAND CRAFTS. One third of all Peruvians live in Lima, but there is little Peruvian about the place. It began as the beachhead of a foreign power and has never learned to change. Lima looks to Europe and America as models, and to the rest of the country only for the wealth to indulge the resulting inferiority complex—a complex evident from the lack of any original style and the uncritical imitation of others. There is truth in advertising: the magic slogan here is *importado.*

The Mexicans have a word for it, this craven staring over the gringo fence—*malinchismo,* from Malinche, the name of Cortés's mistress.

So many changes since my last visit. Gone are the banners proclaiming REVOLUCION and the stenciled busts of Tupaq Amaru, symbol of Velasco's dreams. Instead one sees new signs for old parties brought back to life by the convening of the Constituent Assembly: Acción Popular, headed by Belaúnde, the man the generals toppled; PPC; APRA. One poster says VICTOR RAUL [Haya de la Torre], WITH YOU TO THE DEATH! Not a felicitous choice of words to hail a politician well over eighty and in poor health.

At dusk the Plaza San Martín reminds me of Piccadilly Circus; as daylight fades the shabby nineteenth-century facades retreat behind COCA-COLA and BRANIFF AIRLINES, written large in neon. Where Eros should be there is a florid equestrian statue of José de San Martín, the Argentine general who gave the rather reluctant Peruvian criollos their independence. San Martín retired from history after an ominous meeting with Simón Bolívar, so it strikes me as ironic that the dominant building on the plaza is the Gran Hotel Bolívar.

Outside the hotel is parked a school of vintage Cadillacs, all tailfins and toothy chromium grins; inside I find enervated Americans in a setting of fin-de-siècle elegance. A magnificent stained-glass cupola surmounts the round hall, where coffee is being poured from silver pots while the guests read *Time* and week-old Los Angeles papers. In the "English Bar" a Scotch costs me more than the room at my hotel, and I am watched forlornly by a row of threadbare stags' heads on the paneling.

At a table in the corner a man wearing a tartan sports jacket leans toward his friend: "Say, do I have bad breath?"

"You been turned down by a girl again, Harry?"

"I think it's the food."

———

My hotel, the Richmond, was once a rival of the Bolívar but, like a dissolute member of a good family, has sunk into the lower classes without losing its pretensions. There is still an art-nouveau lobby lit by stained-glass skylights and paved with marble. Draped female statues with dreamy eyes climb the stairs, and gray plastered columns ooze with dusty grapes and foliage.

The dressing table in my room has cigarette burns around the edges and a cracked mirror, the bed is lumpy, and the wooden chair has been painted many times but not recently. In the bathroom there is a lion-footed tub big enough to bathe a horse, a bidet, and a willow-pattern lavatory bowl. All are served by conspicuous plumbing that writhes and groans throughout the night.

23

Lima's other square, the Plaza de Armas, has no neon signs, cinemas, or hotels; merely austere neoclassical government buildings, whose white limestone is relieved by ornate wooden balconies in the Moorish style. There is a delicate seventeenth-century bronze fountain in the middle of the square, a heavily restored cathedral on the southeast side, and, occupying the whole northeast side, the Government Palace. A tall railing keeps tourists and disaffected citizens at bay; behind it is a ceremonial guard of squat conscripts, ridiculous in white Napoleonic uniforms with plumed gold helmets.

This palace, still called the Palacio Pizarro—a name that shows where Lima's loyalties lie—has seen many coups. Most of them have been mere power struggles between factions of the civilian or military élite. But the army takeover of 1968 was motivated by a desire to hasten reforms that Belaúnde and others had promised but were unable to enact. The final *casus belli* was the humiliation of Peru by an American oil company.

By manipulation of title deeds the International Petroleum Company had paid virtually no taxes or royalties on its operations at Talara for half a century. The situation rankled Peruvians, especially as IPC was a subsidiary of Standard Oil (New Jersey), whose corporate income was four times greater than Peru's gross national product. The dispute dogged President Belaúnde throughout his 1963–1968 term of office. His efforts to resolve it caused the Americans to cut off Alliance for Progress funds and exert other pressures on the advice of their intractable ambassador in Lima, who became known among Peruvians as "The Viceroy."

Desperate to settle the issue before forthcoming elections, Belaúnde signed an inadequate agreement with IPC that left the company in an even better position than before. Public anger turned to outrage when the government conveniently "lost" an embarrassing part of the document. On October 2, 1968, the cabinet resigned in a body. The generals, led by Velasco, prepared to move.

Tanks commanded by junior officers of the Velasco clique drove up to the palace in the small hours of the following morning. The guard surrendered and opened the outer gate, but a palace aide refused to unlock the front door. After a brief volley of threats and rebuffs shouted through the studded oak, the rebels decided against smashing the door with a tank, and instead broke in through a guardroom lavatory. Beyond this, at the end of a passage, they were confronted by an iron gate. An officer began shooting quixotically at the massive padlock with his pistol, then noticed a small side door that had been left open. After advancing through unlit storerooms and offices, the revolutionaries at last reached Belaúnde's bedroom. Yelling "Traitors!" at his captors, the pajama-clad president was frog-marched out of the palace and bundled into a waiting van. Within hours he was aboard a flight to Buenos Aires and subsequent exile in the United States.

Thus began the regime that, in its first few years, people described to me as the best government Peru had had since the Incas. But the last time I was here, in February 1975, the revolution was turning sour. The police struck for higher pay; the poor invaded the city center and began to loot; there was rioting; offices of the government-controlled newspapers were burned. The trouble was not confined to the cities. Efforts to keep urban food prices low alienated the peasants, the new owners of the land. And there were other factors beyond the control of Peru: copper prices fell, causing cutbacks in the mines and a resultant strike; the Humboldt Current swung from its course and crippled the fishing industry at a stroke. With the country's major export thus destroyed, there was no money to pay for the arms Velasco had bought to defend the revolution against the real or imagined threat of Pinochet.

24

Lima, as usual, is depressing me; but before heading south to Cusco I decide to visit the Callejón de Huaylas, to see Huascarán and Huandoy, the highest mountains in Peru, and the ruins of Chavín de Huantar. In Inca times one could travel the Andean highway from Quito to Chile without leaving the sierra, but the modern lines of communication tie each mountain basin to the coast; it is easier to go to the Callejón from Lima than from Huánuco, which is much closer as the condor flies.

I walk along the Pan-American Highway north of the airport for two hours before I'm offered a lift. It used to be easy to hitchhike up the coast, but now there are few cars. I still enjoy traveling this way—one meets a variety of people, even if they are all from the motoring class. At last my thumb attracts a Hillman station wagon. (These cars are assembled in Peru by Chrysler, heir to British Rootes.) The driver is a textile salesman, a friendly sort, and he is going all the way to Chimbote, from where I can ascend the Santa canyon to the north end of the Callejón. We share an interest in the weaving of ancient Peru, which he takes as an inspiration in his trade. The logo on his business card is a Paracas figure of a cat.

There are faded government slogans on the walls of the faded khaki and pastel towns we pass through: CHINO! THE PEOPLE ARE WITH YOU . . . LET US

DEEPEN THE REVOLUTION ... WITH VELASCO ... Some have been deliberately erased, others merely scoured by the blowing sand.

"Poor Velasco," says the salesman. "Peru is a masochistic country. We kill our heroes. All our heroes are failures."

"I thought Velasco died naturally, from a bad leg?"

"Maybe. But many say he lost his leg to lead poisoning: six bullets from the CIA. One way or another Peru broke him. You're not a *Yanqui?*"

"No, Canadian."

"If you were, I'd make you get out."

———

Chancay, Huacho, Huaura, Pativilca: the names of the vanished natives live on in the dusty mestizo towns. At Paramonga the salesman parks suddenly below a bluff.

"You must see the Fortress." I can hear the capital *F*.

We scramble up to a huge adobe edifice commanding the green valley, the sea, and the desert, which starts abruptly where the irrigated land leaves off. Five great terraces with corner bastions support a cluster of fallen buildings. Tradition has it that this was a fort of the Chimú, built to defend their southern border. No one really knows. It was probably a temple as much as a fortress (nothing was wholly secular in ancient Peru) and may in any case predate the Chimú. The Chimú did, however, build an enormous adobe capital at Chan-Chan, near modern Trujillo. The ruins cover eleven square miles and are said to be the largest ancient mud-brick city in the world, greater even than Babylon. The Incas abandoned Chan-Chan after their conquest of the coast, but they apparently kept up the Paramonga "fortress." When the conquistador Miguel de Estete saw it, the building was still in good repair: "a fortress with five blind walls, with many painted devices inside and out, and finely carved gates in the Spanish manner with two tigers at the main entry . . ."

The "tigers" were most likely pumas, but one wonders what "gates in the Spanish manner" could have looked like. Sections of the adobe have been recently restored. On some of the original parts I can see traces of painted stucco, but the only recognizable "devices" are the work of Peruvian vandals: the usual hearts, arrows, and obscenities.

Paramonga has a history typical of the coast. The valley has seen early hunters, fishermen, the kingdoms of Moche and Chimor, the empires of Cusco and Castile. But unlike the case of the sierra, there was little continuity between pre-Conquest and colonial times. Cieza de León also saw the fortress in good condition, but the valley was empty by 1547: "There are no Indians here at all to profit by its fertility ... all we saw were empty woods and thickets." The stage was cleared for the conversion of the coast to the hispanic way of life, sugar cane, and slavery. The Spaniards brought black slaves and forced some Indians down from the mountains to create coastal plantations where the desert kingdoms had once thrived. The irrigation canals built by the ancients were gradually repaired—there are some still functioning today that are up to two thousand years old. During the nineteenth century the economic importance of the coast began to overtake the highlands (although not until the 1960s would the area of irrigated land equal that once cultivated by the Inca and Chimú). From the 1830s until the 1930s, criollo rulers of the young republic, afraid that highland Runa might yet try to oust them, encouraged this trend and called for the immigration of "superior races" to counter the "Indian problem." White settlers, mostly from Ireland and Italy, answered the call. Some (like the Goulds in Conrad's *Nostromo*) came as capitalist investors, others as penniless would-be entrepreneurs. But the advantages of white skin and ambitious temperament soon converted vagabonds into aristocracy.

Peru gave Ireland the potato and in return got William Grace, a fugitive from the great blight. He started as a Lima shop boy in 1850, rose to become a powerful banker, and began buying up the sugar estates of insolvent Peruvians. Among his purchases was Paramonga.

The entire north coast soon fell under the sway of Grace and his two rivals, Larco and Gildemeister. These three effectively usurped the throne of the ancient kings of Chimor and amassed more wealth than those monarchs could have dreamed. They acquired a labor force by control of water rights—squeezing out smallholders and converting them into a proletariat. Land seizures by other whites in the sierra similarly forced many Runa into debt peonage down on the sugar estates. All these workers were housed in old Spanish slave barracks and rows of shacks. Order was kept by thuggish private police forces, and when things got out of hand (as they sometimes did) the army could be counted on to come and shoot the "troublemakers."

But William Grace and his colleagues were not only raising sugar: their oppressive methods gave APRA the proletarian soil in which to plant ideas that blossomed, for a while at least, into South America's first modern political mass movement. The party developed the idea of replacing the archaic hacienda regime with workers' cooperatives. After the disputed presidential election of 1931, in which APRA was fraudulently kept from power, party supporters rioted in Trujillo and massacred the army garrison as revenge for past atrocities. From that day on, army and APRA became implacable enemies; but ironically, APRA would become more and more conservative over the next forty years, while the army under Velasco would implement reforms originally conceived by APRA.

======

Paramonga is now deceptively peaceful. From the top of the fortress I can see the Pacific, living its name, gray and still as a sea of moondust, the only life some pelicans, who fly with legs dangling and wings like pterodactyls'. On both sides of the bluff are green expanses of cane, and beyond, the tall stacks of the mill that processes cane wastes to make Suave, a lavatory paper that does not live up to its name. All this now belongs to the Paramonga Cooperative.

"Mas movilizados que nosotros!" says the salesman: More *mobilized*—more advanced or efficient—than ourselves. That is his opinion of the ancient builders of the Paramonga ruin.

= 25 =

Northward. Between Paramonga and Chimbote the foothills of the Cordillera Negra, the Andes' western range, pounce upon the shore. The sand desert is replaced by one of heaving, crumbling stone. There is less dust in the air; the sun's heat gives a flickering motion to the hills. Though barren, these are colorful: a scatter of light and shadow, yellow and black, with bruises of purple and green where minerals stain the rock.

We enter the dreary outskirts of Chimbote, where the hills are briefly driven back. Five years ago this city of a quarter million produced the world's largest fishing catch. But it was a peculiar kind of fishing. Sardinelike *anchoveta* were trawled in the cold Humboldt Current, unloaded from the boats by conveyor, and dumped directly in rendering plants, to become oil and fertilizer, mostly for export.

Despite the recent disappearance of the anchoveta, Chimbote still smells like a long-dead carp.

======

First guano and now fishmeal: ironic that a country with stagnant agricultural production should have produced the richest natural fertilizers ever found. Guano (from Runasimi *wanu*, "dung") was also a product of the anchoveta—thick deposits of droppings from the host of seabirds who fed on them.

In Inca times, these birds were protected and the guano was mined at a rate calculated not to exceed its accumulation. Even so, thousands of tons were transported annually to the highlands, where the guano was used to shorten the growing season of maize and thus allow unprecedented yields from irrigated terracing. Systematic use of fertilizer was unknown at this time in Europe, and the practice was soon forgotten in Peru after the Conquest. But in the nineteenth century science "discovered" fertilizer; mummified pelican droppings were again suddenly in demand.

What followed could well form the plot of a morality play devised to expose the effects of an unbridled free-market economy on weak countries and fragile environments. Exploitation of guano far exceeded deposition, and the human tragedy of the workers was shocking even by the barbarous standards of the day. Highland Runa died so fast on the acrid, arid islands that labor had to be found elsewhere. Chinese coolies were enticed by contracts that specifically excluded guano work, but they found themselves in chain gangs on the islands nonetheless. Many committed suicide (when they had the chance) by jumping into the sea. In one particularly savage episode, 720 Easter Island natives were brought to Peru; 620 died in the labor, and the remaining 100 took smallpox back to their island when they returned.

The resource became a government monopoly, but the concessions were operated mostly by British businessmen. An Englishman visiting Peru described his fellow countrymen as "gaining fortunes after such a fashion as only . . . a corrupt government could sanction or connive at." The money flooding into the Peruvian exchequer paid for a few flashy engineering projects—including Meiggs's Central Railway—and a military buildup that culminated in the War of the Pacific (1879–1883), in which Chile defeated Peru and Bolivia. Peru emerged totally bankrupt from the absurd conflict and was forced to sign over the entire guano operation to a consortium of foreign bankers headed by none other than William Grace. (Grace, who had never really become Peruvian, was by now a United States citizen.)

Not long after the guano deposits were finally exhausted, the fishmeal process was discovered. From about 1950 Chimbote became the center of a similar onslaught on the anchoveta shoals. So many fish were "harvested" that the seabirds died in thousands from starvation. The perfidy of the Humboldt Current merely hastened the death of the coastal ecology.

It is easy to criticize the Peruvians for making the same mistake twice; but the real blame must lie with a dominant world civilization based on the short-sighted profit motive and the frightening myth of constant expansion. The plot of the guano story is perennial: in Bolivia during the same period a few tin barons got fabulously rich, thousands of Indian miners died, and Europe built up a canning industry at bargain rates; in Canada today, Indians and farmers are pushed off their land while oil companies make big profits feeding big cars with gasoline.

The Incas, who had no concept of progress, planned for eternity.

CHIMBOTE

I first saw Chimbote in 1971. Thanks to the earthquake of the previous year the city was architecturally egalitarian: the permanent buildings in the center had been destroyed, but the shantytown of reed mats and sheet metal, where 80 percent of the people lived, survived like the proletariat after a purge of aristocracy. Even now, not much has been rebuilt.

Had he lived to see it, the irony would not have been lost on José María Arguedas, who set his last novel here while struggling with a decision to kill himself. *El zorro de arriba y el zorro de abajo* (roughly, *Top Dog and Bottom Dog*) expresses the obvious dichotomies of rich and poor, foreign investor versus Peruvian worker, factory laborer against fisherman. But it carries a deeper historical meaning: the expression of Peru's split personality, the internal conflict of Runa against hispanic, mountains versus coast. Chimbote, with its mixed population of scornful coast-dwellers and ingenuous Indian migrants seeking work, was the symbol for Arguedas of all that is wrong and rotten in Peru. He depicts the row of whores' shacks along the beach, where the girls sit under naked bulbs, legs apart, showing their wares, "shaved or not." Peru has thus been raped, first violently by the Spaniards, and then repeatedly— unable to resist—by the heirs to Spain's empire, the criollo élite and the British and Americans, the gringo conquistadors.

Zorro is not Arguedas's best book: it is the work of a man half mad with despair. But he is able to articulate the reasons for his state of mind in a way that draws the reader ineluctably toward the same black vision. This was not, as one might suppose, the work of a young idealist; Arguedas was nearly sixty when he shot himself in 1969. He had written some of South America's best modern novels, translated many documents and poems from Runasimi, written poems in that language (his mother tongue), and become an internationally known anthropologist. It seems that the deeper grew his understanding of Peru's dilemma of identity, the more the same sickness took root within himself.

His death came just as hope for change was stirring in Peru; but then most suicides occur not in midwinter, but in early spring.

27

My copy of the *South American Handbook* is out of date. I was planning to take the Santa railway to Huallanca at the north end of the Callejón de Huaylas. But I learned at breakfast that the line was another victim of the earthquake. It seems that the tracks have been taken up and the railbed is now being used as a road. Moreover, my informant (a cook with a filthy vest and a forearm so covered in scales that it looked like a large fish) suggested this "road" is dangerous. Peruvians seldom remark on the hazards of roads. . . . Still, a detour will be tedious and probably no safer.

I wait all morning at a service station on the edge of Chimbote for a vehicle going my way. Gasoline architecture varies little around the world: this place has two greasing bays, four pumps, and an office full of oil tins and girlie pinups. Blondes, of course. Latin Americans' ideal of beauty has nothing at all to do with racial fact. Advertising, pornography, and images of Christ all share a taste for pallid Aryans. They like the girls a little heavier than the current gringo vogue: skinniness is too suggestive of poverty.

A salient concrete roof shades the pumps. The only clues to my where-abouts are the sign for PETROPERU and the fact that urine defeats diesel in the contest of smells.

The sun chases me and the shadows beneath the roof. Outside, greasy asphalt shimmers and stinks, soft as toffee, a mosaic of embedded bottle caps.

After siesta a three-ton Ford arrives. A sticker on its windshield says: VIRGINITY CAUSES CANCER—GET YOUR VACCINATION HERE. The driver is a young, intelligent man with a shock of black hair and supple movements. He offers me a place on top of the load, says the road is perfectly safe, and makes me promise one thing: "Lie absolutely flat when we come to the tunnels or you'll lose your head. There isn't clearance for a fart in most of them."

"How many are there?"

"Sixteen."

For a long time we wind through a former sugar hacienda, now a co-op; we stop often to pick up small loads and people wanting short rides. The usual yellow haze veils the sky, intensifying the heat, robbing the landscape of contrast. Wherever is water, is color—greenery and flowers: frangipani, bougain-villea—infrequent and insecure, like patches of paint left on a peeling fresco. Dust coats everything near the road; even the trees and gaudy houses seem camouflaged for desert warfare.

There is harvesting in the fields, which have been burned to remove the dense, rasping leaves from the cane. Workers wearing only briefs slash rhythmically at the charred stems with machetes. Their bodies run with sugar, soot, and sweat; the air reeks of molasses.

Have things improved for these workers since the reforms? The answer, as far as I can tell, is a much-qualified yes. At first the rhetoric of worker control alarmed the supervisors and technicians on these estates. They threatened to resign en masse, and were placated only by the gift of disproportionate power in co-op affairs. This alienated the laborers, who went out on strike after calls from their APRA union bosses. Then there came an uneasy truce presided over by "military coordinators," resented by both sides. The situation was more complex than the architects of the land reform had realized—many of the cane cutters were seasonal workers, and the co-ops' fulltime members were reluctant to share their new wealth with these outsiders as the army insisted they must. Now the army has backed off and the co-op members have become a proletarian élite; but recent drops in world sugar prices will no doubt threaten their prosperity.

———

At last we leave the desert plain and enter the lower Santa canyon, so rocky that one sees no life here, even beside the river. I long for the sierra. Already Chimbote is a memory of only three colors: khaki land, houses, and sky, and rock islands white with guano standing in a black sea.

The old railbed soon leaves the valley floor, which becomes too wild, and clings to the canyon wall on a ledge blasted from the rock. It is seldom more than six inches wider than the truck on either side: the former railway was narrow-gauge. Abandoned mine workings pock the cliffs like rodent burrows; long tongues of debris depend from their small black mouths. The tunnels are indeed low, unlined and jagged inside. According to the other passengers, more than one traveler has had his head "smashed like a melon."

In twilight we reach one of those tiny hanging pampas that one finds so unexpectedly in the Andes. "Pampa" in Peru has a less specific meaning than in English: it is the Runasimi adjective for "flat," and a noun for any flat space, no matter how small. There are a few huts here, some chickens, children, and dark green orange trees. Though we are a thousand feet above the river, its water is brought from upstream by a long channel cut into the valley wall.

The driver stops and shouts up: "Flat tire. Good thing it happened here!" Yes, very. I climb down and walk to the edge of the gorge. The sky has cleared with the height we have gained and is navy blue with approaching night. All around are folded masses of rock torn by shadow. At the bottom of its dark, dry vee, the river's violence makes it conspicuously white.

The spare is flat (of course), and the puncture is on the inner dual, requiring removal of both wheels. It takes half an hour of hammering and cursing to break the bead from the rim; but it's not until the tube has been patched and replaced that the real work begins. The problem is the pump, one of those tiny plunger jobs suitable for bicycles. It needs lots of spittle inside before yielding any air. The driver, his helper, and one of the more vigorous passengers take turns at a hundred strokes each. I remember an earlier flat tire, on the Huancayo road in 1975, the driver shouting exhortations to his helper—a dull-witted and potentially rebellious teenager—exhortations satirizing government propaganda: "Pump for Peru! I'll tell Velasco how valiant you are. Work hard so the country can afford to buy him a wooden leg."

It is now quite dark. An hour's pumping has failed to inflate the tire to within a quarter of its working pressure. Lights can be seen in the distance coming down the mountain. The driver says, "That's strange. The road is one-way going up today." As with several roads in the Andes, traffic is supposed to switch directions on odd and even days. One of the pumpers hopes for a new Dodge truck with compressed air, but the wish is unfulfilled. Ten minutes later another violator of the traffic code arrives (or is it we who are wrong?) and he does have air.

I return to the *canasta*, the extension of the truck box that overhangs the cab, and get comfortable on my back among some sugar sacks. The stars seem very close, blotted from time to time when tunnels sweep overhead.

Much'aykusqayki Pacha Ruwaq,	Blessed Maker of the World,
Qhawarillaway	Watch us
Sumaq qoyllur ñawiykiwan.	With your eyes, the glorious stars.

I must have slept. Around midnight, very cold, the driver shakes me awake: "This is Yuraqmarka. We can eat here, and there's lodging." He leads me through the darkness to a restaurant. An old woman is shuffling about, half asleep. It takes her ten minutes to bring a candle. I ask how much I owe for the ride. Nothing, the driver says, but he wants the miniature flashlight I lent him while the tire was being repaired. I have to refuse, and feel mean: I need it for camping and there are none available in Peru.

The woman serves an execrable cold dish that was once hot: *seco de cordero*, an old foe of mine, but I am hungry enough to eat it. Seco is usually made from sheep neckbones braised in a gravy flavored with *cilantro*, coriander leaves. It sounds harmless enough, but so much cilantro is used that the result is cloying and sickly, like rotten parsley. The flavor is utterly different from coriander seed, a main ingredient of curry powder.

"Lodging" turns out to be a tin shack behind the restaurant. Two of the four beds are already occupied by bulky forms, from which come snores and gusts of alcoholic breath.

My first sight of the day is the avalanche of refuse that begins at the back door of the kitchen and drops away into the ravine: plastic, tins, corncobs, offal, and rags. Three very hairy black pigs are scuffling for the edible items. Yuraqmarka means White Town; I had imagined a pleasant sierra village, but daylight reveals a collection of metal huts that is little more than a truck stop. I go inside the kitchen, looking for water, and do not immediately realize that what appears to be an old coat hanging from the ceiling is in fact a sheep's haunch, invisible beneath a regiment of flies. The insects settle on me as I wash. Their feet are cold and moist.

=====

The old railbed joins a true road at Yuraqmarka; the truck carrying advice to virgins has left for the north. After the vision of the kitchen I am content with a cup of tea for breakfast. The only other customers are two men conversing intently through the forest of empty beer bottles on their table. One is tall, thirtyish, European-looking, but obviously, from his neat polyester shirt and slacks, a well-to-do Peruvian; the other, a sallow mestizo with Asiatic eyes and blighted four-day stubble. He wears—or, rather, appears to live in—a wrinkled suit and a shirt with no collar.

The tall one (also the soberer of the two) speaks: "Gringo! Where are you going?"

"Huallanca, and Huarás."

"So are we. Come and have a drink with us." I take my tea over to their table.

"Carlos García Cárdenas *a sus órdenes!*" the tall one says, "and my fellow traveler Policarpo Ruíz Huillca." I give my name, we shake hands. Their touch is soft and clammy and reminds me of the flies. (Handshaking in Latin countries is always frequently and lightly done, with the loose grip that Anglo-Saxons believe shows lack of "moral fiber.")

"I am from Lima," García says, in the voice of the Peruvian *Herrenvolk*; "my . . . friend here lives in Carás, in the Callejón." Ruíz looks up, belches, swallows quickly, says nothing. "He's a justice of the peace."

At this Ruíz comes to life, nods at the Limeño as if he were far away, and leans toward me conspiratorially: "He's a PIP. You understan'?" The voice drops to a whisper. "Policía de Investigaciones del Perú!"

The PIP is the élite plainclothes police force. It has political functions (not always those of the government), a reputation for corruption, and a taste for power. Its members are supposed to operate undercover, but are usually too swaggering to be inconspicuous. The acronym is pronounced, appropriately, as *peep*.

"Peep," the judge continues, "you'll see. When a truck comes we'll get a ride. No problem. Nothing to pay. Peep!'" He flashes his hand as if he held a badge. García looks embarrassed. Ruíz calls for more beer. I decline.

"From what country?" García asks.

"England originally—I live in Canada."

"You're my friend!" Ruíz interrupts, seizing my hand and continuing to hold it in a flabby grasp. "This gentleman is a PIP! If anything comes by . . . he'll stop it for us. . . ."

"So, what do you think of us two 'bad functionaries' of the government?" (García must be making ironic reference to the newspaper campaigns of Velasco's day calling on people to denounce corrupt officials.)

"That's not for me to say."

"Have a beer. I'd feel much better if you'd join us."

"No, really I'd rather not."

"Yes! Waiter, three beers!"

"No, please. I'll have a soft drink instead."

"You don't drink?"

"Never before lunch."

" 'Never before lunch'—you gringos have such rules, such discipline. We Peruvians . . ."

"There are plenty of gringos who drink."

"But not you, Ronald?" The "peep" persists.

"Not when I'm traveling. I seem to lose the taste for it."

"You don't smoke marihuana, do you?"

"Of course not." I don't like this line of questioning.

Ruíz revives again and leans across: "What country you from?"

"He's from England . . . and Canada."

"Ah," Ruíz sighs, "England. England is the mother country of Canada and the United States. That so? Just as Spain is the mother country of Peru!"

I reply without thinking: "It's not really the same. Spain isn't the mother country of Peru in the same sense. In North America most of the people have originally come from Europe, but Peruvians are mostly native, descended from the Incas. . . ." The look on Ruíz's face tells me how he has taken my effort to instill national pride. He knocks over his chair and shoots to his feet with impossible speed.

"There are no Indians in Peru! *No Indians in Peru!*"

Huillca, his Runasimi matronymic, must be a terrible shame to him.

———

At eleven, a truck comes at last. Ruíz is now at the incapable stage. García and I hoist him up the tailgate and the passengers inside haul him over the top. He props himself in a corner, crimped at the middle like a furled rug.

A woman sitting on the floor nearby has a large basket holding about a hundred eggs; when the driver puts the motor in gear the truck lurches and the judge's foot goes in. *"Ay, señor!"* the woman wails, pushing him away. He has smashed at least a dozen—equivalent in value to a laborer's daily wage, or two bottles of the beer that has brought him to this state. But the woman does not dare ask compensation and none is offered.

Later there is poetic justice: Ruíz tries to climb out of the moving vehicle and his fedora blows away in the wind.

=== 29 ===

Judge and "peep" decide to stop at Carás, where the Callejón proper begins. It is already early afternoon; I continue to Huarás by colectivo.

There has been plenty of rain here. From Carás south the valley is a study in greens and reds: silver-green maguey and eucalyptus saplings, emerald stands of young maize, bottle-green alfalfa; the adobe walls and houses are russet, and so are the wounds of paths and erosion channels on the land.

"Callejón" (Spanish for "alley" or "corridor") is an apt name for this long valley running between the two cordilleras. The Cordillera Negra is a sad range. Its eighteen-thousand-foot heights are too low to capture eternal snows; too low, even, to receive much of the scanty moisture that remains in the winds sweeping up from the sea. For that reason it is black, and the ranchers of sheep and llamas on its slopes are forced into conflict with the farmers of the valley whenever drought sears their pastures. But the White Cordillera, which forms a great wall to the east, is magnificent. Clouds are hiding the twenty-two-thousand-foot summits of Huascarán and Huandoy, but as I watch, the vapors swirl and part to reveal a kaleidoscopic world of illusion, dazzling against the blue-black sky. I cannot tell what is cloud, what ice, what blowing snow; and when the sun catches the glaciers their refulgence stabs my eyes.

Climbers look on these mountains the way some men regard beautiful women: as objects to be wooed, conquered, and then left. Only a new ascent, like a new sexual practice with an old lover, will tempt the mountaineer to a longer dalliance.

In the case of mountains I am the "pedestal" type, content to worship them from afar. The Runa call the mountains *Apu*, "Lord," the same title that was applied to the Lord Inca and the four Apus who ruled over each quarter of the Tawantinsuyu. To Runa the mountain is an ancestor, a protective deity, as well as a kind of underworld in which life and flesh are held in reserve. All life is cycled through the mountains that preside over an ayllu, just as water is recycled by the process of condensing on the peaks and running down through the streams and irrigation channels of the ayllu lands. Apus are "fed" with offerings of coca, alcohol, and food. Only if an Apu is given the proper respect will he provide for his community's needs. When José María Arguedas was doing anthropological research in Puquio, he was given this description of the Apu concept by the head of a Runa ayllu (in that region, the Apu as a spiritual entity is more often called *Wamani*):

> The Wamani is really our second God. The Wamani exists in all the mountains; all high places have the Wamani. He provides the pasture for our animals, and to us he gives his veins, the watercourses.

The mountains can also be dangerous, not only to foolhardy climbers, but to anyone living in the shadow of their influence. The 1970 earthquake dislodged a great mass of partly frozen mud and rock from the upper slopes of Huascarán. The *aluvión* hurtled down the mountainside, reaching a speed of more than sixty miles per hour. At one place in its path a sudden rise in the topography was sufficient to launch the whole slide into the air. It is said that it flew over a small Runa settlement, inflicting no physical harm, though several people were deranged by the sight and sound of it passing overhead.

A large town near the valley bottom was not so lucky: the mass dropped on Yungay like an Old Testament judgment. All the buildings and twenty thousand people were buried. When the first relief helicopters arrived they saw an unbelievable sight: sticking up from the middle of the waste of boulders, ice, and clay were the tops of four palm trees, still in place, marking the corners of the central plaza.

Until now, the road has been straight, but at Yungay it must snake its way between colossal boulders. The driver and other passengers cross themselves repeatedly. I see only a raw landscape like the bed of a dry river, in which some hardy shrubs are starting to grow.

The valley rises gently from Carás at seventy-five hundred feet to Huarás at ten thousand. The slope is barely perceptible, except perhaps by the drowsiness brought on by gradual rarification of the air. People are more numerous as we draw near the city. Everywhere Runa are returning home, the men dressed dowdily in shabby Western clothes, the women bright and traditional in flowing skirts of crimson, blue, or black. Both sexes wear battered felt hats that look like Humphrey Bogart hand-me-downs. The rest of the female costume has changed little in its essentials since the Indian writer and illustrator Felipe Waman Puma captured it in his great work, *El Primer Nueva Corónica y Buen Gobierno*, which he wrote between 1585 and 1615. Now, as then, the women wear the handwoven *lliqlla*, a shawl and carrying cloth, fastened in front with a large pin or brooch still called *tupu*. Beneath the lliqlla and skirt are frilly blouses and petticoats elaborately stitched in a style that must have been introduced during the eighteenth century. Those with fields to guard carry the slings that were once an Inca war weapon but are nowadays used for killing birds; those with livestock wear homespun lariats around their waists.

Munankichu willanayta	Do you want me to tell you
Maymantachus kanichayta?	Where I'm from?
Haqay urqu qhepanmanta,	I'm from behind that hill,
Clavelinas chawpinmanta,	Amid the carnations,
Azucenas chawpinmanta.	Among the lilies.
Castillamantam warak'ay,	My sling is of Castilian fabric,
Merinomantam seqolloy:	And my lassoo of merino wool:
Enteramente durable,	Very long-lasting,
Enteramente aguante.	Very strong.

Night has fallen when we reach Huarás. Unshaded lightbulbs shine dimly from the doors of one-room shops and bars. Some people are dancing to waynos played on scratchy phonographs. No matter how gay the tune, Andean music always wrenches me: there is a desperation to the gaiety that evokes the tragedy of Peru.

$$=== 30 ===$$

HUARAS, 10,000 FEET

My hotel has ominous cracks in the walls but I am told this is a good sign. The thinking goes that if a building has made it through one earthquake (albeit with cracks) it will survive another. There are two floors arranged around a long rectangular patio; the rooms are windowless, cell-like, but clean. Those upstairs open onto the frail balcony that runs around the inside of the patio.

This morning I made a discovery in the bathroom. Someone had thoughtfully left some old newspapers on the floor; I was staring at one absentmindedly when my gaze was arrested by columns in a different language. The columns were headed by the silhouettes of two Runa in Cusco dress and the words KAYPIN RIMAYKU. The dateline was February 19, 1975, and the byline Demetrio Tupac Yupanqui. I wondered whether the writer's name was a nom de plume or evidence of royal Inca descent. Yupanqui, originally an Inca title, is a fairly common surname in Peru, but this is the first time I've seen it combined with Tupac, as in the name of the tenth Inca ruler.

I study the article at breakfast, with the help of a pocket Runasimi dictionary. The headline means "Here We Speak"; the first paragraph opens with the words *"Wayqipanaykuna: Revolucionpa hatun qullanami, wiraqucha General Velasco, tukuy imata sut'inchan."* "Brothers and sisters: the great leader of the Revolution, General Velasco, is manifestly in complete control." There follows an account of the disturbances in Lima. APRA and the American Central Intelligence Agency are accused of complicity; but, according to the article, the people finally took to the streets against the counter-revolutionaries, chanting "Death to APRA! APRA and the CIA are shit!" The passage ends: *"Chino, wayqichay, llaqtaqa qanwanmi kas-kan!"* "Chino, little brother, the people are with you!"

Thanks to the unifying effect of the Tawantinsuyu, Runasimi replaced dozens of smaller native languages; it is still spoken by half the population of Peru today, with scarcely more variation between most dialects than existed in nineteenth-century Britain. When San Martín declared Peruvian independence in 1821, he issued his proclamations in both Spanish and Runasimi, and he made Runasimi an official language of the new Peru. But this fit of Indianist idealism was soon reversed by Bolívar, the archetypal criollo. Thereafter, Lima ignored Runasimi in the hope that it would disappear. But it did not, and in 1970 the Velasco government announced the intention to make the Inca language official in Peru once more. A standard alphabet was devised, new dictionaries and grammars published, and an ambitious program set up for teaching Runasimi in all schools. If sustained, these reforms could have given Runa culture a new self-esteem, and Peru a focus for national identity.

"You understand Runasimi?" I am addressed in faultless Spanish by a gaunt, scholarly gringo wearing heavy glasses.

"Some. Do you?"

"Like yourself, some. Where are you from?"

"Canada."

"So are we. Montreal." I tell him I live in Calgary, still speaking Spanish so as to avoid offending a Quebecker with English or (perhaps worse) my decrepit French.

André and Suzanne are both anthropologists making a clandestine study of the aftermath of the land reform. Suzanne, slim with dark hair to her waist, very French, powerfully attractive, speaks English softly with an accent that is a delicious cliché of innocent sensuality. André's English is as impeccable as his Spanish.

A few years ago he lived for some time in an ayllu of the southern Andes: "They didn't accept me for a long while. Part of the trouble was the priest—also an outsider of course. He got one of the village girls pregnant. They drove him away and pulled down the church!"

André's research involved social structure and irrigation. He found that the community was composed of four quarters, oriented in the same way as those of the Inca Empire, and still called suyus. The most surprising discovery was that one suyu still carried the name of the Inca Empire as a whole: Tawantinsuyu.

"I could not make sense of this at first. Why should the name of the whole apply to just one quarter? Then one day they had the annual ceremony of cleaning out the irrigation channels. The main canal entered the community lands from the direction they call Tawantinsuyu. Perhaps that canal was built by the Incas when this ayllu was incorporated into their state. Maybe that's why this quadrant has the name of the whole—it was the connection, the umbilicus, between microcosm and macrocosm."

===== *31* =====

Suzanne is away today (alas) visiting a co-op. André and I decide to walk to the ruins of Willka Waín in the foothills of the Cordillera Blanca, about two hours from Huarás by foot.

It has rained during the night and the morning air is crisp; the dung-laden earth smells like a rabbit hutch. Paths between the rude stone walls of the fields are shaded by eucalyptus and *molle* trees spattered with tiny red peppercorns. Maguey cactus line the tops of the walls. Women pass, heading for market in Huarás; some have a pig or a sheep following on a rope. Their fingers are heavy with bronze rings, and they spin constantly as they walk, dropping the twirling distaff and recovering it with unconscious skill.

Behind us is a fine view of the city and the Black Cordillera beyond. Damage in the earthquake was severe: there are neat rows of prefabricated wooden huts on the north side of town. Like most "temporary" structures they seem destined to stay.

André talks almost continuously about the land reform: "People who don't know Peru think a land reform is easy, that all you have to do is divide the land among the peasants. But here in the sierra there were two main groups of peasants with conflicting claims—the serfs who lived on the estates and thought the land should be theirs, and the surrounding ayllus from whom the estate was probably stolen in the first place and who thought the land should be returned to them."

"Did many ayllus remember what they had lost?"

"Sure they remembered. Some have documents going back centuries. But the biggest land grab was after Independence. The villains were Bolívar and other 'liberals' who thought like him. The Spanish Crown, for all its faults, recognized communal and aboriginal title. Not many people know that the Indians still owned about half the land in Peru when Independence came. But Bolívar thought the Indians would 'progress' only if they were forced to learn the values of private property. Ayllu title was abolished, and any lands not registered in individual Indians' names within two months were declared forfeit to the republic. You can imagine what followed. No one bothered to tell the Indians what had happened to their rights. Whites bought property from the government and moved in on it. If there was resistance the army came and shot the Indians."

"I believe the same thing happened in Oklahoma."

"The same thing has happened just about everywhere."

The Willka Waín temples are enigmatic: squat blocks of masonry honeycombed with tunnels and small rooms. To us they look like lesser versions of the Chavín monuments, but apparently they are thought to date from the Wari period because of the pottery types found at the site. We see little of the interiors—I forgot to bring my flashlight, and a box of Peruvian matches is a poor substitute.

A boy sells us prickly pears for lunch. André goes on to describe the Velasco government's ingenious but naive attempts to reconcile the different peasant groups by trying to swaddle them within a type of co-op called a SAIS (pronounced *Sy-ees*), an Agrarian Society of Social Interest. The idea was to keep former haciendas territorially intact so as to avoid breaking up viable economic units, but ayllus with claims on the land were given a say in the SAIS management and a share of the profits. Unfortunately the trauma of the reform, often involving various kinds of sabotage by the previous owner and the problem of amortizing payments (through the government) to that owner, meant that profits were rarely to be had. And there was the ethnic divide between estate dwellers and ayllu Runa. Although most serfs were originally of ayllu descent they had become semi-hispanicized: the old mistrust between cholo and indio made cooperation difficult. The ultimate goal of the SAIS system was integration of former haciendas and surrounding native communities; most Runa just wanted their land back and perceived the SAIS idea, with some justification, as yet another attack on their ancient communes. However, there were cases where ayllus had their property returned without being obliged to join a SAIS.

"The reform came fifty years too late," says André. "There are too many people now and not enough land, no matter how you slice it."

The land reform was implemented by the now discredited and forgotten SINAMOS, the National System for Support of Social Mobilization. Set up enthusiastically in 1971, SINAMOS soon became as unwieldy as its name. The young idealists who staffed it set out to "organize" the peasantry—only to find the peasants already organized but with highly disparate aims and a general suspicion of the government. In two years SINAMOS alienated almost everyone: in 1973 its offices in several cities were sacked and burned by motley crowds of landless peasants, landowners, APRA supporters, and ayllu Runa.

The Andean peasant has so often been portrayed as docile, submissive, easily bossed by Inca and Spaniard alike. But this is only the appearance he presents to the non-Indian world. In the criollo/mestizo towns he is *humilde*, truck-ling, adopting a mask of inoffensive stupidity. But in the ayllu he—and equally she—is dignified, ceremonious, and standoffish toward outsiders. When the criollo world pushes too hard there may be a sudden flare of anger that results in violence, although seldom the gratuitous violence of the Euro-pean.

In 1885, the Runa of the Callejón de Huaylas rose up against the whites and mestizos. The action was prompted by many abuses but particularly by the treatment given to the Indian *varayoq* (community mayor) Pedro Atu-sparia. He had complained to the authorities in Huarás about injustices against his people. The authorities promptly threw the insolent indio in jail and cut off his long, braided hair—an unbearable affront. The Runa overran garrison and city, and then took all the towns in the valley. There was some looting of the most rapacious hacendados and merchants but little bloodshed or rapine.

The army sent from Lima to quell the revolt behaved quite differently: in a bloody reconquest of the Callejón more damage was done to the property and persons of the hispanics by the soldiers than by the Indians. Minor lead-ers of the rebellion were shot, but Atusparia, championed by Indianist sympa-thizers in the capital, was spared. Later he was quietly poisoned.

But his name is not forgotten in the valley today; he was made a local Tupaq Amaru in the rhetoric of Velasco's reforms. There is a SAIS Atu-sparia.

Walking back into Huarás at dusk, we pass a shuttered building. Over the door there is a faded, damaged name: SINAMOS. André points out an irony I hadn't noticed: *sin amos* is Spanish for "without bosses."

32

CHAVIN DE HUANTAR

A bus takes me south to Recuay and then east to the continental divide. The pass is actually a long tunnel through the mountain wall, a connector be-tween worlds. On the Pacific side it is snowing hard, but on the other side, despite the altitude of fourteen thousand feet, it is sunny and warm. Near the tunnel's mouth there is a shallow tarn from which runs a torrent one could step across. This stream swells rapidly to become the Wacheksa River; at Chavín it will be joined by the Mosna, which in turn joins the Marañon, which becomes the Amazon.

The bus crosses the young Wacheksa dozens of times as it falls like a pinball through endless hairpin bends, before settling for a route on the left bank.

Five hours after leaving Huarás the bus makes one of its frequent stops. I notice beside the road a wall familiar from book illustrations: we have arrived. Although the altitude is about the same as Huaras, the vegetation here is far lusher. A passion plant is growing on the masonry, its long scarlet flowers and pendulous fruit crassly suggestive of male organs. The corner of the ruined temple that juts toward the road is made of long stone slabs laid in narrow courses. At one time it had a row of grotesque feline heads projecting from tenons. One of these heads remains in situ; it gives me a demented three-thousand-year-old grin as I turn toward the nearby town.

Twentieth-century Chavín has a mean, scruffy look. Its streets are unpaved, muddy, more suited to the numerous pigs than to the human inhabitants. On a large house near the plaza someone has scrawled: "Mr. Mayor, why haven't we got water or drainage?"

I ask myself the same question when I see the inside of the Hotel Inca.

———

In 1880, in a pueblo much like this, was born a boy whose name would become linked with Chavín. He was short and stocky, the descendant of Aymara people from the Lake Titicaca region settled by the Incas in the mountains behind Lima. Though his parents were poor peasants, on both sides of the family he was related to the ancient native nobility of the area, the kurakas of Hanan and Hurin Yauyo. He grew up speaking a dialect of Aymara and some Runasimi. All his life he would pronounce Spanish poorly, though he soon learned to write it well. He had an Aunt María who worked as a maid in the Presidential Palace. Recognizing his genius, she brought him to the capital and enrolled him in a school, where he learned to suffer the insults of classmates who called him indio.

Julio César Tello went on to medical school and later won a scholarship to Harvard. There anthropology seduced him away from medicine; he continued his studies in Oxford and Berlin, and at the Sorbonne. Returning to Peru, he founded several museums, became member of parliament for his native Huarochirí (despite strong opposition from the landed family who usually held the seat), and was instrumental in writing the first antiquities laws. He began digging at Chavín in 1919. From those excavations, and many others throughout the highlands, he recognized the importance of Chavín as the first pan-Andean horizon.

(A story goes that while Tello was digging here, a criollo politician came to visit the excavations. "Hey, you, where is Dr. Tello?" the Limeño called out to a figure he took for a Runa workman. "In that hut over there, *señor*," the "indio" replied, doubling around through the back door to meet the astonished criollo coming in the front.)

Archaeologists are still disputing the origins and nature of the horizon first defined by Tello. Researchers have spent a disproportionate amount of effort on the coast (because it is so much easier to work there) and have consequently looked for beginnings of the mountain cultures in the desert. For a time it was thought that the Cerro Sechín ruins were earlier than Chavín, but this is now discredited, and so is the old idea that Chavín was somehow inspired by contact with Olmec Mexico. The discovery of Kótosh has shown that sophisticated cultures existed in the northern highlands long before Chavín and Olmec times. Tello himself thought that Chavín showed influence from jungle cultures, and this theory is being supported by the best modern work.

How, then, to explain the sudden appearance of pottery, architecture, and sculpture in the Chavín style at already existing towns over most of Peru? Using analogies such as Islam, there has been a recent trend to favor a religious model for the Chavín expansion. (It's a standing joke that archaeologists trot out religious explanations when facts are scarce.) Proponents of this model see Chavín not as the capital of a state but as a pilgrimage center; they point to the example of Pachacamac, on the coast near Lima, which was indeed a kind of Mecca for a thousand years without ever being the capital of a powerful state. It is suggested that the temples of Chavín, like those at Pachacamac, were built by hordes of pilgrims under the direction of a few priests.

But there are fundamental differences between Chavín and Pachacamac. The latter is, as one would expect, a repository of heterogeneous artistic endeavor, not a source. And its adobe architecture could conceivably have been erected by unskilled crowds given proper supervision. Chavín, on the other hand, is built in hewn and sculpted stone, and there is a sophistication and unity in its architecture that is unequaled anywhere else in Peru at the time. Such work can only have been produced by a polity capable of maintaining numerous fulltime craftsmen over a long period.

Chavín *was* almost certainly the center of a great religion (*chawin* is a Runasimi word for "center") just as Cusco was, or Tiawanaku; but I think it unlikely that the faith spread without a simultaneous political expansion. Missionary evangelism for its own sake was virtually unknown in pre-Conquest American religions. The New World never divorced the soul from the body, and therefore felt no need to "save" the one and burn the other. Amerindian religions were syncretic, not dogmatic; new beliefs might be added to old. There were never outbreaks of the psychotic zealotry that has brought so much trouble to the world since its escape, in various forms, from Arabia and the Holy Land. Peru was too subtle and diverse a land for the monomania of desert prophet or Nebraska Baptist.

As to the nature of Chavín beliefs, we have some clues. Chavín art brims with a superabundant animism, a dreamwork of living forms. Graphically meticulous figures are built of human, bird, serpent, and feline elements: wings have eyes, arms become snakes, hair sprouts teeth. It is a lost world of metaphor and archetype, but the carvings yield insights into how this world was apprehended. One bas-relief shows a (mainly) human figure holding a giant wachuma cactus, the psychotropic San Pedro. Though wachuma is a dry-land plant, other carvings suggest influence from the ritual patterns of the jungle. The more realistically portrayed animals have all been identified as denizens of the selva: the feline is a jaguar, not the puma of the Andes; the bird is the monkey-eating harpy eagle, not a condor; and the snake is the giant anaconda of the swamps, unknown in the highlands physically, but present to this day in the form of the *amaru*, the chthonic serpent of Andean mythology.

Modern jungle peoples make elaborate and precisely controlled use of hallucinogens. Drugs are consumed in the context of rituals for divination in hunting, for contact with the dead, or to enable a shaman to take animal form. Was the sudden florescence of Chavín (so mystical and baroque after Kótosh) the result of contact between organized mountain dwellers and the formidable shamans of the jungle? Are the baleful eyes of Chavín sculpture—with pupils enlarged, eccentric, and upturned—in a state of psychedelic trance?

33

Last night my bed was filled with fleas, and my head with the above speculations. Breakfast at a co-op restaurant on the plaza is unexpectedly good: fresh rolls, two eggs boiled correctly to my instructions (!), and several cups of coca-leaf tea. Coca is traded from the slopes above the jungle but is no hallucinogen. The effect is like coffee laced with amphetamine; just what I need this morning. As I eat, the sun creeps down the mountainsides above the town. By the time I reach the ruins on their wedge of land between the Mosna and Wacheksa, the old stones are gilded with the day's first warmth. Birds and crickets are celebrating.

Long morning shadows emphasize the terraces, sunken plazas, stairways, and platforms exposed by excavation. There is the genius for landscaping, the feeling for the wholeness of architecture and its setting, that one finds at Monte Albán, Teotihuacan, Huánuco, or Machu Piqchu, at all the great cities of ancient America. The ruins are dominated by a truncated pyramid called (inevitably) El Castillo. It is two hundred and forty feet square at the base and still reaches a height of forty-five feet at one corner. On the side overlooking the ancient plaza the pyramid has a fine portal of white granite with black stone columns covered in bird motifs. Behind this, recessed stairways of granite ashlars rise toward the summit. At one time friezes of bas reliefs circled the building—many of the flat stelae now in museums around the world were once mounted on these walls.

The Castillo contains a labyrinth on five levels; parts of this network have been open to the public for years, although many rooms and galleries are still choked with rubble. I persuade the site guard to unlock the labyrinth's iron door. The electric lights strung inside are "temporarily" out of order; forewarned, I have brought candles and my flashlight.

The tunnels are about a yard wide, six feet high, roofed with stone slabs resting on corbels. After several right-angle turns I am shown a room filled with stone heads that formerly adorned the temple walls. The heads are about twice life-size, wizened and grotesque like gargoyles. Human features prevail on some, others are more feline; several are covered in writhing snakes, while a few represent a single serpent's head like the carvings of Quetzalcoatl in Mexico. By candlelight the room with its occupants has the aspect of a bizarre and slightly sinister shrine; but in fact the heads were simply stored here after being found in excavations. However, penetrating farther into the maze, I am introduced to the original dweller of the labyrinth.

A long corridor opens suddenly into a tall chamber, revealing a fearsome monolithic statue. The figure is about fifteen feet high, slender, shaped like a dagger stuck in the floor (whence its nickname, El Lanzón). Huge fangs resembling walrus tusks droop from the corners of a mouth upturned in a sardonic grin. The hair is alive with snakes, and crowned by a lofty headdress of storied serpent heads with glowering eyes and overlapping teeth. Such is the Great Image or Smiling God, a personage perhaps none other than Pachakamaq, Creator of the World. Later, at his shrine near Lima, he became as much an abstraction as the Christian God; but here he has stood, cloaked in primeval metaphor, since before the Chavín temples were built. For he presided originally at the focus of a parabolic plaza, and only later was encased by the Castillo and its labyrinth.

Above the statue there is a small hole, which connects with a higher level of tunnels and rooms. It has been suggested that concealed priests made oracular utterances through this opening, thus giving the image the power of speech. Perhaps, but I think Chavín was more an Eleusis than a Delphi. Modern-day shamans use singing and peculiar vocal effects to direct the course of their initiates' visions. The degree of control is said by witnesses to be astonishing: if, for example, the jaguar is summoned, all persons present will agree on the apparition's behavior; the experience is utterly convincing. Such techniques performed in the temple of Chavín would have had overwhelming power. One can imagine that after consuming San Pedro, the worshipper would be shown friezes depicting the beings with whom he was about to communicate; then the descent into the labyrinth, the chants pulsing through the tunnels and ventilation shafts, rising to a crescendo at the moment of confrontation with the Smiling God.

―――――

In 1940, Julio Tello set up a small museum at Chavín. There he placed most of the sculptures he had dug up and those he had rescued from buildings and patios in the modern pueblo. In 1945 calamity struck. A landslide of mud and rock descended on the ruins, burying the temples and sweeping the museum and its contents down the Mosna gorge. Fortunately Tello had taken some pieces to Lima and made casts of the rest. Since then the site has again been cleared, but he did not live to see it. Tello died in 1947; in accordance with his wishes, his remains lie not under a cross in a graveyard, but in the patio of the National Museum he founded, beneath a great crocodilian obelisk from Chavín. At the base there is a small plaque with an inscription in Runasimi.

NEXT DAY, NOON
A long morning waiting for transportation in the plaza. Two buses came and left, impossibly full.

2:00 P.M.
At last a ride—in the back of a brand-new truck belonging to Caritas, the Catholic aid agency. The driver is going to Lima direct, and reckons the journey optimistically at eighteen hours.

There is no load to prevent the vehicle's bouncing viciously on its new springs. I share the spare wheel (the only seat) with a Frenchman from Provence. He wears a large backpack and a sturdy pair of hiking boots, and is sixty-four years old.

"I am a cabinetmaker. All my life I want to see the Andes, but for years my wife is very sick. Eight years she is confined to her bed and I have taken care for her.

"Now she has died and I can travel. And you know I almost can't admit it, even to myself, but it is such a relief to leave that house. How is such a thing possible when you have loved someone so much and for so long?"

We cross the divide and ride all night in the darkness of the vehicle's box, lulled by the sound of the tarpaulin overhead, but unable to sleep. It is bitterly cold. The Frenchman never complains. When the truck stops for fuel in Recuay I hear a woman's voice singing a bilingual wayno in a bar:

Me voy de tu casa,	I'm leaving your house,
Mana kutimuq,	Never returning,
Mana vueltaq,	Never coming back,
Noqa ripukusaq . . .	I am going away . . .

= 34 =

LIMA

"The Chilean woman is whore and pays the hotel with her aging *chucha*." This graffito (which I didn't notice when I was here before) whispered its unkind message as I shaved this morning. Near it, in minuscule on the grout between tiles, someone has written neatly in English: "I'd give my right arm to be ambidextrous." I notice these little things the way one does the morning after a night of excess. The journey from Chavín has left me feeling as if I had been under the truck, not in it.

I've noticed the Chilean woman; she is fortyish and attractive, and often gives me what I take for a purely friendly smile while she gossips with the desk clerk. Maybe she is a whore, but if so seems the type, beloved of fiction, with a heart of gold. It can't be easy being a prostitute, or Chilean, in Lima. Ever since the War of the Pacific Chileans have been regarded here the way Germans are in France.

The snack bar where I have a glass of orange juice and a fried-egg sandwich for breakfast has the menu painted on the wall above the counter:

Toast and butter—S/40
Toast and marmalade—S/45

I have been here long enough to know that it means exactly what it says.
Toast with butter *and* marmalade is too great an extravagance to appear on
the list. For this I must pay 55 soles.

"*Expreso!* . . . *Comercio!* . . . *Prensa!*" A boy of twelve, with bare feet
and a soiled gray school uniform, thrusts the headlines of the morning papers
under the noses of munching businessmen. I buy one of each. In northern
Peru we could find only *La Prensa*, whose editorials irritated me so much that
Mary made me stop reading them.

In 1974, Velasco expropriated the major papers, vowing to create a press
of the people by entrusting them to sectors of the new society. The *Expreso*,
for instance, went to the educational associations; the *Comercio* became the
organ of the land co-ops. The policy met with protest from champions of civil
liberty, but Velasco made the point that the old press had largely served the
interests of the oligarchy.

The reforms appear to have been in vain. The front page of today's *Expreso* is graced by a bikini-clad member of the *gente dorado*, the golden people (read: "idle rich"); and the editorial is as vacuous and shrill as those of the
paper's British namesake. Only the *Comercio* is tolerable reading. It still carries articles announcing amazing potato yields by SAIS Such-and-such, but
there's no obvious party line and it has a good section of syndicated international news. The Runasimi columns, however, have disappeared.

———

The Ministry of Education is where I begin a search for Demetrio Tupac
Yupanqui (the *Kaypin Rimayku* columnist) and the fate of bilingualism. The
building is a monument to the Latin American belief in the power of architecture to create institutions. Built twenty years ago, it absorbed a budget that
could have provided many local schools. The entrance hall is daubed with
colossal murals in the Mexican Expressionist style. Like most modern Peruvian art, they lack conviction or vitality and betray a borrowed idealism no
deeper than the paint.

No one here has heard of the Academy of the Runasimi Language. I am
directed to the Casa de la Cultura (Department of Culture) nearby on Avenida Abancay, with similar results. But a helpful secretary finds me the address of something called the Institute of Aboriginal Languages.

The Institute is in an old deserted patio as quiet as the inner cloister of a
Cambridge college. Tarnished bronze plaques announce several apparently

moribund government departments. Aboriginal Languages is upstairs in Room 6A.

A petite middle-aged woman wearing enormous spectacles regards me across a desk strewn with papers and professional magazines. On the walls are posters for some avant-garde films in Runasimi; outside, the traffic roars unheard, silenced by a tall window paned with thick, old-fashioned glass that distorts the image of the street.

"Can I help you?"

"I am looking for the Academy of the Runasimi Language."

"This is it, or rather, this was it." She smiles, sweeping with her hand the small, untidy, yet comfortable office and its great window: "We are down to a very small staff nowadays. Just myself and the director. He only comes part-time."

I explain that I am from Canada, a country that also has two official languages, and that I am interested in the problems of bilingualism in Peru.

"Yes. On paper Peru is bilingual, but recently . . . with the economic crisis and everything . . . not much is being done. For two years we had a very strong program. Schoolchildren had to take Runasimi before they could learn any foreign language. But there were difficulties finding enough teachers. Now it's all been dropped. No funds.

"Between you and me, *señor*, too many people were against it, especially here in Lima. Teachers and pupils went on strike; the government couldn't afford confrontation over a thing like that."

Even the official status of Runasimi is now in doubt. Apparently the Constituent Assembly, dominated by APRA, voted to drop it, but the military insisted that it remain. Ironic that Haya de la Torre should be voting thus. In his younger days he was a champion of *indigenismo*; he coined the term "Indo-America" to replace "Latin America" for countries like Peru, with large native populations.

= *35* =

The museum of Peruvian gold in the Lima suburb of Monterrico leaves me sad. There are amazing things here: a puma skin with a three-dimensional head, human forearms complete with hands (an echo of Kótosh?), ceremonial knives and drinking vessels, llamas, all in cast or beaten gold. But I doubt if the entire collection (one of the largest in the world) amounts to a hundredweight, and most of it is wrinkled repoussé resembling crumpled paper rescued from the waste basket. When the Spaniards sacked Cusco they removed one and a half *tons* of gold from the outside walls of the sun temple alone. The finest pieces at Monterrico serve only to remind me of the loss—the destruction of a civilization's whole oeuvre in its most exalted medium. Everything—the reliefs, the life-size figures of people, animals, and plants, the great disk of P'unchaw, "The Day"—all are now piles of absurd yellow bricks in concrete bunkers.

Gold and silver had no monetary value to the Incas: they were substances of beauty and religious meaning, the "sweat of the sun" and "tears of the moon." An economic system based on value arbitrarily attributed to metal made no sense to the native Peruvians. Waman Puma cleverly depicted the cultural gulf in a drawing showing Inka Wayna Qhapaq questioning a Spaniard. The mutual incomprehension is symbolized by the fact that each speaks his own language. *"Kay qoritachu mikhunki?"* ("Do you *eat* this gold?"), asks the Inca, and the Spaniard replies, *"Este oro comemos!"* ("Yes, we eat this gold!").

36

It does not take long to walk out of the few blocks that constitute presentable Lima and enter the real city of cracked paving, dust, and urine smells. At the end of Nicolás de Piérola, only two hundred yards from the glittering Plaza San Martín, I pass a traffic circle with a vulgar statue in the center. At one time there must have been flower beds and grass here, but now there is only trampled earth and bits of newspaper smeared with human shit. I turn right and head toward the Puente Militar, which crosses the Rímac. Just before the bridge is the Coliseo sports arena, a great vault of corrugated yellow plastic sheets stretched over a metal frame. A high perimeter wall of bare concrete surrounds it; tickets are on sale at a tiny barred embrasure.

The music known to the world as Peruvian is hard to find in Lima. One could spend weeks and hear nothing but pop, salsa, and criolla ballads. Most Limeños are busy wearing the mantles of culture that confer status: the upper classes are anxious to appreciate the Bee Gees (or any other kind of foreign pap); the lower classes with Runa backgrounds and upward mobility in mind are cultivating a taste for cancion criolla and musica tropical. But there remains a stratum of recently arrived mountain migrants who long for the culture left behind. Early in the mornings, before *gente decente* (respectable, i.e., hispanic, folk) are about, these people tune their cheap transistors to the stations that deign to play Andean melodies and Runasimi songs. And on Sundays they congregate at the Coliseo to hear mountain bands give live performances.

———

This is *hora peruana*, Peruvian time; the show was scheduled to begin an hour ago, but the audience is just now trickling in. Once inside I notice that the plastic vault is peppered with holes where birds? balls? bottles? stones? have entered or left. The jagged perforations create an infernal star-chamber, a yellow firmament flecked with a khaki constellation wherever Lima's sky intrudes. Acoustically the roof—unnecessary, surely, in a city where it never rains—has even less to recommend it: the music has not yet started, but the shouts of vendors, who climb with their trays of chocolates and roasted beans among the tiers of wooden benches, echo, re-echo, and blend like the confused wave patterns that follow a passing ship.

The first act is a ten-piece band called the Familia Robles. The parents can't be more than thirty-five, but the ages of the children suggest that they are indeed a family. The youngest, a girl of six, beats a tambourine; the others play guitars, mandolins, fiddles, a drum, and two *qenas*, Peruvian end-blown flutes of ancient pedigree. Qenas have no mouthpiece and are hard to play but, once mastered, produce the clear, melancholy tones so characteristic of the Andes. The music of the Robles family, insofar as I can hear it, is less than authentic; but they make the most of the cuteness of the small children and this the audience loves. The echo is so severe that several different notes assail the ear at once like airport announcements. The crowd doesn't seem to mind at all. High fidelity is almost unknown in Peru, volume always preferred to clarity. The people come here for the ambience, the being with others of their kind. They know most of the tunes by heart anyway.

Where have they come from, these Runa adrift in the foreign metropolis—these young girls, fourteen, fifteen years old, plump, shy, giggly, sitting beside crewcut soldier boys? With no other prospects, many must have answered those advertisements one sees on doorways of well-to-do houses all over the sierra: *Se necesita muchacha para la capital*—Girl needed to work in the capital. Not that there are no girls available in Lima, but the mountain servants will work longer for less and, because they have no one to run to, will stay. Washing, cleaning, cooking, raising children who will one day scorn them; and always, of course, the fear of sexual advances from the *patrón*, late at night (the señora asleep), liquor on his breath—whisky, perhaps, a bottle of which is worth twice the girl's weekly wage.

But this is Sunday afternoon, time off for the servant girls and their Runa conscript beaux. The boys are trying to act sophisticated: dressed in thin sweaters, flannel trousers, and black plastic shoes; shorn to the scalp of their long dark hair; bronze ears and cheekbones sticking out; not much Spanish.

Ripuy, ripuy nispalla qanqa
   niwachkanki,
Pasay, pasay nispalla qanqa niwach-
   kanki.
Uralla chayamuptinqa
   ñoqallayqa ripukusaqmi.
Ingratitudes nispalla qanqa niwach-
   kanki.
Sabiendo mi mala suerte
   ñoqallayqa ripukusaqmi;
Avionlla chayamuptinqa
   ñoqallayqa pasakusaqmi.
Chay chay yana ñawichayki,
Chay chay suny chukchachayki,
Sonqoyta suwallawachkan.

Go away, you keep telling me to go
   away,
Move on, move on, you keep say-
   ing.
When the time comes I shall
   leave.
Ungrateful, you keep on calling
   me.
I know my bad luck,
   and I shall leave;
When the plane comes
   I shall go away.
Oh, those dark eyes of yours,
And that long dark hair,
Are stealing my heart away.

There are older people, too: pigtailed matrons, perhaps market vendors, and sorry little men who might sell blankets on the street. On the stage, bands come and go; each plays only two or three songs. Most are disappointing, but I am delighted by a shy quintet from Andahuaylas: two violins, two qenas, and a magnificent Andean harp. This instrument's wide-bellied sound chamber and thirty-six strings give it a five-octave range. Its music has two parts, one for each hand, bass and treble; a good performance sounds something like a duet for double bass and lute. But the technician, whose churlish haste throughout the show speaks of his contempt for the music, unhooks the microphone that should be placed near the harp's apex, and drops it into the sound box through one of two round holes. All I can hear is a distorted booming.

———

Outside, dusk is turning Lima from brown to gray. A market has sprung up at the unsavory traffic circle nearby. Each stall plays a battery-operated record player at full volume: waynos, salsa, and rocanrol are locked in aural combat.

An organ grinder on the corner is completely inaudible, but his monkey draws a crowd. The monkey has a woolly coat, prehensile tail, and permanently startled expression; it collects money from bystanders with a quick brown hand, bites the coins as if testing for counterfeits, then drops them into a tin.

=== 37 ===

Tupac Yupanqui's house is in an upper-middle-class suburb. The streets are clean, lined with a few parked cars and dusty palm trees. The two-story houses are compact but comfortable, almost touching one another on narrow lots, but each one different. Chinese restaurants and grocery stores on the corners of the main blocks remind me of similar districts in North American cities. The house is easy to find: over the door is a large sign in Runasimi—
YACHAYWASI.

A dark girl, about eighteen, with fashionably permed hair and tinted glasses, invites me in and bids me wait on the inevitable plastic sofa in the hall. His daughter. Tupac Yupanqui comes briskly down the stairs.

"*Yachaywasi?* That means 'school.' I give free lessons here for anyone who is interested."

"Free?"

"I make it my life's work to disseminate the language of my ancestors."

"So—excuse my asking—Tupac Yupanqui is not a nom de plume?"

"No, *señor!* My family is from Cusco. I have to live in Lima because I'm a journalist, but we are descendants of the tenth emperor, Tupac Inca Yupanqui." He has indeed the classic hawklike profile of the Runa, high cheekbones, straight black hair brilliantined to his scalp, and the eyes that are called in a Cusco wayno *kapuli ñawi*, black and shiny as the wild Andean cherry. He wears a well-tailored suit.

I ask about *Kaypin Rimayku*. He laughs.

"Times have changed. I used to have half an hour every day for Runasimi broadcasts on radio and television, but that's been stopped now, too. Now I write against the government. I do a lot of work for this outfit. . . ." He shows me some of his writing in the fortnightly *Opinión Libre*, a right-wing journal.

"Surely these people aren't sympathetic to Runasimi?"

"Well, no, they only take pieces in Spanish, but these days . . . Besides, they're against the military dictatorship, and that's the main thing." Tupac Yupanqui becomes evasive, agitated. Perhaps there is some personal crisis here, of ideology or identity. To foment Runasimi is generally considered a radical activity, but the author of all that revolutionary rhetoric in *Kaypin Rimayku* now seems conservative, or at least pragmatic. Probably the latter: ever since the Conquest, most members of the native nobility have swum with the tide, and it is probably still a good strategy in Lima's present turbid waters.

He changes the subject: "Look, I'm teaching a class in five minutes. Would you like to sit in on it?"

There are five students at the Yachaywasi; only one is a Peruvian. The rest are bored expatriate wives of embassy officials. At least they have the originality to choose Runasimi over macramé or découpage. Carlos, the Peruvian, is a young mining engineer. His mother's family is from Huancayo and spoke Runasimi originally. He sees the language as a family and national heritage and thinks it might be useful if he gets a job in the sierra. Rare sentiments indeed.

The lesson is by the old-fashioned rote method still used in Peruvian schools. The scion of the Incas writes some simple phrases on a blackboard and we have to chant them in unison:

"*Allillanchu?*" ("How are you?")

"*Allinmi.*" ("I'm fine.")

"*Maymantam kanki?*" ("Where are you from?")

I find my mind wandering back to a very bad prep school, from which my parents rescued me only when they found out that the Latin master liked to hold my hand. (I was ten at the time.)

The lesson breaks into a discussion. Like many Peruvians, Carlos has the idea that English and Runasimi are very similar: "Isn't it a fact that the adjective goes before the noun in English?"

"Yes."

"Well, so it does in Runasimi! Another thing: In Spanish we say 'How are you called?' but in English you say 'Woz jour name?' Right? In Runasimi it's the same: '*Imatam sutiyki?*'—'Woz jour name?' "

There are many such coincidences, but the ones I like best are the insults. When I was walking near Huarás with bespectacled André, some Runa girls called him *Tawañawi*, which translates literally as Four-eyes. André rose to the occasion with "*Sikiyta muchay!*" ("Kiss my arse!"). This the girls had a mind to take as an invitation, and only André's patent ingenuousness allowed us to escape without giving offense. I have a copy of the Runasimi school grammar prepared for the Velasco government by Guardia Mayorga. In it one finds the following somewhat Confucian proverb:

Yaw, opa, tutayaq wasipi supi maskaq.
(The fool searches for a fart in a dark house.)

Beyond a few superficial resemblances, Runasimi has nothing in common with any European language. Its agglutinate grammatical structure depends on a formidable array of suffixes, which give a subtlety and precision of expression that can be achieved in English or Spanish only by much wordier constructions. (Because of this property, Runasimi has often received the ignorant criticism that it lacks vocabulary.) In theory, as many as twelve thousand modifications can be appended to any noun. Here are three basic ones for *wasi*, "house":

Wasi-yki	Your house
Wasiyki-kuna	Your houses (*-kuna* forms all plurals)
Wasiykikuna-manta	From your houses

Many related verbs can be created from a single root:

Qhaway	To look at
Qhawakuy	To look at oneself
Qhawachiy	To show (make look)
Qhawamiyay	To spy on, overlook
Qhawapayay	To contemplate, admire
Qhawariy	To oversee, care for

Languages describe the world; like art styles, they emphasize some facets of reality, ignore others, and create categories of their own for which there may be no "objective" reason and no parallels in another tongue. Languages shape, and are shaped by, culture as a whole. When people lose their language for another, profound distortions may affect their vision of the world: as if Hieronymus Bosch were suddenly forced to paint in the style of John Constable.

In two areas the linguistic gulf between the Runa and the hispanic Weltanschauung is especially wide: sex and property. Spanish culture and language are steeped in gender-consciousness and an obsession with material worth. There is scarcely a neuter word in Spanish; even the inanimate world is arbitrarily divided into male and female. It is impossible to talk about someone without indicating his or her sex. One cannot conveniently refer to "my friend" without revealing whether the party is an *amigo* or an *amiga*.

Most European languages share this characteristic, although English has lost some gender determinatives and is increasingly under pressure to lose more. In Runasimi there is no gratuitous gender: he, she, and it are expressed by the single pronoun *pay*. An individual's sex is not conveyed in a conversation unless there is some reason for mentioning it. There is no deliberate avoidance of the question—it is simply irrelevant. This is a cultural statement: people are *persons*; there is no impertinent fascination with their sex. When needed, separate words for man, woman, mother, father, and so forth, are available.

Culture mirrors language. The aggressive dignity of the woman market vendors, the tough female butchers, the ribald Chaucerian wit of the Runa women on buses—all reflect a society that, though it does differentiate male and female roles, is more sexually egalitarian. Both sexes freely pick partners at village dances and are equally likely to initiate sexual advances.

Consequently, Runa men lack the machismo obsession of Latin males: they aren't wolf-whistlers or bottom-pinchers. In Runasimi there are no such words as "whore," "bitch," "cuckold": the sexual repressions of southern Europe are absent from the culture and inexpressible in the language.

European languages are also fraught with subtle validations of materialism. Consider the semantic relationships of "God," "good," and "goods." Spanish goes even further: the old word for gentleman, *hidalgo*, is a contraction of *hijo de algo*—"son of some*thing*" (not "some*one*"). The verb "to have," which is widely used (one "has twenty years," one "has thirst"), does not exist in Runasimi. To indicate possession one must use a suffix meaning "with." To say "I have a house" one says "*Wasiyoq kani*," "I am with a house." Notions of private ownership are as underdeveloped in the language as in ayllu life, but the Runasimi vocabulary for the native economic system is full and precise:

Ayllu	Community
Ayni, mink'a	Reciprocal labor
Mit'a	Labor in turns
Sapsi	Common land
Rantiy	To barter, exchange

After the lesson, Tupac Yupanqui gives me a lift back to the Plaza San Martín in his Volkswagen.

38

On my last night in Lima I find a folk concert of a different kind at the genteel Teatro Municipal. There is no working-class atmosphere here. The performers and most of the audience are students, members of the upper stratum of Lima society who feel secure enough in their convictions or (white) ethnicity to appreciate Runa culture. The ambience is intellectual, self-conscious. The material is treated with the clinical reverence Parisians might give to acoustic blues.

A little poetry is read, some of it in Runasimi:

Usuta	The Sandal
Sapaq hanaq pachakuna,	Every sky,
Puyu wayrakunam	Cloud, and wind
Watuykita muchapayanku,	Kisses your rope sole,
Sumaq usutallay, seqollay;	O pretty sandal of mine;
Qanmi raprayoq llantuta qollanki	You give wings to the shade,
Puñuq mayu hina ñanman	To the still river of the road,
Chaycha	And so
Hirkakuna rampachakun	On each mountain
Mosqoyniykita oqarinampaq.	There is a pedestal for your
	dreams.

The musical groups give long, sometimes apologetic introductions, explaining their approaches to the music. The experimental musicians are the most apologetic of all, conscious of censure from purists but nonetheless interested in extrapolating from traditional forms.

But the star performer is a young Limeño who plays outstandingly on the *charango*, solo, in pure Lake Titicaca style. The charango is a tiny instrument shaped like a miniature guitar, with a sound box made from the segmented carapace of an armadillo, stiffened with layers of lacquer. The player both strums and plucks the fifteen strings, and the tone they yield is high-pitched, metallic, penetrating.

The charango and Andean harp are rare examples of successful union between native and Spanish traditions: stringed instruments were among the few innovations that Andean culture was glad to receive from the West.

The player is criollo, but the music Aymara; it earns him a standing ovation and several encores.

=== 39 ===

To Ayacucho by road (barring acts of God) takes thirty hours, by air thirty minutes. I've made that bus trip twice before and feel no need to do so again.

The sun has not quite risen. The Boeing 727 banks over the sea, then heads for the gray foothills of the Andes. Lima, half hidden beneath a veil of yellow pollution, sprawls like a monstrous lichen on the desert.

In 1940, Peru's capital had five hundred thousand inhabitants. Now there are more than five million.

Sitting next to me, in the window seat I would have liked for myself, is a sallow priest with lizard eyes. From the way he is emptying packets of sugar into his tea, I am sure he must be Peruvian. As a prelude to asking me for my sugar, he introduces himself. I am wrong about his nationality; like all Spaniards in Latin America, he is very anxious to correct me.

"I am from Burgos, Spain, with the Jesuits. The order sends me on inspections of the 'colonies' from time to time. Alas, I have to visit the brethren in Ayacucho almost every year. Don't you find Peru terribly primitive?"

"It's a sad country."

"Son hombres primitivos!"

I lean across to look out of the window. Below there is a heaving mantle of white cloud from which rise two great icebergs splashed by the early sun.

"Do you know the names of those peaks?" I ask the priest, who sucks, rather than sips, his tea.

"All that," he says without looking, "is the Cordillera of the Andes."

"Yes, I know, but those two mountains . . ."

"They are just the Andes."

===

Beyond the continental divide the cloud begins to break and dark green ichu pastures, dappled by shadows of the clouds that remain, appear below. Black puna tarns flash silver when they catch the sun. The green turns to brown and brown to bone as the plane drops toward the arid chalky hills surrounding Ayacucho. Strangely, the views from the aircraft are little different from those I remember when arriving overland—the sixteen-thousand-foot passes from which the road descends offer much the same perspective of the intermontane basin. The city is near now, threaded on the bright green meander of the Rio Watata that gives it life; nowhere can I see, or even imagine, an airstrip large enough for jets in these rounded hills.

Suddenly the pilot starts throwing the jet around as if it were a bush plane. He banks over a farmstead—so close I can count the chickens—and drops onto the top of a long, flat mesa not much wider than the runway it presents to the sky.

The morning is bright and cool; the airport an austere, airy structure of concrete columns, absurdly large for a town of only thirty thousand. A long white car full of batlike figures collects the Jesuit. I ride into town in a wretched old Dodge taxi whose driver takes corners much too fast. The car has window fringes, an icon of the Virgin beside one of Che Guevara, and a windshield sticker showing a wolf dressed as a Wild West gunfighter, with the caption: PAY UP OR DIE!

The erratic drive is caused at least partly by large stones littering the road. The driver explains that students are rioting: the roads and airport were blocked during the night, and the runway was cleared only half an hour before my plane came in.

I find a cheap, clean hotel near the plaza. The entrance is a stone archway that leads to a patio with a tall tree, flowers, and singing birds in cages. The proprietor, an immensely fat and morose woman made up like a fallen opera star, calls a boy to carry my suitcase.

Only when I climb to the first floor do I notice that the tree covered in scarlet blossoms is a poinsettia.

= 40 =

AYACUCHO, 9,000 FEET
EL PUEBLO UNIDO JAMAS SERA VENCIDO!
THE PEOPLE UNITED SHALL NEVER BE DEFEATED!

Youthful voices are chanting in the plaza; soldiers with riot sticks, helmets, and a few tommy guns watch sullenly from the surrounding colonnades. The students are ripping up cobblestones to block traffic and to use as missiles. A pickup truck that tries to run the gauntlet gets its windshield shattered by a paving stone and is forced to retreat. After this, the soldiers gather at the corners of the square and seal it off. The ensuing deadlock lasts all morning: the students in possession of the plaza and adjacent university buildings; the army containing the disturbance, but afraid to move in and quell it.

Eventually, Peruvian common sense prevails. Noon approaches; the heat of the sun, reflected from buildings and the white hills beyond, beats heavily into the open square. Lunchtime cooking smells waft across, unmindful of demarcation lines. The antagonists gradually melt away to shade, food, and siesta.

After the midday lull, the army gains the initiative by reappearing in the form of a thirty-piece brass band inside a large bus. The band takes formal possession of the square by driving round and round, playing full blast with the windows open. The music—a curious blend of martial tunes and Andean melody—sounds something like early ragtime. Each musician has his sheet music pinned to the collar of the man in front, and the instrument of the man behind braying into his ear.

The disturbance was caused by the sacking of a dissident professor.

———

The radiating walkways and wedge-shaped gardens of Ayacucho's plaza focus on yet another "liberator." But in this case there is some local relevance: Antonio José Sucre achieved the decisive victory over royalist forces in South America on the Quinoa pampa, some twenty miles from here, in 1824. In those days Ayacucho was called Huamanga; after Independence, the new name was transferred to the city from a small village on the battlefield. *Aya kuchu* is Runasimi for "corner of corpses," a name retained from an earlier battle on the same ground in Inca times.

Ironically, the Spaniards founded San Juan de la Frontera de Huamanga (to give its full title) to defend themselves from the last independent Incas in the mountain stronghold of Willkapampa (Vilcabamba). The *frontera* was the constantly fluctuating border of the Neo-Inca state, from which Manku Inka II and his heirs made guerrilla raids into Spanish-occupied Peru. Their resistance continued until 1572, when a severe epidemic decimated the Inca forces and enabled Viceroy Toledo to capture Tupaq Amaru I.

But that old war—a true struggle for Runa independence—has been long forgotten, and Ayacucho is now a shrine (albeit seldom visited) to the criollo myth. The airport and a huge obelisk on the Quinoa battlefield were built with oil money given by Venezuela, the homeland of Sucre and Bolívar.

———

By the time I finish coffee, the life of the plaza has returned to normal. Street cleaners are removing the litter of the morning's skirmish from under Sucre's metallic gaze; shoeshine boys are back on the benches; and next to the monument a street photographer has set up his tripod, box camera, and the stuffed pony on which children are enticed to sit for snapshots. The creature looks like a crude and rather sordid tribal fetish. Obviously the skin came not from a pony but from a foal that died soon after birth—the long legs are oddly stiff from the wooden poles inside them, the eyes and muzzle have been garishly touched up with shiny black paint, and the head is tightly bound by a red plastic bridle that suggests fetishism of a different sort.

Under the low Roman arches of the colonnades vendors spread their wares on the cool flags. They are selling Lima papers, magazines, and an eclectic choice of paperback books: *Confessions of an Alcoholic Teenage Girl*, *Learn Quechua* [Runasimi] *in Ten Days, How to Raise Guinea-Pigs for Food & Profit*, and Marx's *Manifesto of the Communist Party. Time, Newsweek*, and *OH!* (a Lima skin magazine) are displayed next to the black-and-white Trotskyist *Peasant Voice* and the equally austere *Amauta*, a left-wing weekly originally founded fifty years ago by José Carlos Mariátegui.

Mariátegui, whose boyish good looks smile from every poster of the Peruvian Communist Party, was, besides Haya de la Torre, the outstanding political theorist and writer of this century. Although he died at thirty-five from bone cancer, his *Seven Interpretive Essays on the Peruvian Reality*, published in 1928, is a classic of Latin American political journalism.

$$=\!\!=41=\!\!=$$

WARI

Tires, fuel drums, and smoky little eating houses—this morning I waited amid the familiar clutter of a Third World truck stop on the edge of Ayacucho. It seems I am too late a riser—the traffic to Quinoa market had already left, and it was only by good luck that I was offered a lift by three elderly members of the former landed gentry. They didn't want to talk politics; instead they pointed out landmarks along the way: the reservoir for the city's water supply, in which a badly decomposed horse was found last week, and the "priests' leap," a bend in the road where a carload of clerics plunged into a rocky stream thirty feet below. (The victims escaped "miraculously" unhurt—a miracle much aided, I was told, by the padres' relaxed condition induced by libations of pisco.)

It has taken only half an hour to cover the fifteen miles to the ruins. The fine asphalt road, yet another gift of the Venezuelans, cuts through ancient Wari and continues to the monument at Quinoa—and a few miles beyond, just enough to give the illusion that the paving surges across the puna, while in fact it changes abruptly to a muddy track.

The landscape is suddenly brilliant, like an overexposed film, after the tinted glass of the Ayacuchans' old Pontiac. A fierce sun burns in a sky light blue from airborne dust, the blue turning almost to silver where it touches the gray-white hills. The first impression is of London bombsites seen as a child. Fragments of walls rise above more than a thousand acres of rubble. But here, instead of nettles and old lilacs, prickly-pear cactus and molle trees cluster around the masonry, the outcrops of red boulders, and the stone piles made over the years by Runa farmers trying to return parts of the old metropolis to the plow. Dry stems of last year's barley poke forlornly from a soil of dust, stones, and potsherds. How anything grows here is a mystery to me: there is no water for irrigation, and very little rain.

I find it hard now to imagine these disconsolate ruins as the capital of Peru in the Middle Horizon, a period contemporary with the rise of the Frankish kings in western Europe. Europe at that time had the wheel, the horse, iron, and writing—all lacking in Peru. Yet Charlemagne, the first Holy Roman Emperor, had to move his small court every few months as the surrounding country became exhausted by his presence. The rulers of Wari, on the other hand, maintained a large urban population in an arid mountain region, built garrison cities at strategic points throughout their realm, and created a road network and supply system equal to their needs. These roads were sufficiently well made that they remained in use until the time of the Incas, who restored them and incorporated them into the Tawantinsuyu network centered on Cusco.

There have been two recent excavations. Those of the University of Huamanga (it keeps the old name) lie beneath an expanse of corrugated iron dancing in the heat. Here is revealed an extraordinary complex resembling a subterranean city in miniature—a collection of chambers and "towers" built with slabs of hewn stone. My first thought is that these were burial chambers; but though the structures do resemble underground versions of the Oxamarca ch'ullpas, not a single bone or potsherd has been found in them. It is as if they have been not only rifled in the past, but scrupulously cleaned out. Most of the "tombs" are about four to six feet square and the same in height; the "towers" consist of two or three of these chambers superimposed. The featureless, smooth slabs of each wall, floor, and roof bring to mind modern office buildings made of prefabricated concrete sections. Yet there is one distinctive feature, as inexplicable as the structures themselves: the lid of each chamber has a small round hole, sometimes in the middle, but more often near an edge, where it connects with a drainlike groove cut into the inside surface of the wall with great precision. This groove descends to connect with a hole in the floor when there is another chamber below. Were these holes for

ventilation? For the free movement of souls? Or were they perhaps for sup-
plying the dead with beer—a custom still observed at "Catholic" cemeteries
today?

A team from New York has been digging in a residential sector of the
city; their trenches are protected from the weather more aesthetically by roofs
of ichu grass thatched over rustic frames. Here, too, are underground buildings, but these are one- and two-story houses almost identical with those of
modern times, and it seems that originally they were entirely free-standing
but became buried by later deposits. The depth of the rubble here—as much
as fifteen feet—indicates that the city was densely populated over a long period of time. Buildings collapsed and were leveled, and new ones raised
above. The plan is chaotic, medieval, very different from the orderly grid pattern adopted at Wari's own garrison towns such as Wiraqochapampa (near
Cajamarca) and Pikillaqta (near Cusco). But there is an overall arrangement
of buildings into crowded compounds and clear evidence that specialized
trades were located according to wards: vast quantities of turquoise may be
found in one area of the site, obsidian in another—concentrations that reveal
where the artisans lived and worked. Right at the bottom of the deepest
house excavated so far there is a remarkable find: a wall of large, finely cut
stone blocks that obviously bears no relation to the buildings above. Such a
wall must belong to an early ceremonial building; it implies that space originally occupied by temples became preempted for housing in later times. In
other words, the city became secularized as its population grew: as if the
careful planning evident in the provinces, and at the great contemporary city
of Tiawanaku, broke down under an influx of inhabitants. Did Wari, in this
respect, foreshadow modern Lima?

Farther into the site I reach the underground complex called, strangely,
Monjachayoq (Place of the Little Nuns). It consists of long, well-built tunnels roofed with cut slabs. Again one sees the curious drains or ventilation
holes, but they seem too small and infrequent to provide an adequate air supply. These tunnels have the appearance of being subterranean when built,
rather than covered by later deposits. Were they something like the labyrinth
at Chavín? It would be tidy to think so, but the oddest thing is that the corridors are blocked at intervals by walls; these are identical in construction (and
therefore presumably contemporary) and divide the tunnels into discrete sections with no way in or out. Only the openings made by looters give access, to
reveal that the Monjachayoq (now, at least) is empty.

Wari is disturbing. Everything seems turned upside down, rifled,
cleaned out, as if evidence were deliberately removed in the past to hinder the
prying of archaeologists.

The heat pounces on me as I emerge from the cool recesses of Monjachayoq. Myth has it that the underground system runs all the way to the Capillayoq sector, the best-preserved walls overlooking the highway, half a mile from here. If only it were so, but I must find an overland route—no easy matter through the maze of thorns and rubble.

There are trees like baobabs here—they have the same thick trunk and tapering, fleshy branches that earn the baobab its nickname: "the upsidedown tree." But the branches have no leaves, and the small lattice of shade is already occupied by two donkeys standing motionless with that exploited look that donkeys have. I feel bad when they run away, but I'm glad to take their place and eat a much-needed lunch: rye buns, olives, and cheese from Ayacucho market, and a bottle of water, which by now is warm.

Farther on there is a clump of molle trees growing around a monolithic slab. The stone measures eight feet by sixteen, but is only nine inches thick—a remarkable feat of quarrying. A raised rim suggests that it may have been a shallow basin, but, like most things at Wari, the stone lies here, inexplicable, without any apparent relation to the debris all around.

Capillayoq (Place of the Chapel) puts me in mind of a sprawling castle, and such it may have been (again: "may have been"). At any rate, it commands the steep gorge of the little Viñaque River and the switchback road climbing up from the bridge. The tapering walls are still thirty feet high, almost ten feet thick at the base, rather crudely made of rough black stones set in clay mortar. Perhaps they were once stuccoed and covered in painted designs; if so, no trace remains.

It is late afternoon now; a rising tide of shadow starts to creep between the hills. Black clouds have gathered above the puna on the rim of the horizon; lightning flashes in their darkness. Up there it is probably hailing, while I wilt in the heat. *Así es mi Perú.*

=== 42 ===

The whine of gearboxes and popping of exhaust remind me that market in Quinoa is over; I had better catch a ride back to the city. Halfway down the rocky trail from the ruins there is one of those curious votive rocks that one finds all over Peru—the wak'as so vigorously attacked by the early friars. But I can still make out a system of water channels carved into the living stone, and there is a basin about two feet deep, which holds a quantity of stagnant rainwater. While I am looking at this a herd of goats passes: a bustle of dry hooves driven by a ragged little girl, who stares at me, brows knit.

Two trucks, full even by Peruvian standards, ignore my wave. A third stops. The canasta above the cab has ten cramped figures in it, and there is a solid rank of youths astride the sides of the truck box. One calls out in Runasimi: "*Gringu! Maytam rinki?*" ("Where are you going?")

"*Ayakuchuman.*" The unexpected reply meets with approving laughter. I climb the ladder fitted to the vehicle's side like a fire escape, and, once up, see not an inch of empty space. But some girls make room for me on the edge. They are traveling with a woman in her early thirties, wrinkled by sun and good humor, the mother of eleven. These are her four eldest.

"Teach us some English insults," say the girls. I keep the selection as clean as possible, thinking the mother will not appreciate anything too risqué, but when I translate she says: "Hasn't English got anything stronger?"

The girls repay me in Runasimi and some bilingual carnival songs:

Huamangina religiosa,	Religious Huamanga girl,
No me lleves a la misa,	Don't take me to the mass,
Por qué no vamos a las Watatas?	Why don't we go down to the river Watata?
A bañarnos *qalasikis*.	And go swimming bare-arsed.

A jug of chicha starts, or rather continues, to circulate; before long I am in a state of empathy with the rest of the passengers, who have doubtless been drinking all day. The brew tastes like a mixture of ginger beer and sour milk. Questions:

"How much does it cost to fly to Canada?"

"Are you married?"

"Why not?"

"Watch out for her," a woman shouts, referring to the mother of eleven. "She's after you." (Laughter sweeps the truck.)

"No, I'm not! There's my husband over there." A shy man, to whom time has been kinder than to his wife, grins and shakes his head. More laughter.

"What were you doing at Wari?"

"Just looking. I'm an archaeologist."

"*Arqueólogo.* What's that?" The word is translated into Runasimi: *ñawpa pacha yachaq*—"person learned in ancient times."

"How old are the ruins?"

"More than a thousand years ago," I tell them, "Wari was the capital of Peru."

=== 43 ===

AYACUCHO (HUAMANGA)

In the late sixteenth century, a remarkable man received here the instruction in Spanish that would enable him to write the most significant chronicle of the Conquest and its implications. Felipe Guaman Poma de Ayala (or Waman Puma, a better spelling of his Runa name) was born at about the time of Inka Atau Wallpa's death. He grew up in the village of Suntuntu, not far from Huamanga, and came to the city to be educated—when already an adult—by his mestizo half-brother, a Franciscan, of whom he wrote:

> All his life he stayed with the poor in the hospital of the city of Huamanga, and made much penance and slept little . . . and had a cockerel as a clock . . . to wake him for prayers and for visiting the poor who were sick . . . and many birds came to sing to him in the morning to receive his blessing and the mice made themselves humble before him. . . .

There is something of Saint Francis himself in Waman Puma's portrait of his teacher, a "saintly hermit," who must have given the chronicler his profound belief in the Christian ideal. But the more Waman Puma came to understand of Christianity and the men who had brought it to his country, the more the Conquest seemed to him some ghastly cosmic mistake—a reversal of the natural order, which had to be put right. If it was true that the Spaniards had invaded the Tawantinsuyu to bring the word of the Son of God, why was it that this good news had been attended by nothing but destruction, suffering, and death? Christianity was, after all, a creed of reciprocity, of doing unto others, an ethic already inherent in Andean life, but the men who called themselves Christians—these *corregidores, encomenderos,* and renegade priests—knew only how to take; and they took from the Indians their country, their gods, their wealth, wives, and daughters, and in return gave the plagues that took the Indians' lives.

"To write is to weep," wrote Waman Puma; how could it be otherwise for a Runa who had somehow survived the Andean apocalypse? The Runasimi for "apocalypse" or "cataclysm" is *pachakuti,* "world reversal." Throughout his long and bitter account Waman Puma repeats the same refrain: "The world now is in reverse, and there is no remedy in this kingdom of Piru."

It took Waman Puma more than thirty years to write *The First New Chronicle and Good Government*. During this time (c. 1585–1615), he wandered the lonely broken roads of the Tawantinsuyu, working here and there as an interpreter, listening to the laments and stories of the increasingly few old Indians who remembered how things had been. Somehow he obtained ink, pens, and paper, and managed to preserve himself and his manuscript (which ran to almost 1,200 pages, including 450 drawings) through dangerous times—times that in another land saw William Shakespeare writing plays.

Waman Puma's work is more than a chronicle. It takes the form of a letter addressed to the Spanish emperor, informing the monarch of the history of Peru (and the world), of how the Tawantinsuyu was governed in the past, and how it should again be governed along Inca lines if order is ever to be restored. Much of the time Waman Puma is really talking to himself, trying to understand what has happened: From where has come this alien universe that is irrupting into his own? How can it be explained, understood, and above all, contained?

This extraordinary soliloquy, carried on in a Spanish just sufficiently grasped to be readable (and occasionally lapsing into Runasimi), but with a mind-set that is entirely Andean, gives Waman Puma's work tremendous significance. The inconsistencies, the bizarre restructuring of events and the startling anachronisms, are not, as was first thought, evidence of ignorance or mental disorder, but a window into a mind primarily educated in the pre-Columbian tradition—a mind organizing the catastrophic events and consequences of the invasion in the way in which the Incas tried to interpret them.

Space and time are a single, related concept in Runasimi, represented by one word, *pacha*, which can also mean "world" and "universe." The image of time familiar to Waman Puma was static and spatial: one could travel in time as one travels over the earth—the structure, the geography, remaining unchanged. To him it does not matter that he shows Inka Wayna Qhapaq, who died in 1525, talking to Spaniards, who did not arrive until 1532. Wayna Qhapaq was the last Inca to rule an undivided empire: *he* is therefore the archetype, and it must be he who asks the Spaniards, "Do you eat gold?"

In Andean thought both world and time were divided into four sectors or directions unified under a presiding fifth principle. The Tawantinsuyu— "the indivisible four quarters"—was united and presided over by Cusco, the center. Similarly, history was divided into four previous ages, presided over by a fifth, the present. In his book, Waman Puma organizes the history of both Old and New worlds according to this scheme. The Old Testament and the pre-Inca times are each divided into four equivalent and parallel ages. The "present" age in Peru begins with the appearance of Manku Qhapaq, the first

Inca, a being of supernatural origin. And in the Old World the "present" starts with the birth of Jesus Christ. Thus *The First New Chronicle*.

The second part of the work—*The Good Government*—departs into political philosophy as it seeks to impose Andean principles of order on a chaotic present and an inauspicious future. Waman Puma's lecture to the Spanish king is one of the most detailed and cogent rejections of colonialism ever written by a member of a conquered nation from within an indigenous world view.

> You should consider that all the world is of God, and that thus Castile is of the Spaniards, and the Indies [America] of the Indians, and Guinea [Africa] of the Negroes—that all these peoples are the lawful owners of their lands . . . so one Spaniard or another should not intrude on other nations, because they are Spaniards from Castile, and by the right and law of the Indians they are called *mitmaq Castillamanta samuq* [foreigners, those who come from Castile]. The Indians are the natural owners of this kingdom, and the Spaniards are the natural owners of Spain: each is the lawful proprietor in his own realm.

Waman Puma then goes on to restructure the whole greatly expanded world of which he has become aware into a new Tawantinsuyu—a world of four quarters in which Peru, Europe, Africa, and the East are each one suyu. And to ensure that his ideas are carried out:

> I offer, firstly, a son of mine, a great-nephew of Tupaq Inka Yupanki, as prince of this kingdom [Peru], and, secondly, a black prince in the kingdom of Guinea; thirdly, a king of the Christians of Rome [Europe], and fourthly, a king of the Moors of Grand Turkey—the four to be crowned with their scepters and robes; and in the middle of these four parts shall stand the Majesty and Monarch of the World, King Philip.

The "Monarch of the World" is to have symbolic and metaphysical power only: "The Monarch has no jurisdiction: he has beneath his hands the world." He is, in other words, a god-king—an idealized abstraction based on the concept of Inka as archetype, as divine and impartial protector of the world. Waman Puma is asking for self-government. His new world order is something akin to the modern British commonwealth, in which the monarch reigns but does not rule; the four suyus are to be governed by their "natural," that is, native, lords. And he goes even further, proposing to King Philip that those Spaniards whose presence in Peru is unavoidable (clerics, for example) be confined to their towns under a kind of apartheid, so that their vices and foreign ways will be unable to disrupt Runa society.

===

By his own account, Waman Puma was over eighty when he returned to Suntuntu after years of wandering. He found his village virtually abandoned, the houses in ruins, and the fields overgrown. Those few of his kin still alive neither recognized nor welcomed him. So, in the middle of the rains, he set out again—this time for Lima, where he hoped to find a traveler he could trust to carry his book to Spain.

The contents of Waman Puma's book, if understood, would probably have been about as well received in Castile as the writings of Che Guevera at the Reagan White House. But it seems likely that no high Spanish official ever saw *The First New Chronicle and Good Government.* The manuscript lay unknown and unread for three hundred years, until its discovery at the Royal Copenhagen Library in 1908.

=== *44* ===

The Apollo Restaurant, where I have been coming for breakfasts, is a place of gaudy wall hangings and high-volume disco music. The patrons are a mixture of middle-class Peruvians and what the *South American Handbook* calls "budget travelers," a hearty, hairy crowd, mostly German and French. But the fare is good by local standards: banana pancakes soaked in cane syrup, washed down with coca tea. Progress has discovered this ancient stimulant; the leaf—a sacred thing to Runa—now comes in a tissue tea-bag with a cardboard label attached.

There is one group of regulars who never touch hot beverages of any kind and seem to compensate for this by ordering extra helpings of syrup, which they eat with spoons. They are four young men, identically dressed in white shirts, dark ties, and slacks; all blond, crewcut and blue-eyed. (The Englishman with whom I share a table offers the opinion that they must be clones.) They have about them the humorless sincerity of missionaries or morticians.

===

At home I have a record of Peruvian music on which there is a magnificent harp solo. The accompanying notes say that the piece, recorded in 1964, is by Antonio Sulca, a blind harpist from Ayacucho.

I find him standing in a stone doorway with one of his young sons. They are selling kerosene from a large drum. He looks frail, though stockily built, and old beyond his years, which I guess at about sixty. His face bears the pockmarks of a childhood disease; opaque wraparound sunglasses hide the sightless eyes. His mouth seems heavy, expressionless, as if weighed down by habitual sadness.

"Are you Antonio Sulca, the harpist?"

"At your service, *señor*," he answers formally in Spanish, offering his hand in somewhat the wrong direction. His palm is gnarled and soaked with kerosene. I wonder if these hands can still play the intricate music I have heard on record.

Did he know, I ask, that in 1964 a gringo taped some of his music, and that one piece, a stately *harawi*, was released by Folkways of New York on an anthology of Peruvian mountain music?

"It could be, *señor*. Some *norteamericanos* have come here with tape recorders, but no one told me a record was made." Maybe he doesn't remember—it was, after all, many years ago—or perhaps, indeed, no one told him: Third World musicians have no union and hence, it seems, no copyright.

I explain my interest in Andean culture and ask if I could hear him play.

"If you can come back this afternoon I will play for you; you may bring a tape recorder if you wish."

Now, of course, I wish I'd brought a cassette machine from Canada. But I find it difficult to travel light as it is. My suitcase, containing camera, notebooks, camping equipment, and a minimum of clothes, already weighs sixty pounds. I spend the rest of the morning trying to borrow a tape recorder from fellow guests at the hotel. No luck. Then I remember the "clones."

One of them is having his shoes shined in the plaza by a barefoot boy. He has a bored expression and a handshake like a lobster's. He also has a small cassette machine and, after struggling with himself, agrees to lend it.

"We're with the Mormon Church, you know," he says. I profess surprise. He tells me something of his work: two months' crash course in Spanish at Salt Lake City, followed by knocking on doors and shaking hands in a country totally strange to him.

"We don't like tourists very much," he adds, looking at me with some distaste. "They make our mission so much more difficult."

"How come?"

"So dirty and immoral. They give the Peruvians such a bad impression of foreigners."

Returning to the Sulcas' shortly after two, I am admitted through heavy wooden doors to a patio cobbled with river pebbles. Inside are some chickens, a pig, two dogs, a well in the middle; barnyard smells. Barefoot children stare at the gringo.

Sulca takes me across the yard and into a lofty, windowless room with thick adobe walls and a brick floor smelling of damp. The peeling walls are pastel green; on them hang a mandolin, a violin, a cracked mirror, and an old calendar picture of a little (blond) girl clutching flowers. A cloth partition divides the family's sleeping quarters from this, their living room. Along the far wall, in the gloom, is a row of simple wooden chairs; against one of them leans a great harp, its mahogany belly gleaming like a new ship.

The old man feels his way to the harp, lifts its narrow end from the chair, and sits down. Caressing it lightly with the inquisitive touch of the blind, he shows me how it is designed and played. His instrument is a fine example of the Andean harp, thought to be derived from Castilian instruments of the sixteenth century, or perhaps from Celtic harps brought by Irish Jesuits. It has thirty-six strings and a very wide sound box, this a Peruvian modification, giving it the boatlike appearance and a powerful bass. The bass strings carry a separate part, often in a rhythm different from that of the melody but subtly related to it.

So far as anyone knows, the ancient Peruvians did not have stringed instruments but had developed a variety of flutes, panpipes, drums, and trumpets. By about 1600, they had added the harp and charango to their pre-Columbian repertoire; and during the Andean renaissance of the eighteenth century, violins and mandolins were also adopted. Though of European origin, these instruments are generally played on the ancient five-note (pentatonic) Peruvian scale. The resulting sound—if I am pressed for a comparison—is reminiscent of Celtic and Oriental music, with occasional flourishes inherited from the Spanish invaders.

While tuning, Señor Sulca begins to talk about his life. Blinded by smallpox when he was seven, he turned to the sense of hearing. Soon he was playing his brother's mandolin, and then a violin of his own. One day he heard a musician from one of the Runa ayllus of the Ayacucho hinterland:

"I liked the sound of that harp. I asked the harpist to teach me how to play. He was generous with his time. At first I repeated only what I heard; later I started composing waynos and harawis of my own. People called for me to play at fiestas, weddings, funerals, in their homes. Once I went to Lima and performed on the radio. That was when Velasco had the government.

"Have you heard of José María Arguedas, gringo? He used to come here, to this same house, to listen. He always spoke to me in Runasimi, like a brother. He used to call me Sonqo Suwa, which in our language means 'Stealer of the Heart,' and ever since I have performed under that name. Now they tell me he is dead."

Sulca falls silent, then begins to play. I recognize the solemn, formal notes of a harawi—melancholy, epic music that from Inca times has been played to lament departures, tragedy, and death. The piece is "Garsila," the same one that is on the Folkways record. His fingers have lost none of their skill over the years; if anything, there is a greater assurance, a deftness that has grown from skill to mastery.

A woman comes in and shuts the door. The darkness gives the music stature, something of the prominence it must have for Sonqo Suwa. The strong bass becomes palpable, more felt than heard; higher notes sparkle, each crystalline, a particle of light, a manipulation, as it were, of the thin sunbeams piercing the old door. The sunbeams are woven into intricate, fleeting structures in the mind, then begin falling in fanlike patterns as the rhythm quickens and the harawi is followed by its wayno fugue. The melancholy is mitigated but not altogether dispelled. There remains an edge of desperation to the dance: the despair of an old culture catching scent of death.

Kuka kintucha, kuka kintucha,	O coca leaf, choice coca,
Qamsi yachanki ñoqap vidayta;	You know my life and destiny;
Kay runaq llaqtampi waqallas- qayta,	How I wept in foreign parts,
Kay runaq llaqtampi llakillasqayta.	How I suffered in strange towns.
Mamallayqa wachakuwasqa,	My mother bore me,
Taytallayqa churillawasqa,	And my father begot me,
Para puyupi chawpichallampi,	In the middle of the rainclouds,
Para hina waqanallaypaq;	So I would weep like the rain;
Para puyupi chawpichallampi,	In the middle of the storm,
Puyu hina muyunallaypaq.	So I would wander like the clouds.

PONTÍFICAL
MVNDO

las yñs del piru
en lo alto de espana

cuzco

castilla en lo auajo
de las yñs

castilla

en este

1. "Pontifical World. The Indies of Peru above Spain. Castile below the Indies."

Waman Puma's conception of the relationship between Peru and Spain according to the Andean duality principle of Hanan (Upper) and Hurin (Lower). Each country is shown as a Tawantinsuyu—four quarters with a capital in the center. Peru is higher, closer to the sun, and therefore full of gold, the "sweat of the sun."

AGOSTO
CHACRAIAPVI
quilla

tiempo de la braussa – hayllin mi ynca –

hacca

2. Inca communal agriculture. In August, *Chakra Yapuy Killa* (Month of Plowing the Fields), teams of men turn the sod with the *chaki-taklla*, foot-plow. Women break up the clods. Those unable to work supply the others with beer and food. The work is accompanied by uplifting *haylli* songs.

GOVERNADOR DE LOS PVENTES DESTER.no
CHACASVIOIOGACOSIVGA
GVAMBOCHACA

vedor de puentes   puentes

3. "Chaka Suyuyoq, governor of the bridges of this realm."

An important member of the Inca bureaucracy.

4. "Wayna Qhapaq Inka:
Kay qoritachu mikhunki?
('Do you eat this gold?')

Candía the Spaniard:
Este oro comemos!
('We eat this gold!')"

Economic incompatibility. Gold
to the Incas was a sacred substance, "the sweat of the sun,"
with no monetary value.
Waman Puma shows their won-
derment at the Spaniards' consuming desire for it.

*"Inka Wana-
kauri
Maytam rinki?*

*Sapra auqan-
chikchu
Mana hucha-
yoqta
Kunkaykita
kuchun."*

"Inca Wana-
kauri
Where are you
going?
Our evil bearded
enemies
Are cutting

Your innocent
neck."

Tupaq Amaru I is beheaded in
Cusco. Below the scaffold a
group of Inca mourners sings a
lament.

HIJO DE LOS P DOTRI

nantes mesticillos y mesticulas
lo lleua un harriero es pañol
alquilado a las ciudades delos
rruys delima me dia do
zena deninos lo lleua

6. "Children of the doctrinal priests—little mestizos and mestizas. A mule driver is taking them to Lima. He is carrying half a dozen children."

———

Priestly miscegenation.

FRAILE MERZENARIO VA

son tan brabos y jus ticieros y mal
drabalos yns y hazetra ubjar cõ
un palo en los trines y no en las do
trinas no agoue
me dio

7. "The mercenary friars are so ill-humored and demanding; they mistreat the Indians and make them work with the stick. In the doctrinal settlements of this kingdom there is no remedy."

———

The friars operated the *obrajes*, sweatshops for the production of cloth.

8. "The poor Indian parents defend their daughter from the Spaniard."

A Spaniard seizes an adolescent girl from her parents.

9. "Don Philip III, king and monarch of the world. Ayala, the author, personally presents the Chronicle to Your Majesty. Your Majesty asks questions, the author responds."

Waman Puma imagines himself presenting his book to the Spanish king.

10. View across the Ollantaytambo valley from the Inca ruins. Note terracing of valley floor and lower slopes. The ancient quarries are on the mountainside at top right in background.

11. The polygonal masonry increases in scale as one climbs the terraces of Ollantaytambo. Enormous stones, still on their working platforms, can be seen directly above the main door. The wall of six megaliths is visible in profile at top right.

12. Ollantaytambo: detail of niche in the back wall of what was once a corridorlike building on the fourth terrace.

13. Ollantaytambo: the monumental door. The two upper stones, displaced long ago, have been restored flush with the wall since this photograph was taken.

14. The Cumbe Mayo aqueduct near Cajamarca.

15. *Ch'ullpa*, or funerary tower, at Oxamarca.

16. Saywite: boulder carved with zoomorphic and architectural figures.

17. Raqchi: the temple of Wiraqocha.

18. Cusco: curved wall of the Qorikancha.

19. The terraces of Saqsaywaman seen from Suchuna hill.

20. The author at Saqsaywaman.

21. Kusilloq Hink'inan, the Monkey's Perch, on Suchuna hill.

22. The *mixto*, near Huánuco.

23. Antonio Sulca and harp. Mermaids are a common motif in the folk art of Ayacucho.

24. Girls from a Runa village near Ollantaytambo.

25. Maiden of Inca times, drawn by Waman Puma. In parts of the Andes the dress of women has changed little in four hundred years.

QVINTA CALLE
CIPASCONA

26. Cusco: the church of La Compañía, built on the site of the Amarukancha.

27. Cusco: Hatun Rumiyoq Street.

28. The masonry of Hatun Rumiyoq.

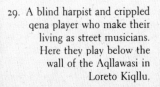

29. A blind harpist and crippled qena player who make their living as street musicians. Here they play below the wall of the Aqllawasi in Loreto Kiqllu.

30. The main building at Huchuy Qosqo. Ground level was originally some four feet lower than at present. The building is remarkable for preservation of an upper story of Inca adobe, which was almost certainly painted in a variety of colors and motifs.

31. Entering Machu Piqchu by the Inca road (visible at left foreground).

This morning there is a white Land-Rover with British license plates parked outside the Apollo. Two gringos nod at me as I enter the restaurant. The one facing me has unruly red hair, a matching beard thin and long like a goat's, and the mischievous eyes of an extrovert. The other is older, mid-thirties, dark, clean-cut; intent on a pancake.

"Is that your car outside?"

"No, it's 'is." The redhead points at the pancake-eater.

"Must be a nice way to travel."

"It is when it doesn't give you problems," says the owner with his mouth full. Richard bought his car in England, drove it through Africa, shipped it to Buenos Aires, and is now making his way north. Howard, the redhead, is a paying rider, an Australian heading south.

"I met Richard 'ere in Lima. He'd come up from Chile. I said, 'You can't leave Peru without seeing Cusco and Machu Piqchu,' so I talked him into a side trip an' taking me along."

I decide to be brazen and ask if they've room for a third paying passenger. Richard is hesitant: the car is rather full. But my tent is the clincher. (There is room for only one person to sleep in the car; Howard has been enduring what he calls "brass monkey" conditions under a piece of plastic.)

11:00 A.M.

Richard stops for gas at a filling station on the edge of town and checks everything: oil, water, tire pressure, including the two spares. The road has already risen above the city to reveal a panorama of sagging tiled roofs and never-quite-straight adobe walls. The hills beyond are milky and amber, darkening to purple in the distance. The late-morning sun is hot; no breath of wind disturbs the flicker dancing here and there above a metal roof.

At the roadside control, the young policeman is deep in a magazine with flashes of pink on its cover. A radio pulses with a modern wayno.

Empresachallay Felix Barbarán,	Bus line Felix Barbarán,
Apurachawta, aparullaway.	Hurry! Carry me quickly.
Warma yanaysi suyallawachkan	They say my lover waits for me
Ayakuchulla kuntrulchallapi.	At the Ayacucho checkpoint.

We climb steadily all morning, at first gradually, then up to the puna by a road like a flattened corkscrew. The Ayacucho basin is now nothing but a small, pale navel in a body of military green. Rain turns to sleet at the junction with the road to Puquio via the Inca ruins of Willkaswaman. I would like to make this detour, but some Runa huddled in a shelter say the road is bad; Richard decides they are probably not exaggerating.

We are now following the route taken by Squier more than a century ago, but in the opposite direction. E. George Squier was in the great nineteenth-century tradition of traveler, amateur archaeologist, and amateur diplomat. His excavations of Mississippi earthworks were published in the first monograph of the fledgling Smithsonian in 1848. Prescott's *History of the Conquest of Peru* had come out the year before, and it sparked in Squier a longing to visit that mysterious and almost unknown land which Prescott himself had never seen. The two men were already friends, and shared the affliction of failing sight. Through Prescott's influence, Squier obtained diplomatic commissions to Central America and Peru. These provided him with the backing for his archaeological treks. He was almost blind when he arrived at Callao harbor in 1863, but the undemanding schedule of a diplomat in Lima gave him the rest cure prescribed by his doctor. Before long Squier was enjoying "glimpses of dark eyes and ivory shoulders" behind the shutters of the house across the street.

Having discharged his commissions (about which he remains diplomatically vague), he set out on a prodigious tour, accompanied by an artist, a surveyor, and some rascally muleteers. His route took him down the coast to Arica (then still part of Peru), and up over the cordillera to the Bolivian altiplano. There he examined the ruins of ancient—and modern—Tiawanaku. (In the cemetery Squier surprised a pack of dogs devouring the fresh corpse of a child; when, outraged, he remonstrated with the priest, the cleric replied: "What does it matter? They are only Indians.") He then worked his way north to Cusco, where he spent several months, and from there returned to Lima via Ayacucho on a mule trail that cannot have differed much from the course of the present road.

The shelter of stones and ichu at the Puquio turn-off may well be a rare relic of the *tampu* (*tambo*) system, a network of posthouses that still functioned in a reduced way when Squier was traveling. The Incas had built tampus a day's journey apart on every road to provide lodging, food, and llama fodder for all travelers on official business (about the only business there was). The colonial and republican governments made inadequate efforts to keep the system working, and Squier found the posthouses few, filthy, and staffed (if at all) by drunken officials who laughed in his face whenever he produced his documents from the government in Lima. After wasting several days fruitlessly haggling with such functionaries for mules, he wrote:

> The influence of Spain in Peru has been in every way deleterious: the civilization of the country was far higher before the Conquest than now. The modern voyager would consider himself supremely fortunate were he to find one in a hundred of these tambos still in existence.

2:00 P.M.

The sleet hardened into a brief flurry of hail. Now a fierce sun appears and quickly changes the puna from white to green as the frosting transpires in the thin air. Great herds of llama and alpaca outnumber the flocks of bedraggled sheep. Occasionally one sees a Runa woman, conspicuous in a loud pink jumper, alone on a crag watching her animals, or perhaps lost in contemplation of the landscape, but always spinning—dropping the spindle, catching it up, dropping, without a thought.

4:00 P.M.

The Land-Rover climbs breathlessly in second gear toward the sixteen-thousand-foot pass between this watershed and the next. Puna gives rise to a country of black shale escarpments encrusted with snow, dull under a battleship sky. Perceived through senses awry with altitude, this colorless world becomes sinister and prone to sudden reversals of light and perspective, as though we are wandering in a three-dimensional photographic negative.

At the very crest of the pass there is an *apachita*, a cairn built up over centuries by travelers. All Runa who pass it add a stone and a wad of chewed coca leaves, symbols of the fatigue left behind and offerings to the Wamani, the spirit guardian of the place.

The descent comes into view, and opposite us ice-topped peaks stretch across the horizon like a row of worn teeth in a cracked and blackened jaw. Below, on the road ahead, four trucks listing under their loads are vainly trying to pull one another out of slush and mud left by a recent snowstorm. Richard clicks the Land-Rover into four-wheel drive. We fishtail between the stranded hulks whose names are: Valentina, Tupac Amaru, Heart of Jesus, and My Destiny.

= 46 =

Last night Richard cooked. Richard doesn't delegate cooking any more than driving: "I know this stove, it's tricky at altitude."

It must have been almost fifteen thousand feet where we camped. (Richard likes to choose desolate locations away from settlements: he can't stand the crowd of onlookers that would otherwise gather to observe gringos.) Boiling chocolate was not too hot to drink immediately, and my goosedown sleeping bag was chilly because there was insufficient air to give the fibers a good "loft."

Somewhere in the small hours the chocolate forced me outside. The cold was so bitter I remembered old Canadian tales of urine freezing before it hits the ground. But the night sky was the finest of my life. There was no darkness, only a mass of steadily burning stars, receding into space, yet distinct as particles of dust caught in a sunbeam. The Milky Way flowed opulently from horizon to horizon, worthy of its Inca name, Mayu, the River. On such a cloak of stars one can see the "negative" constellations that the Incas recognized—dark patches of cosmic dust such as Yana Llama, the Black Llama (called by us, prosaically, the Coal Sack), with his two shiny eyes, Llamaq Ñawin, a pair of stars in the Southern Cross.

===

This morning we scrape ice from the tent, but as soon as the sun reaches camp the day warms quickly. No wonder the Incas worshipped the sun: the thin atmosphere of these highlands holds little warmth. Even at midday one feels a chill when entering a shadow or when a cloud hides the face of Inti. The Incas' idea of hell was a sunless altiplano where there was nothing to eat but stones.

Down from the puna and through the small town of Ocros, where Squier found the tambo "alive with fleas innumerable." Then another climb before beginning the long descent to the Río Pampas. We cross this river on a metal bridge, which has replaced the forty-five-yard suspension span of Inca design that was the only crossing in 1865.

Here in the Pampas canyon we are ten thousand feet lower than yesterday's high pass. It is semitropical, but arid; the air hangs stifling between sedimentary cliffs sparsely covered in cactus and thorns. There are some stony groves of fruit trees along the bank; we buy fresh oranges and avocados.

I am not feeling well when we stop for lunch. While the others are getting water from the river I experience a sudden disorientation, sit down, and begin to sway from side to side. Then I notice the Land-Rover rocking on its springs. An earth tremor. (Contrary to popular belief, it does not give me an erection.)

Three thousand feet above the river the mountainsides become wetter again, watered by the clouds that sail down the valley at dusk and dawn. The people here have forgotten how to make even the rudest terrace: cultivated clearings are so steep that a careless move while hoeing could easily tumble the farmer from his field.

———

Next day: another puna dotted with grazing llamas and their owners' scattered hovels—casts of red earth beneath untidy scalps of ichu. At noon we descend to Andahuaylas, a town of one long street cupped in a bowl of nibbled slopes and eucalyptus. The tall "gums" remind Howard of home.

At the edge of town there stands an old adobe church with sloped-in walls like those of Inca buildings. The door is bolted and has the appearance of being seldom otherwise.

Antawaylas ksurañataq	The priest of Andahuaylas
Kasarakuy niwaskasqan,	Keeps telling me to get married,
Icha yachan, icha manam	Maybe he knows, maybe not,
Ch'isi tuta purisqayta.	Where I went last night.
Sakristanta maskachkani	I'm looking for the sexton
Chakin makin pakinallaypaq,	To break his hands and feet,
Warma yanallay kasarakuqtin	Because when my beloved wed another,
Amen, amen nisqanmanta.	He said: Amen, amen.

═══ *47* ═══

ANDAHUAYLAS

The birthplace of José María Arguedas: had we not walked the main street looking for supplies, we might have missed the small tarnished plaque. What led him from birth here, in 1911, through a distinguished career as novelist and anthropologist, to suicide in Lima in 1969? Some have looked for the answer in his childhood.

José María was three when his mother died, and he was left in the care of an Indian woman while his father moved to Puquio to become the district judge. The boy grew very attached to his foster mother, whom he called Mamita. She gave him the unsentimental tenderness of the Runa, Runasimi, and a mystical understanding of the world. His father remarried and sent for José María three years later. The white boy with chestnut hair had become a Runa inside: he did not like his stepmother and stepbrothers, and they did not like him; they threw soup in his face and made him eat in the kitchen with the servants.

At age twelve he ran away from the judge's household to his grandmother's farm. There he had to work in the fields with the Runa peons, but he enjoyed that, and participated in their rituals and fiestas. He had none of the graces or appetites of criollo adolescents: while his stepbrothers were out serenading señoritas with masturbatory rhythms on their Spanish guitars, José María sat in verminous huts listening to the ancient music of the Andes.

His grandmother taught him to read and write and soon recognized his exceptional intelligence, for the boy consumed book after book, making up for his lack of schooling and acquiring a remarkable command of Spanish. But he still wrote letters in Runasimi to his Mamita in Andahuaylas—a neighbor read them to her and wrote down her replies. She was José María's only real parent and he kept in touch with her until her death.

Arguedas went on to secondary school, a job in the Lima Post Office, and a university career. He fell in with a group of radicals who frequented the Café Romano and read Mariátegui's *Amauta*. Though never doctrinaire, Arguedas became strongly anti-fascist; he earned himself a jail term by helping to dunk one of Mussolini's generals in a water trough when the Italian made an ill-advised visit to Lima University.

After release from prison, Arguedas kept a low profile as a schoolteacher in the southern sierra. There he worked on *Yawar Fiesta*, his first novel, which is set in Puquio. On the first page he establishes the dichotomy between the town of the criollos around the plaza and the surrounding Runa Puquio of four ayllus. Later, in scholarly articles, he showed how much of the social structure of Inca Cusco survives in the four-part division of that town.

Unlike other indigenista writers, Arguedas had lived in both Runa and criollo worlds, and they appear equally real in his books. If anything, the native characters are the more skillfully drawn. His flawed childhood gave him unusual insight into the divided self of Peru; but this insight was to cost him his own equilibrium and ultimately destroy him.

His Mamita had given him the sensitivity of the Runa but not the defenses. He had been too young to put on that insulating mask which the non-Indian sees as sullenness or stupidity. All his life sadness and joy would move Arguedas to uncontrollable tears. Simple chores of living sometimes became terrible obstacles. Sleep was often impossible, and he would wander for hours in the middle of the night. Like a Runa, he loved the nonhuman world and talked to animals as if they were people (something hispanic Peruvians generally do not); but the sound of dogs barking in the street could send him into a nervous state, unable to write. And that was the worst, because writing was the only effective catharsis.

Hawan kallipis allqulla allwachkan,	Out in the street a dog is howling,
Kurria warmacha qhawaykamunki.	Run, little one, go and see.
Ch'isi tutalla musqoychallaypi	Last night in my dreams
Yawar qochapi nadallachkasqani.	I swam in a lake of blood.

There is much of Waman Puma in Arguedas. The Indian who learned Spanish, the criollo who grew up Indian: both spent melancholy lives trying to understand and reconcile the Peruvian dichotomy. For Arguedas, as for Waman Puma, to write was to weep.

48

We have made good time today. By noon we are in sight of Abancay, the last town of any size before Cusco. In sight, that is, from a puna bluff five thousand feet above the settlement. A tiny web of streets describes a regular pattern on the far bank of the Antabamba River. To the south, east, and west, mountains rise as far above us as Abancay lies below.

A white Mercedes van approaches from the pass, curiously silent. It coasts to a halt behind the Land-Rover. The number plate is German, and, as if that were insufficient proclamation of the vehicle's ethnicity, above the windshield is written in Gothic script: PANZER.

"Can you help us please? We are coming down off the pass, I hit a bump and there is this terrible sound. I look and I see the radiator is falling on the fan." The forlorn owners of Panzer are Dieter, who looks more like a French chef than a German—swept-back hair, trim goatee, white trousers—and his wife, Inge, dark and frauish. Dieter opens the hood with the air of a policeman asking us to identify a body. The radiator has a circular gash through several of its coils, and the cast aluminum fan has lost all its blades but one.

"Maybe if we take the pieces to Abancay they can do something there?" Dieter asks. Richard is silent for rather too long.

———

The mechanic at the only garage examines the radiator and mutters "*Difícil.*" He suggests we try the stove mender.

REPARACION DE PRIMUS is painted in childish red letters above the door of a small dark workshop. Inside there is no furniture, not even a bench, and no equipment except a hacksaw, three spanners, a bellows, a pile of charcoal, and an old-fashioned soldering iron. Carcasses of stoves are scattered about like the remains of some ghoulish robots' feast. An acrid taste of burning charcoal rises from a hearth in the middle of the floor. The laconic young primus expert reaches for his bellows and tells us to come back in an hour. He points out an adobe hut on the hillside where he says a Señor Barrios will be able to help us with the fan.

Barrios's establishment is part scrap heap, part barnyard. A large sow is nursing her young in the cab of a Dodge truck circa 1950, the most recent hulk in his collection. Barrios is a stout mestizo with an entrepreneurial eye; he beckons us into the tumbledown hut, which is filled, to my utter surprise, by a gleaming lathe.

"How on earth did you get that up here?"

"On a truck." (It looks far too heavy for the small lorries that can negotiate the mountain roads.)

"And how did you unload it?"

"*Con muchos indios.*"

He looks at Dieter's handful of fragments, goes outside to a junk pile, pulls out a fan: "Thirty-eight Ford. I can make it fit."

Back to the hut, where there is also a drill press: a few new holes (using the broken pieces as a template), and *voilà.*

"Fifteen dollars, please."

Back at the primus shop we find the radiator propped against the wall, holding water. The repair is elegant: all the damaged fins have been neatly cut away and the broken coils sealed with caps of solder. The charge is three dollars—labor comes far cheaper than parts.

It is dark when we get back to our eyrie. After a celebratory bottle of Dieter's pisco, Howard wants to know: "How come your van's called Panzer?"

"Ah. Everyone is asking that. A few years ago we drove through Cambodia, and we got caught in some shelling—we want to see Angkor Wat but the war got there first—we survive so we call her Panzer, which just means in German 'tank.' But some people have other ideas: when we crossed into Ecuador from Colombia, the border guards gave us the Nazi salute!"

===

It rained heavily in the night. Howard, on the lower side of the tent, awoke in a pool of water. The rain ceases just before dawn; we get up with first light.

The cloud has dropped no more than a few yards below our level; it hides everything beneath, stretches like an ocean to the horizon; mountains rear from it like volcanic islands. A wispy surf breaks almost at our feet; one feels capable of walking across it to the rising sun. But the sun, in climbing, changes the ocean to smoke and fire.

=== 49 ===

ABANCAY

Here Arguedas set his equivalent of Joyce's *Portrait*, that is to say, *Los Rios Profundos*, an account of growing up in a Catholic boarding school, of how the narrator's young personality is deformed by the social and cultural conflicts of Peru. Arguedas chose an exile different from that of Stephen Dedalus, an exile alternating between the two mutually exclusive nations inhabiting the geography of his country and his soul.

But we are here today for supplies. Richard has offended a shop proprietress by asking *"Tiene huevos?"* ("Have you got eggs?") I explain that for such a request one must use the impersonal construction *hay* (are there): "eggs" is the Spanish equivalent of "balls."

Unabashed, Richard asks for meat and is shown a tin of Paraguayan corned beef that has obviously been rusting on the top shelf for years.

"I'd rather go hungry than eat that stuff," he says. "One time in Africa I bought a can like that. There was a big gob of white fat on top of the meat inside; I was just going to flick it off with my fork when it got up and walked away—some kind of worm, don't ask me how it got there."

A man in the store volunteers that a cow is about to be butchered at the far end of town in the new slaughterhouse.

===

It is an easy place to find. Women are waiting outside with baskets; small boys are craning to see into the glassless windows. They are shooed away, but soon slink back with the stray dogs, who also know that bloodshed is afoot. The place is indeed new: there is as yet no roof, and the tops of the mud walls are protected from rain by maguey leaves laid like Spanish tile.

Two men are sitting on a cow; a third is sharpening a long kitchen knife on a stone. The cow is bawling, its eye wild with terror.

"*Larguense!*" The man with the knife threatens the boys, who scatter once again. Then, like an inexperienced matador, he begins stabbing the cow at the base of the neck. At last he finds the exact spot between the vertebrae, and the knife sinks to the hilt. The animal shudders once and is still. Blood flows into runnels in the floor from its open mouth.

Richard says, "It'll be quite a while before they get this cut up into steaks." And so, meatless, we leave Abancay.

=== 50 ===

SAYWITE

Two hours from Abancay are some of the most extraordinary monuments in Peru: the Saywite Stones. They sit on a mountain saddle, a raft of flat land tossed high in the vertical landscape. Even now, overgrown with thickets of yellow broom, red heather, thorns, and bamboo, the spot has not lost the quality of a sacred garden. The slopes still ripple with contours of ancient terracing, and in the clefts water still trickles through the silted remains of baths, channels, and fountains.

But the stones: no description can convey the otherworldly charm of these two carved boulders. They seem like sculpted asteroids fallen intact upon the earth. The larger stone, beside which Richard parks, is about twice the size of the Land-Rover. Its decoration is entirely geometrical: planes, curved surfaces, and two stairways side by side, the one too big for human feet, the other too small. A system of water channels originates in stone basins on the flat top. Grooves run from these basins down the side and bifurcate twice, ending in an upper and a lower pair of cups cut into the side of the rock. This layout, with its four-part division, could be a model of an irrigation system or a Runa community, or a device for divination in which the course followed by a liquid (blood? beer?) is taken as an augury. Most likely it comprises all three ideas and others, now unknown, besides. The two pairs of cups perhaps illustrate yet another principle of Andean order in space and time: the division into *hanan* (upper) and *hurin* (lower) halves, or moieties. It probably has its origins in the geographical facts of life in Peru—hanan groups are the first to receive the irrigation water that runs through their land. Powerful social constraints must be imposed to ensure that hurin people, living lower down, get their share of the life-giving fluid. The two groups therefore intermarry. But the duality extends far beyond the practical to form a structure of symbolic order as fundamental as the Chinese *yin* and *yang*: the Andes are hanan in relation to the coast and jungle; the present is hanan in relation to the past; male is hanan, female hurin; and so on. Lower does not necessarily mean inferior; the Creator, Wiraqocha, is hurin because of his association with water, while Inti, the Sun, created by Wiraqocha, is hanan because of his association with light and heat. (To Waman Puma, the Spaniards were hurin and the Incas hanan; when he wrote that the world was "upside down" he meant it quite literally: the triumph of Spain, ruling from Lima on the coast, over Cusco was a reversal of cosmic order.)

Appropriately, perhaps, the great boulder has now cracked in two, along the line of a cavity in the back originally closed with a stone slab. The cynical Squier decided this was where an oracle dwelt in the form of "thirsty priests . . . imposing on the credulity" of the worshippers and quaffing the libations of beer poured into the basins. More likely it was the tomb of a mummified ancestor.

The other Saywite stone, several hundred yards from the first, presents a very different character. The boulder is approximately spherical, some twelve feet in diameter, and sits on low terraces, which also support the remains of a small temple. The stone's lower hemisphere is smooth except for protruding knobs around the equator. These, before they were defaced by zealot friars, were probably puma heads. The upper hemisphere is richly carved in high relief—an extraordinary collage of animal figures, platforms, terraces, and miniature buildings. Throughout the zoomorphic and architectural fantasy runs a system of tiny channels, far more complex than the layout on the larger stone. The carvings are well preserved except for the faces, smashed long ago in the extirpations of "idolatry." Most can still be recognized as pumas, lizards, monkeys, and snakes.

Was this, as some have suggested, the model of a province? And do the figures represent the totems of ayllus living there? Or are they perhaps models of constellations on the celestial vault? Recent studies of ancient Cusco's social organization suggest that all these speculations may be valid: heaven, earth, and human communities were all articulated in an intricate symbolic order.

Saywite, at any rate, was the abode of an important wak'a or wak'as. There are modern traditions linking the place to the appearance of Our Lord of Pampamarca—ostensibly a manifestation of Christ but, like all foci of Andean pilgrimage cults, an ancient deity thinly Catholicized. It is said that the

Pampamarca Lord was found by a little girl while he was resting under a bush at Saywite. He looked like a *wiraqocha* (a god or white man), wearing silver sandals and sweating blood. Twice the priest and people of Pampamarca hauled the wiraqocha to their church, and twice he escaped and returned to the bushes at Saywite. Only after a third and more magnificent procession was the recalcitrant "Christ" persuaded to remain in Pampamarca as its Lord. Perhaps also relevant to the Saywite Stones is the legend that one of the Lord of Pampamarca's four "brothers," the Lord of Huanca, *turned to stone* while trying to escape from a zealous congregation intent on capturing him for installation in their church. What is claimed to be his petrified image is still venerated at the great rock of Huanca, from beneath which issue four springs credited with miraculous powers.

The Spaniards' evangelization of the Andes was a failure: they imposed a nominal Christianity that was co-opted by Andean belief as surely (perhaps more so) as Christ's original message had become distorted by the pagan creeds of Rome and Europe. The religious landscape of the Andes is still a country of supernatural rocks, springs, and huacas. Even the depiction of these Lords as white men is not of Spanish origin. Wiraqocha, the Creator, was associated with white for several reasons: white is the color of water, the foam of the sea (which is what wiraqocha literally means), fat, Mayu (the celestial river), spittle, and semen—all symbols of the life force. The belief of course gave the first Spaniards some psychological advantage, and they played up to it by making images of Christ that show him as a blond, blue-eyed gringo.

=== *51* ===

From Saywite our road drops quickly to the Apurimaq, Great Speaker or Lord Oracle, the grandest river of highland Peru. The name reflects the river's status as a powerful wak'a, and the fact that in the wet season its voice can be heard for miles.

We enter the gorge early, having spent the night on the heights. The configuration of the mountains produces dramatic variations in sunlight and rainfall: one side of the canyon is lush with grasses, shrubs, and flowers, but opposite there is only a waste of gray stone and tubular cactus. Vertical strata of harder rock protrude like ancient fortifications from the canyon walls and cast long shadows in the morning sun. Downstream, distant ranges recede behind curtains of haze hiding inaccessible Willkapampa, the land of the Neo-Inca state.

In the Incas' early days the Apurimaq was the natural boundary between Cusco's domains and those of the Chanka confederacy, a remnant of the Wari Empire. The two rising states clashed early in the fifteenth century; Inka Pachakuti was victorious and won the Chanka to his scheme of empire. He flung the greatest of the Peruvian suspension bridges across the chasm, and began the furious expansion that would take his descendants to triumph in Quito and nemesis in Cajamarca. The arterial road that followed the conquests became, ironically, the route by which the "wiraqochas" struck at the Tawantinsuyu's heart. The Spaniards arrived here in early November to find the bridge burned, but the Apurimaq, normally impassable, failed the Incas in their time of need: the year 1533 was uncommonly dry, the Speaker's voice had fallen to a murmur, and the white men forded on horseback.

This year there have been early rains; as we stop on the new concrete bridge we must shout to be heard above the roar and the eerie booming of large stones swept along with the current. These surface from time to time, glistening like the backs of porpoises.

The remains of the old *chaka*—better known to the world as the Bridge of San Luís Rey—are disappointing: some crudely mortared nineteenth-century abutments seem to have smothered whatever there may be of Inca work. The first Europeans to see the bridge described how it was made of henequen fiber ropes, braided like a woman's plaits and as thick as the body of a man. Three main cables formed the floor, two slighter ones the balustrades. The five were joined by smaller ropes and rawhide straps, and the floor was surfaced with wooden planks. Estimates of the span vary; Squier gives a figure of 148 feet with a further 40 feet of cable buried in rock at either end.

Under Inca rule, the Chaka Kamayoq (Overseer of Bridges) saw that the cables were renewed every two years. Several local ayllus fulfilled their mit'a obligations by making and installing them. The materials were provided by the state. After the Conquest, the maintenance of bridges grew more onerous as time went by. Like most of the Indians' tributes, the task remained the same (or increased) while the population and economic base declined. And the materials now had to come from the ayllus' own land. Waman Puma exhorted the Spanish king to build more bridges of stone and lime "because then it is done and finished in one go . . . a great mercy to the poor Indians." But no permanent structure replaced the Apurimaq chaka until 1890. Meanwhile its state of repair became unpredictable. When Squier crossed, the whole thing was sagging ominously to one side and the main ropes were only four inches thick.

Several times during the colonial period the great bridge broke. Around one such disaster Thornton Wilder wrote *The Bridge of San Luis Rey*, a novel set (with much geographical and historical license) in eighteenth-century Peru. The story, very briefly, is as follows:

Brother Juniper, a philosophical Franciscan, stops to rest before crossing the bridge and is thus saved from death. He hears a terrible rending twang as the chaka lets go and propels the antlike figures of his five traveling companions to the river hundreds of feet below. *Why those five?* he asks himself. What have they done with their lives to merit that?

And so the pious and ingenuous monk, seeking proof of the wisdom in divine purpose with which to impress his Indians, compiles a book of information on the lives of the victims. (Two of them, it turns out, are the mentor and the bastard son of La Perricholi, the "Chola Bitch" from Huánuco who for a time was the greatest actress in Spanish America, and the mistress of the elderly, but sprightly, Viceroy Amat.)

Like any competent theologian, Brother Juniper concludes that the wicked of the group have received their just deserts, while the good have been rewarded with an early call to Paradise. Brother Juniper is himself rewarded for his inquiry into the ways of the Almighty: he and his book are declared heretical, and both are burned by the Inquisition.

———

Though he could not have read Wilder's tale (published in 1927), Squier's artist had heard enough about the Apurimaq chaka to inspire in him the greatest dread of crossing it. Being a strong swimmer he decided to make his own passage at a calm spot in the river farther downstream. Squier lent him an "India rubber life preserver" and arranged to meet him in a tambo near Saywite. And that was the last he saw of the artist, despite days of frantic searching.

Months later, back in the States, Squier received news of the man's fate. It appeared that crossing the river had been easy; in fact the water was so delightful that the swimmer left his clothes on a rock and enjoyed a longer dip. While he was doing so a sudden wind gust blew his things into the water. He dived several times, looking especially for his shoes, but only succeeded in bruising himself on the rocks before crawling ashore "naked as our father Adam."

Poor Mr. H (as Squier coyly identifies him) wandered for three days in search of human habitation. The ravine was virtually unpopulated because its hot climate was conducive to fevers, which the few inhabitants conceived as malevolent beings of whom they lived in constant fear. The artist became terribly blistered by the sun, scratched by thorns, and bitten by venomous flies. When at last he did find an occupied hut, the Indians panicked and began pelting him with stones, in the belief that "the dreaded fever had made its palpable appearance."

The letter with the news concluded thus: "I venture the prediction that Mr. H will never again flinch from the imaginary dangers of the swinging bridges of Peru."

═══

Lunch at Rimaq Tampu, Oracle Tambo, now a ruin. Here five Spaniards were killed in a skirmish with one of Atau Wallpa's generals before their entry to the capital. The walls of the palatial building are well preserved: a regal flight of terraces constructed in the exquisite "cellular" style of Inca masonry, which looks like capped honeycomb.

Beyond Rimaq Tampu we cross the swamp of Anta on a twenty-foot-wide stone causeway, made for the feet of men and llamas, but capable of carrying regular motor traffic despite the fact that it seems to have received little upkeep since the Incas built it.

═══ *52* ═══

Cusco, 11,500 feet

Howard and Richard have left to camp on the hills, and from there they plan first to visit the Holy Valley and Machu Piqchu. I am deliciously alone in the streets of my personal Mecca. Nothing evokes the memory like smell and sound: dusk is upon the city and the eye rests while odors of street cooking, eucalyptus smoke, and urine pissed against old stones remind me I am here. Shrunken in a doorway, a blind man plucks a tune I recognize from a cracked mandolin; I can scarcely hear him above the rush-hour buses taking people home from the main plaza:

Valicha lisa p'asñawan,	Where will you now find,
Ñañachay deveras,	Little sister of mine,
Mayñas tupanki?	That naughty wench Valicha?
Qosqo uraytañacha,	She's already down in Cusco,
Ñañachay deveras,	Little sister indeed,
Maqtata suwasian.	Stealing young men away.

So many tourists, so many more than I remember. As the Peruvians go home, foreigners take possession of the city's core. Raucous English, French, and German replace the burr of Spanish, the muttered lilt of Runasimi. Even in Cusco Runa speak furtively, apologetically, as if their language were not official but still under the viceregal interdict. Those natives who remain display bronze knickknacks, weavings, and "Inca" pottery in the colonnades around the plaza. Tourists are haggling loudly: theatrical gestures of disgust at prices already so low they inspire parsimony in the rich the way meekness aggravates the bully. A handwoven belt for the price of a cup of coffee, a fine poncho for the cost of a night in a clean hotel: these are the modest demands of the Runa vendors. But the tourists have the idea that all South Americans are like Arab rug-sellers, that if ten dollars is asked, then the article cannot be worth more than five. Some Runa understand this and play the Levantine game; others quietly fold their weavings away—if ten dollars is too much for a month's skilled work on the loom, better not to sell at all. The sad result is that quality declines to meet the unsophistication of the buyers. If the gringo cannot appreciate that the fine weave with the intricate *pallay* designs takes three times as long to produce as the merely competent, then *Carajo!* We shall make what the gringo chooses to afford. . . .

The phenomenon of tourism: the moneyed gringo on a two-week tour who feels as though a *National Geographic* article has come to life around him; the self-styled adventurer searching for gold and lost cities, but somehow (thank God) his itineraries exist only on napkins scribbled in the Paititi Bar; the hippie mystic on pilgrimage—Cusco, Crete, and Katmandu—seeking the aura of past ages and the local sacrament: cocaine, wine, temple balls; the vagrant scholar (myself?) who turns the pages of this land and thinks perhaps he understands it, but really is looking only at pictures, adding captions gleaned from books. All of us are poaching on a dying civilization to still the hunger of our own.

Cusco responds with her mimesis. In Le Paris café one can enjoy the company of fellow travelers while contemplating posters of motorcycles bestrode by California nudes. At Govinda, the Hare Krishna restaurant, bread "baked with love" is served by shaven-pated Argentines. In El Tumi one listens to a Mantovani arrangement of "El Condor Pasa" while dining on pepper steak, chips, and—the ultimate chic—frozen vegetables. All the time ragged beggar children press dirty noses against the glass; and in El Muki discotheque a dark audience of Inca niches watches the foreign contortions in mute contempt.

Returning to Cusco is like arriving in Peru: I have forgotten the bad side and must learn again to ignore it.

I know where I will stay. Leading off the plaza is Loreto Kiqllu, Cusco's most perfect Inca street—narrow, straight, like a railway cutting, faced with eight hundred feet of majestically sloping walls in coursed masonry. The corner debouching into the square is rounded, and the long porphyry blocks, hard as granite, bulge in a way that suggests resilience, as if they swelled with the weight of the wall. Some little way down the street, a colonial doorway has been hacked through the austere charcoal masonry. Two wooden doors hang here, old, massive, studded with iron knobs, and surmounted by a crudely carved coat of arms, the boast of an overnight hidalgo. Above them, written in wrought iron, is the word "Hostal."

Inside, eight simple rooms are arranged around a glass-roofed patio. "Would you like a room with the Inca wall?" asks the proprietor, a petite, girlish woman whose voice echoes like birdsong under the skylight. The room she shows me is painted white on three of its walls and contains mahogany furniture and a brick-red carpet. The fourth side is the interior surface of the wall I admired from the street: the same charcoal-gray porphyry running through the room like a night express passing an unimportant station, its rank of trapezoidal niches dark recesses, the windows, as it were, of an unlit carriage. The stonework shows nothing of five centuries: the builders might just have left and the Incas not yet moved in. Well-placed lamps throw the convex surfaces of the blocks into half squares of light and shadow; the fit is so perfect that the joins, emphasized by their beveled edges, seem merely scribed, as if the wall were not an assemblage of stones but a monolith sculpted to give the illusion of masonry. The old claim that a knife blade will not enter anywhere is an insult to this craftsmanship: there isn't space for a cigarette paper.

"Some people don't like the lack of windows in this room," the woman says, "but others like the wall."

53

Supper: a steak at El Tumi. Then, to clear my head of Mantovani (or whatever it was), I find a Chinese restaurant and bar on Saphi Street, where I drink beer and listen to a fine harpist, a white-haired, blind old man dressed in a baggy black suit that looks like an undertaker's hand-me-down. Some French tourists keep demanding "El Condor Pasa"; I ask him for a harawi. His soft voice is a little frayed with age:

Mana sonqoyki qhewiqchu?	Does your heart not pain you?
Mana waqaykunki?	Do you not weep?
Sikllallay kaspa,	You are my beautiful flower,
Koyallay kaspa,	My queen,
Ñustallay kaspa.	My lady.
Unuy wiqellam apariwan,	The water of my tears is sweeping me away,
Yakuy parallam pusariwan.	Carrying me like a flood of rain.
Chay lliqllaykita rikuykuspa,	The sight of your shawl,
Chay aqsuykita qhawaykuspa,	The glimpse of your skirt,
Manañam pachapas ch'isiyanchu;	Keep time from passing;
Tuta rikchariptiypas,	I lie awake all night,
Manataqmi pacha paqarinchu.	But still it is not yet morning.

I make my way home, tipsy, across the now-deserted main plaza. The facade of the Jesuit church at my street corner is brightly lit, but the somber bulk of the cathedral looms darkly on the left like an unwelcome memory.

In Inca times the plaza was twice this size and divided into two symbolic halves: Kusi Pata, Square of Joy (a part of which survives as Plaza Regocijo, behind the row of shops opposite the cathedral), and Auqay Pata, Square of War, the present Plaza de Armas. (There are several other versions of this name: Wak'ay Pata, Holy Square, and Waqay Pata, Square of Weeping—I must ask if any of these are used by Runasimi speakers today.) As at Cajamarca, it is hard now to imagine the violence this place has seen.

Inka Wanakauri,	Inca Wanakauri,
Maytam rinki?	Where are you going?
Sapra auqanchikchu	Our evil bearded enemies
Mana huchayoqta	Are cutting
Kunkaykita kuchun.	Your innocent neck.

Waman Puma records these lines sung by a crowd of weeping Incas as they witnessed here the beheading of Tupaq Amaru I in 1572. Wanakauri was a carved stone believed to be a petrified ancestor of the royal ayllus. The image was kept in a hilltop shrine near the city, and in the old days was carried into battle against the enemies of Cusco. By addressing Tupaq Amaru as Wanakauri the crowd is lamenting the passing of the entire dynasty in his person. The Spaniards set the Inca's head aloft on a pike for all to see, but soon buried the relic when they discovered that a multitude assembled every night to worship it in silence. From these events arose the widespread legend of Inkarí (Inca-Rey, Inca-King), a millenarianist belief that the head of the Inca is growing a new body underground: when the process is complete Inkarí will return from *ukhu pacha*, the inner world, and restore the old pre-Conquest order in a final triumphant reversal of worlds—a pachakuti. For, according to Andean thought, the past is not irrevocable but exists in its entirety, latent in the hurin world beneath the surface of the earth.

But there was also a more literal sense in which the Inca line survived. The Spaniards killed Tupaq Amaru and his son, but a daughter survived to marry Felipe Kunturkanki, the kuraka of Tinta, a town eighty miles south of Cusco. (His name, You Are Condor, itself implies royal descent, the condor being a totem of the Inca rulers.) The name and memory of Tupaq Amaru were kept alive in this family for more than two hundred years. In 1780, José Gabriél Condorcanqui (as the old spelling has it) assumed his ancestral title and raised the great rebellion that came close to ending Spanish rule. Many Runa thought Inkarí had returned; with the desperation that creates messiahs, followers of Tupaq Amaru believed that if they died in battle they would rise from the dead to fight again beside their Inca. The revolt continued to sputter for two more years after the death of its leader in 1781, but its ultimate failure was the turning point between the old and the new Peru: ironically, it hastened the criollo Independence by exposing the weakness of the Spanish Empire, and by revealing to the whites the real threat that Runa might again rule the Andes.

Tupaq Amaru II was cruelly executed, with most of his family, in this same square, which had witnessed the death of his great-great-grandfather two centuries before. He was forced to watch as his wife (who had been a major power in the rebellion), uncle, and eldest son had their tongues torn out and were subsequently garrotted. The Spaniards reserved a special fate for the Inca himself: his limbs were attached to horses, which were then spurred in the four directions, "a spectacle never before seen in this city." But the Inca's body resisted this symbolic rending of the Tawantinsuyu. The horses were unable to dismember him; Tupaq Amaru was returned to the gallows, where he was disemboweled while still alive and then hacked to pieces by the executioner. Though it was the driest time of year, a cloud suddenly formed to obscure the sun, there was a great squall and such a downpour that "even the guards" ran for shelter. A Spanish eyewitness wrote: "This is the reason that the Indians declare the sky and the elements grieved at the death of the Inca, whom the inhuman and impious Spaniards were killing with such cruelty."

The execution was followed by a thorough purge of the remaining Inca nobility. All who had not fought on the side of the Spanish Crown were executed, imprisoned, or shipped to exile in Spanish Sahara. The old kuraka system (indirect rule through native chiefs and princes) was abolished. Ethnocide was added to genocide: Indian names, dress, language, even music, were banned. The extermination of the latter-day Inca royalty was complete, the way cleared for the eventual seizure of power by the criollo republicans.

The Runa nation became headless, but has continued to resist assimilation by drawing on its tremendous mythic resources. The death of the second Tupaq Amaru inspired with a new sacrifice the legend of Inkarí: weavings made in Runa villages today show the sinuous motif of the amaru crowned by the figure of a man resisting four rearing horses.

=== 54 ===

In the morning I did nothing but shower and eat a late and leisurely breakfast in Le Paris café (the coffee and bacon overcame my dislike of the ambience).

===

Hangover and altitude are a wicked combination. I am spending the afternoon in the Café Ayllu, where the decor is more tasteful and the music classical. Beethoven, Bach, Handel spill into the somnolent siesta-time plaza from the open door. The proprietor must have indigenista sympathies: a bookshelf behind the counter offers books and periodicals on Runa life. I buy a copy of *Gregorio Condori Mamani: Autobiografía*, the life story of a Cusco *cargador* dictated to a Peruvian anthropologist in 1973. (Cargadors are human mules—"porter" would be too mild a word—who ply the markets and steep streets of the city with colossal loads attached to their backs by a tump line across the chest. I once saw such a man laden with an upright piano.) The text is in the original Runasimi with a literal Spanish translation on facing pages. Condori is in many ways a modern man: he has worked as shepherd, soldier, and factory hand, but when he saw overhead his first airplane,

> I remembered what my uncle Gumercindo once told me, that
> when only a few days remain before the end of this world there will

come an *alqamari*, which has the head of a condor and the feet of a llama, to us the Runa, the people of the Inca, to warn us to prepare for the ending of this world. . . . The Inkarí is living now in ukhu pacha, since the time when that señor priest Pizarro killed him, and on that last day of the world he will come out and gather to him all the Runa.

I am content to read, and the waiters, who are washing the windows, content to let me. A young student comes in; somehow he has me marked for an anthropologist.

"Are you interested in some texts on Peru? I must sell them to pay for my tuition." He looks as though he needs the money: threadbare tweed jacket, rather smelly patched trousers, and a broad, sad face to go with his Aymara name, Carlos Taypi. He sits down and produces some worn books from a satchel, among them Titu Kusi Yupanki's *Relación de la Conquista del Perú*, an account of the Conquest by the second ruler of the Neo-Inca state. The price asked is high, but I believe Carlos when he says the book is out of print and buy it after a brief haggle. He is that rare "new Peruvian," more numerous since Velasco's reforms, an educated Runa proud of his origins. And he knows his anthropology: he deplores the recent arrival in Peru of a Spanish edition of *Chariots of the Gods*—"A contempt of man, because it divorces him from his great past." Carlos is right—Von Däniken has been particularly garrulous on Peru, and his facile nonsense, by attributing the achievements of the ancient civilizations to spacemen, has given criollos yet another wedge to drive between the Runa and his heritage.

———

Carlos leaves; I pay for my pastry and turn up the narrow streets behind the cathedral—a neighborhood full of the clutter of centuries and the litter of modern life. Two old men in shabby suits are supporting each other like geriatric lovers, framed by a trapezoidal Inca doorway beneath a neon sign saying BAR. They are given a wide berth by a criolla mother and daughter. The little girl wears a fussy turn-of-the-century dress that, like much of the jetsam of European fashions, retains a snobbish function in South America. Lace collar, full sleeves, and flounced hem about the ankles tell the world that this nine-year-old is a *niña*, a doll-like creature kept away from work and play, and especially out of the sun lest she turn too dark. In the shadows hanging from tiled eaves two middle-aged Americans pant up the steep cobbled street, ignoring their pleading wives—"Mind your heart, dear"—with pathetic bravado.

A fragment of Inka Wiraqocha's palace-temple (on most of which the cathedral now stands): small quadrangular stones fitted in gently undulating courses rise and fall, never a straight edge, no mortar, never a gap. Colonial adobe rests on this, the Spanish windows hatched with iron grilles, prisons made by the rich to defend themselves from the kind of society they brought to this land. From an open door comes a stench of liquor and the clack of billiard balls.

I turn a corner and come to the street Hatun Rumiyoq, "Of the Great Stones." Here remains part of Hatun Kancha, traditionally the palace of the Inka Ruka, now housing the Archbishop of Cusco and an art museum. Unlike most of the buildings within the city, these walls are not of coursed masonry but are in the style called polygonal or Cyclopean: enormous rambling shapes in semitranslucent diorite the color of a weathered copper roof. As with most Inca walls, the joins are recessed and finely trimmed, but the surfaces of the stones are allowed to roam: here rough, here smooth, here graced with surprising knobs in pairs suggestive of a woman's breasts, representing, perhaps, the female identity of the earth's crust from which they are hewn. One guesses from this wall that the Incas worshipped stone. With an aesthetic like the Japanese or Scandinavian, they felt no need to smother it in sculpture but made nature into art by the "framing"—the perfect fitting, as precise as the surfaces are rustic: that is the only sculpture they allowed themselves and that is entirely sufficient.

Hatun Rumiyoq includes the famous stone of twelve angles—a megalith whose portrait can be found in any postcard rack—but to my mind those who come to gawk at this one stone (as do most visitors, especially the ones who have surrendered themselves to the selective visions of a guide) miss the artistic achievement of the wall as a whole. Hatun Rumiyoq is no mere assemblage of random stones, but an abstract masterpiece whose shapes have been chosen with a sense of harmony, proportion, and flow, like well-put words. To understand the wall one must *read* it, walk slowly past the individual statement of each stone and the subtle calligraphy of the sunken joins. The builders have given life to rock, or, rather, they have made it possible to perceive the life they never doubted to be there.

=== *55* ===

Cusco was a model in stone of Inca society, Inca history, and the Inca Empire. Each of the main blocks of the city was occupied by a *kancha*—a complex of courtyards surrounded by buildings against a perimeter wall—and most of these were said to be the palace of an emperor and his descendants. The names of these buildings are still known today; modern Cusqueños will tell one which Inca ruler is supposed to have lived where. But there's an obvious problem: how could the city have been so planned in advance that choice building land was left vacant for the palaces of the right number of future rulers? Of course it wasn't. There was no empire until its foundation in the 1430s by Pachakuti, the ninth "emperor" according to the traditional king list. R. T. Zuidema's work suggests that the first eight rulers were not successive chiefs but the contemporary heads of the eight ayllus of early Cusco. (The number eight reflects the classic Andean division of four directions, further subdivided into hanan and hurin moieties.) It seems that when the Incas' ancestors settled Cusco, each ayllu occupied a large area for its kancha—originally (like those of Runa villages today) a combination of living space and farmyard. These became the principal city blocks, the great residential compounds that the Spaniards were to call palaces. The names of the first eight "emperors" were most likely hereditary titles possessed by the heads of these ayllus. Later, with hindsight, the eight were arranged in a prestige hierarchy based on the closeness of their kinship ties with Pachakuti, founder of the Tawantinsuyu. Proximity in space equaled proximity in time, so in Andean thought the pecking order of the eight ayllus could naturally be represented as eight successive reigns: the ayllu related to Pachakuti through his father would have been the "eighth emperor"; the ayllu related through his grandfather, the "seventh emperor"; and so on. The scheme was of course a conscious rewriting of history, not only to give antiquity to the Inca dynasty, but also to express a unified theory of cosmic order: the division of time, space, and man into four directions and the hanan/hurin duality.

The custom of royal sister marriage was adopted after the achievement of empire to perpetuate power in a single imperial family, but Pachakuti, Tupaq Yupanki, and Wayna Qhapaq each built a new kancha (on boggy land in the center of Cusco, reclaimed when Pachakuti canalized the city's rivers), and each founded an ayllu of wives and descendants, who continued to live there with the ruler's mummy after his death.

Besides making—and remaking—history, Pachakuti is credited with refurbishing Cusco, turning it from a Runa farming settlement into a capital worthy of the Tawantinsuyu. He drained and paved the plaza, built his own palace, Qasana, on the north side of it and the Aqllawasi (House of the Chosen Women) on the south. Above all, he rebuilt the holiest part of the city, the Qorikancha (Golden Court), into the magnificent structure that the Spaniards called the Temple of the Sun. Such it indeed was, but Qorikancha also contained chapels to all the sky gods, the sacred rock Qosqo Wank'a, considered the city's ancestor, and perhaps a shrine to Wiraqocha. Originally this kancha had been the doubtless humble homestead of Manku Qhapaq and Mama Oqllo, the first Incas, Intiq Churin, Killaq Wawan, Children of the Sun and Moon.

The city as a whole expressed the Incas' kinship with the sun in a remarkable way: the street plan was designed to represent the stylized figure of a puma, the sun's nocturnal avatar. Cusco is built on a northwest-to-southwest axis, the same orientation as the Andes themselves. (To simplify description I shall call it north-south.) At the north end of the city a steep escarpment rises more than five hundred feet to Saqsaywaman hill. Two streams rise on the moors beyond, flow down each side of this hill, and run parallel in a southerly direction for half a mile. (Their orderly course is the result of straightening by Pachakuti.) Then the easternmost stream, the Tullumayu, turns west thirty degrees and runs for a further half mile before meeting the straight Watanay in a point. These streams still flow in their conduits of precise Inca masonry but have been roofed with concrete slabs to make streets. They are visible in places through iron gratings. The triangular ward enclosed by their confluence is still called Pumaq Chupan, Puma's Tail.

The Temple of the Sun occupies the space between the puma's tail and one of his back legs (if these are pictured one behind the other). The foremost hind leg includes the Aqllawasi and Amarukancha, the residence of Wayna Qhapaq. (My hotel is in part of the Aqllawasi—hence the fine walls—but the rest of the building still houses an order of religious women: the silent, recluse nuns of Santa Catalina.) The main plaza is the area between the puma's pairs of legs; the cathedral is located in his abdomen on the site of Kiswarkancha. Sunturwasi, a round tower that once stood in front of this, may have represented the animal's penis.

The two blocks north of the square constitute the front legs; those blocks farther east correspond to the chest and neck. A street in this area today is called Pumakurku, Puma's Trunk. Above the city rises the feline's head: the hill of Saqsaywaman.

After Pachakuti's reconstruction (if not before), every building, shrine, garden, watercourse, and terrace represented the complex kinship of the Inca ayllus, and the Incas' relationships to the gods, to the natural world, and to other men. The kin network was extended by ritual and mythological constructs to include all mankind within the Tawantinsuyu: it became the basis of reciprocity, the structure and fabric of the imperial state, the veins and arteries of a body whose navel was Cusco (Navel is what Qosqo literally means).

This extension of ayllu institutions to the level of empire resulted in the well-ordered and comparatively humane polity that has drawn so many superficial comparisons with modern bureaucracies, especially socialist ones. But, though the Tawantinsuyu did function superbly as a bureaucracy on the material plane, the concepts behind it were metaphysical, based on a cosmology that linked man to the earth, water, and stars, and had little in common ideologically with materialist utopias.

═ 56 ═

Up early to attend a live broadcast at Radio Tawantinsuyu. (I've always thought that's what Cusco's radio station should be called.)

Loreto Kiqllu is dark and cold between its tall gray walls. (*Kiqllu* is Runasimi for cleft or passage.) The narrow streets of the city serve as latrines during the night; there are the usual whiffs of urine on the crisp air, but also the more substantial problem of shit beneath the cat-ice in the gutters.

Light is already spilling into the plaza from a Wedgwood sky. A diffuse mist gives the surrounding hills—their green slopes, red scars, and eucalyptus—an illusory, Oriental quality like scenery on silk. The square is empty, but the cathedral tolls its great cracked bells relentlessly, not inviting worshippers (the doors are shut), merely asserting its presence. Inside, in the medieval glitter and gloom, there lives a miraculous image, Our Lord of the Earthquakes, a smoke-blackened Christ with a golden sun halo, the usurper of Wiraqocha's temple. Once a year he is carried through the streets like an Inca mummy. But he was powerless against the disaster of 1950: his sanctuary was shattered and the subsequent heavy-handed restoration paid for, ironically, by Spain.

La Compañía, the Jesuit church built on part of Amarukancha, is more cheerful. Time has softened the excesses of its churrigueresque facade, weathered it to a venerable Petra pink that glows in the early light. Spanish colonial society was a culture of appearances and manners, and how clearly this shows in the architecture it produced: only the facade of La Compañía is well made, embellished to the point of bad taste; the rest of the building is a jumble of rubble and misappropriated Inca stones.

The search for a café takes me across the square. Trapped behind the privet hedges of the plaza gardens lie other stolen stones, turquoise megaliths dragged from Hatun Kancha, forlorn as zoo creatures on their triangles of turf. At least they are kinder to the eye than the cast-iron fountain in the center, with its spewing Tritons and life-size swans (painted white with yellow beaks) that seem to have migrated here from a suburban lawn.

Nothing is open yet in the colonnades; I walk down Avenida Sol, the broad modern avenue beneath which runs the Watanay. Just beyond the post office the tall mast of Radio Tawantinsuyu sprouts like a lone pine from a low adobe building. (The new post office, by the way, is the only bilingual building I have found in Peru: lettering above the doors says CORREOS Y TELE-GRAFOS on one side and CHASKI WASI on the other. The *chaski* were the postal runners of the Inca road system.)

———

There are already a few musicians waiting on the small stage of the auditorium, but as yet I am the only spectator. The host of the show, El Waylaychu (roughly, The Bumpkin), gives me a good seat in the front row. More musicians arrive: three well-dressed young men with mandolins; a Runa family I saw busking near the market yesterday—blind father, young wife, and boy of about nine, the wife carrying a harp; two youths with guitars. All are inscribed in a book by an assistant.

El Waylaychu explains: "It's first come, first served. Everyone plays in the order he turns up. We get all kinds—beggars, bar singers, students—everyone goes on the air provided there's time. Sometimes it's good, sometimes bad, you'll see."

The tiny auditorium, no more than fifteen feet by thirty excluding the stage, begins to fill with people and the smell of bodies. The air is stagnant, trapped by the damp-stained soundproof tile on the walls and ceiling. The stage fills even more quickly than the rows of seats. Runa, cholos, mestizos, students, become increasingly squashed among their guitars, flutes, mandolins, and unwieldy harps. There is no jostling, but at 7:30, when the show is slated to begin, shouts of *"La hora! La hora, pues!"* draw El Waylaychu from the studio where he has been hiding. Frantic hand signals through the soundproof window transfer the broadcast from recorded music to the microphone on stage. El Waylaychu, diminutive, Asiatic-looking, with a long, humorous face, speaks so rapidly that I can barely discern the language. It is in fact a disc-jockey patter that switches promiscuously between Runasimi and Spanish.

First on the air is a blind harpist from a community of ayllus near Cusco; he is led to the microphone by his young son. El Waylaychu's patter increases its Runasimi content and brings crinkles of amusement to the stoic, sightless face. (Every harpist I have met so far has been blind: in a country with no social security, music is one of few callings for those who cannot see.) The instrument's belly swells in the middle like the body of a Roman lamp and tapers to a prow at each end; it rests on four short legs. This is a variant I haven't seen before. Juan Chuqi Ninan (Juan Golden Fire) plays more simply than Antonio Sulca, and a few flat notes fall from the battered harp, but the mournful harawi hushes the crowd.

To the next player the audience is less respectful: an atrocious flute player is laughed off the stage with shouts of *"Fuera esa quena!"*—"Get rid of that qena!"

After each performance El Waylaychu reads from a sheaf of personal messages in Runasimi and/or Spanish: congratulations on a wedding; a plea for the return of a lost horse; a sack of potatoes left on a bus; appointments missed because of lack of transport—the daily frustrations of Andean life. These are followed by commercials for the show's sponsors, Cusco Brewery and Inca Motors. (How many of the listeners—chiefly rural Runa—are potential buyers of Toyota trucks?)

Next comes the family trio who arrived just after me. They wear the dress of remote ayllus on the slopes of Apu Ausangate, southeast of Cusco. The woman has a fringed hat like an inverted lampshade, a handwoven lliqlla rich in pallays (among them the figure of Tupaq Amaru), and a long black skirt falling almost to her bare and muddy feet. The man, again a blind harpist, seems prematurely aged by his handicap; his poncho is rich but faded and so is his *ch'ullu*, the knitted cap with ear flaps typical of highland Peru. From their clothes comes the earthy, smoky smell of the peasant's life in huts without windows, furniture, or chimneys. El Waylaychu puts them at ease with puns in Runasimi that I cannot follow. The man plucks sour notes that sound like drunken delta blues; his wife stands with her eyes closed, clasping the boy to her chest; mother and son begin to sing in the high-pitched ululation characteristic of the southern Andes. It's an archaic sound, seldom heard in its pure form even in Cusco, strangely beautiful, but the applause is timid. When the three finish they awake as if from a trance and leave immediately, son leading father and wife carrying aloft the precious harp as they flow through the throng in the aisle. What brought them here, I wonder? Did they come for the thrill of playing to the transistors of their ayllu? (The man asked El Waylaychu if he could say *iskay palabrata*, "two words," over the air; *"Rimayki rimay,"* replied the host, "Speak your speech," and the harpist said, *"Kay waynuta llaqtamasiykunapaq, Ripuy Ripuy nisqata,"* "This wayno is for the people of our ayllu, it's called Ripuy Ripuy.") Or did El Waylaychu see them on the street and invite them to his show? He told me it is getting difficult to find the authentic country music, and it's true that most of the other performers are playing the modern urban waynos, and these are what the crowd enjoys best:

Utuskuruscha presulla hamuchkan	The caterpillar is going to jail
Habaspa sisachallan chutaykusqan-manta,	For taking the young bean flowers,
Llullu habaschata chiptiykusqan-manta.	For munching the tender unripe beans.
Chaynama ñoqapas presulla rich-kani	I too am going to prison
Doncella warmachata chutaykus-qaymanta,	For taking a sweet young girl,
Doncella warmachata llachpaykus-qaymanta.	For grabbing a sweet young virgin.
Ama hina kaychu yanapaykul-laway!	Please, help me!
Kurria willaykamunki abugadul-layta.	Run and tell my lawyer.

The audience gets increasingly rowdy with the uptempo songs. There are shouts, whistles, and impromptu yells of greeting from friends of the musicians. Toward the end of each wayno the crowd breaks into the complicated off-beat handclap that is an integral part of the music. The players respond; an air of fiesta enlivens the shabby auditorium.

I am the only gringo present and unfortunately I disgrace myself by offending the man beside me. He is a mandolin player waiting to go on. Between pieces we have chatted in a friendly way. When it is his turn he asks if he can give me a "dedication" over the air. I've been trying to keep a low profile, and suspect that the dedication is likely to be long-winded and embarrassing, so I decline. But when he reaches the microphone and simply mentions the names of some friends, I realize he had amiably wished to include me and I have snubbed him. When he leaves I try to apologize. It's no use. There is hurt in his eyes: the cultural gulf has opened and there is nothing I can do to bridge it now.

57

To the Le Paris for breakfast, ruing how one can never fail to be the ugly gringo. One reacts unthinkingly (as I always do early in the morning); up pops the obnoxious foreigner and the obnoxious foreigner is me.

But here I meet Big Bill, and talking is a respite from remorse. He is huge, six-feet-five and so broad-shouldered that he must have to pass sideways through most Peruvian doors. There's an air of beach-boy good humor in his tanned face, longish blond hair, and California twang, but by his own account Bill has had a run of bad luck.

"I'm getting over hepatitis—came down with it on the train between La Paz and Arequipa. At first I thought it was just soroche but when I looked in a mirrow I'd turned yellow overnight, man."

"You look pretty fit now."

"I run five miles a day."

"Isn't that overdoing it?"

"Used to run ten. I'm fine now, but when they robbed me at Arequipa station I didn't even have the energy to shout. I was sitting on a bench with my metal suitcase between my feet—it had everything in it: passport, money, travelers' checks, and three hundred rolls of film; I'm a professional photographer and that was six months' work, some of the best work I'd ever done. Anyway, these two guys came up to me and just grabbed it from between my legs. I watched it all happen like it was slow motion or something. By the time I stood up they were gone. All I had left was fifteen soles in my pocket—what's that, five cents?"

Somehow Bill persuaded the Peruvian air force to give him a free lift to Lima, and then talked a taxi driver into taking him from the airport to the American embassy for nothing.

"And then, you know what? Those fuckers said they couldn't issue me a new passport without the twelve-dollar fee up front. And without the passport I couldn't get a refund on my checks. I had to borrow the bucks from the marine on duty. Then the consul kept me sitting in his office for three hours—all the time I'm feeling like shit. While he was out of the room I left a note for the asshole under a book: 'P.S. I've got hepatitis and I licked everything on your desk.' "

"You're staying in Peru after all that?"

"Got to. I was making a photo archive for the Audubon Society—they wired and told me to go ahead and do it over. Anyway, I like it here; I'm in no hurry to go back home. I'm down on my fellow Americans right now.

"There's one thing that gets me about this country, though, and that's the priests. You know, they charge the Indians for baptism, burial, everything. When I went to see the gold chalices they keep in one of the churches here—all of it stolen Inca gold—the fat bastard of a curate tries to charge me a thousand soles just to look at it! When you read about what they did here in the name of religion—and still do—it makes you sick. The Inquisition and all. You know, the Devil couldn't have invented anything better than Christianity to fuck the world around."

"Bill, you've got it worse than you think."

"What?"

"Hepatitis. You're taking a jaundiced view."

"Oh, no. I'm optimistic, man. Most people go straight home. There's a guy here in Cusco who makes me feel like the luckiest person on earth. You must have seen him—I call him the Wizard—the guy with half his face gone and the withered hand."

I have seen him. A leper or perhaps a victim of *uta* (leishmaniasis), he lunges out of the crowd, hideous in stinking rags, and confronts one with the threat of body contact—*Give me something or else. . . .* The hand on his only functioning arm has one and a half fingers, and from the whole finger sprouts a nail almost two inches long, curved like a lacrosse crook. Several times I have given him a few soles and once some food, and of course he accosts me all the more; and there is now an intelligent look of recognition behind the ruin of his face.

"That man," Bill continues, "that man is the most powerful human being in Cusco. Nobody can refuse him: he's the Wizard."

58

Bill has left to go on his daily run. I am still not fond of my own company and decide to retreat into ancient Cusco.

I walk down Loreto, past the hotel, between the great wall of the Aqllawasi and the somewhat lesser wall of Amarukancha. The next street has fragments of early Inca work—still well fitted but of small stones—much broken by doorways of seedy clothing shops and *ahawasikuna*, chicha bars.

The first one sees of the Qorikancha is the famous curved wall beneath the tower of Santo Domingo. The wall describes a parabola, a figure often associated with Inca sun temples—perhaps symbolic of the sun's path across the sky. It stands to a height of twenty feet or so and the straighter section is rusticated in places with bulbous stones and breastlike knobs, but where the curve becomes sharpest the surface is dressed perfectly smooth, and one sees that Inca architects, like the Greeks, had discovered entasis: the wall swells slightly as it rises to correct the optical illusion of concavity that would otherwise be present.

In the seventeenth century, the Dominicans pulled down the Hall of the Sun, the largest Inca structure within the Golden Kancha, and replaced it with the Church of Santo Domingo. But they found the other Inca buildings around the court—the chapels to the Moon, Stars, Lightning, Rainbow, and the apartments of the priests—sufficiently adaptable to their own architectural ideas that they incorporated them into a two-story quadrangle with colonnades: the cloister of the monastery. Stern Inca walls were hidden beneath coats of stucco and whitewash, and violence was done to some of the trapezoidal doors to make them square. The invaders' building was Moorish in style: lofty, elegant—and delicate. And in the case of the Qorikancha, the awaited pachakuti—the reversal of Spanish and Inca worlds—was not long in coming. In 1651 a severe earthquake reduced the whimsical Mediterranean structure to a pile of rubble, from which the Inca walls emerged unscathed.

The Spaniards were never noted for receptivity to the cultures they dominated: not once did they ponder the implications of this. It did not occur to them that there were good reasons why the Incas built so massively and so well. The monastery of Santo Domingo was rebuilt exactly as before—two stories of spindly pillars supporting ponderous, poorly constructed vaulted ceilings. In 1950 Cusco was visited with another pachakuti. All over the city the gimcrack buildings of the conquerors collapsed, and among those that fell was again the cloister of Santo Domingo. The church survived precariously, but a large part of its tower fell onto the curved wall below and dealt it a crack.

———

The Dominican church is cool and dark inside; it takes a minute for my eyes to adjust to the contrast with the brilliant Andean day. A dozen or more altars are arranged around the walls: San José, Santa Rosa de Lima, Santiago Mataindios (Saint James, the Indian slayer), San Sebastián, the Heart of Jesus—bloody icons crying out in silent agony. Before the image of San Isidro, patron of farmers, a Runa man and woman are praying on their knees in Runasimi; two small candles (purchased from the sexton) burn in the gloom.

Qonqor sayaspam	On our knees
Chunka muchaykuyki,	We worship you tenfold,
Dios, wakcha kuyaq.	God, lover of the poor.
Santa Cruzpa unanchanrayku	By the sign of the Holy Cross
Auqaykunamanta qespichiwayku,	Deliver us from our enemies,
Ukhupachamanta qespichi- kuwayku,	Save us from the underworld,
Apu Yaya, hinataq kachun.	Lord Father, let it be so.

The high altar is at the west end, next to the tower. The unorthodox location confirms that here was the holiest altar of the Incas—the shrine of Qhapaq Inti, Almighty Sun, carved into the rock of Qosqo Wank'a, which I suspect still remains behind the embrace of the curved wall.

I pay admission at the entrance to the quadrangle. When I was last here, some years ago, cleaning and restoration of the Inca chapels had just been completed. The work was funded by UNESCO as part of the slow but sure rebuilding program after the 1950 earthquake. During the Velasco years priority was given to the pre-Conquest remains, and a very fine job was done. The restored sections can be distinguished from the original parts only by pressing one's cheek to the wall and looking along the courses. The Inca work, though apparently of rectangular blocks, has in fact no straight lines. Every stone is subtly cupped by the ones below it; the joins undulate slightly when "eyeballed." This is the secret of the building's legendary indifference to earthquakes. A shock can pass through the wall because the stones are not cemented, but they never displace because there is only one way they will fit. The modern masonry is cut with straight edges by diamond saws—one flat surface will always fit another; the difference, once perceived, impresses one with the incredible skill of the Inca masons in matching all these curved surfaces individually. And they had to work in several planes at once. The stones of lesser Inca buildings were fitted accurately for a depth of only a foot or so; the invisible interior of the wall was sometimes left quite rough. (The restorers of the Qorikancha have "cheated" in the same way, filling the interstices with cement.) But the original walls of the Qorikancha are perfect throughout their three-foot thickness—a cross-section hacked out for a doorway in colonial times reveals this. The perfectionism so characteristic of Inca culture was here indulged to the full.

It comes as a shock to see that some of the restoration has been dismantled since my last visit, and that the Inca buildings again frown from behind a fence of spindly columns. I suppose it was inevitable that the schizophrenia of this country should manifest itself in Peru's most symbolic edifice. The criollos, again in the ascendant, have demanded that the Spanish superstructure also be restored, and an uneasy compromise has been reached through the good offices of reinforced concrete and steel. To my mind this is inexcusable: there was nothing remarkable about the Santo Domingo cloister—there are hundreds like it on two continents—but in the whole world there is only one Qorikancha.

I walk out onto the parapet of the curved wall. From here there is a view across Avenida Sol of the hills to the west. They seem in the noon haze like great paws holding down a carcass of blood-red roofs. Below, from the base of the wall, green slopes fall away to the untidy hamlet of souvenir stalls that borders the avenue. The hanging gardens of the temple were once here, stepping down in a flight of terraces to the masonry banks of the Watanay. The cup of the parabola has a single great niche on the inside. This is perhaps the spot where hung P'unchaw, the golden image of the Day, which was said to shine so brilliantly when it caught the rising sun that it became impossible to see. An ugly crack runs through the niche from top to bottom, a rent in the temple's veil caused by the collapsing rubble of Santo Domingo's tower. It is not pleasant to reflect on what may happen when the thrice-built Spanish building comes down, as it surely will, in the next pachakuti.

$$= 59 =$$

I walk back to the plaza by the streets called Romeritos, Maruri, and my Loreto. There is Inca work in all of these. How did Cusco look in its heyday? The early accounts are poor on detail, and the city was burned before learned observers had a chance to see it. Most modern writers, seeing only what remains, have pictured it as a drab city of single-story gray stone enclosures incongruously roofed with rustic thatch. But there is plenty of evidence that Cusco was magnificently decorated with mural paintings, precious metals, and elaborate roofs on buildings as tall as the Andean environment will prudently allow.

Above the kancha walls rose upper stories to a height of thirty feet or more—this can be seen today at the Aqllawasi: the fine stonework reaches twenty feet and there are sections of original Inca adobe brick rising ten feet higher. These adobe upper stories were plastered in red or yellow and painted with bright, intricate designs like those found on Inca pottery and weaving: geometric borders surrounding fluid figures of pumas, butterflies, condors, hummingbirds, and snakes. The Spaniards seldom admired foreign aesthetics, but one who saw the Inca palace at Willkapampa wrote: "The whole palace was painted with a great variety of paintings in their style—something well worth seeing."

Geometric patterns were also worked into the roofs, whose construction was closer to weaving than to simple thatch. Squier found one Inca roof still standing tight after more than three centuries, near the village of Azángaro. The building was round, with high windows and a stone bench around the inside, and the local people called it Sondor Huasi. It was clearly a provincial version of the great Sunturwasi (Round Palace) of Cusco, in which several hundred Spaniards hid when besieged by Manku Inka. Squier described the roof as dome-shaped, resting on a hemispherical framework of curved poles:

> Over this skeleton dome is a fine mat of the braided epidermis of the bamboo or rattan, which, as it exposes no seams, almost induces the belief that it was braided on the spot. . . . It was worked in different colours and in panelling conforming in size with the diminishing spaces between the framework, that framework itself being also painted.

Over this were several layers of reeds, and then "a fleece of finest ichu . . . cut off sharply and regularly, producing the effect of overlapping tiles."

Garcilaso de la Vega, mestizo son of a conquistador and an Inca princess, and author of the *Royal Commentaries*, has been somewhat discredited as a historian. But his descriptions of the Cusco he saw in his youth have the ring of authenticity. He recalled that the roofs were between a yard and six feet thick, supported on painted beams of jungle hardwood, and that they overhung the streets in neatly trimmed cornices that kept the rain from passers-by. The roofs were so tightly woven that when Manku set them alight, some smoldered for weeks. They were almost ideal for Andean conditions: flexible enough to take earth tremors without collapsing murderously like the vaults and tiled roofs of today, thick enough to hold the warmth of the charcoal braziers in the Inca palaces and keep out the damp chill that nightly penetrates the bones of the modern visitor to Cusco.

=== 60 ===

It's time I had a haircut. Yesterday I bought an *anticucho* (a small shishkebab of beef heart) from a chola woman on the street corner, and she gave me the mischievous compliment "*Sumaqmi chukchayki*" ("Your hair is beautiful"), delivered with a giggle.

Señor Kusi, the hotel factotum (do all such people have Inca names?), recommends a barbershop ominously located next to the headquarters of the Guardia Civil.

The place is a block and a half from the plaza. Parked outside is a Mercedes armored vehicle with a water cannon mounted on top. This belongs to the police—once I saw it used to break up a student demonstration—and is scarred all over from encounters with flying paving stones. Usually, however, it serves the worthier purpose of hosing down malodorous streets in the small hours.

One wall of the tiny barbershop is exposed Inca masonry decorated with pictures of exposed blondes. A fly-blown fluorescent tube lights the ceiling; a price list above the spotty mirror advertises three kinds of haircuts: "English Style," "French Style," and "German Style," each for the equivalent of fifty cents. The barber, a cheerful hunchback with a squint, wields his scissors like castanets, slicing at imaginary scalps in the air, then swooping in to remove great tufts of hair with the nonchalance of a gardener assailing a shrub. His victim sits unperturbed, reading a comic. Evidently he is getting a German Style, the standard trim of Peruvian conscripts—everything off but a stubble the length of a three-day beard.

I consider leaving, but the "German" is already shorn and the hunchback steers me with mock obsequiousness ("*Estimado gringo*, please be seated") into the chrome-and-leather chair. I explain I want most of my hair left the way it is, just the lank bits taken off. He interprets this as a request for "English Style," and within five minutes has me sporting a coiffure like that favored by my dreaded school barber: a shock of springy hair on top, short back and sides. Then he sprays me with some rancid alcohol that smells exactly like the *licor* sold to Runa at fiesta time, and any thought of protest leaves me as he shaves my neck with a dull cut-throat.

———

In the afternoon I set off to the market for hiking provisions. I must go to Ollantaytambo and Machu Piqchu before the rains begin in earnest. Yesterday afternoon there was a cloudburst; the steep streets on Pumakurku ran like waterfalls, and the plaza was six inches deep in water for an hour. Then the sun broke through and the city steamed until dusk.

Halfway to the market one comes to the Plaza San Francisco, where tin merchants sell small lamps and ornaments cleverly made from Leche Gloria milk tins. On a stretch of ancient wall are some faded political slogans in Runasimi, relics of the Velasco years: KAWSACHUN LIGA AGRARIAKUNA! (Long live the Agrarian Leagues!). And there are more recent additions: PUKA LLAQTA! PCP MARIÁTEGUI (Red Nation! Peruvian Communist Party—Mariátegui Line). The wall on which they are pasted is actually post-Conquest work. During Manku's siege, after the roofs were burned, Inca warriors ran along the tops of the kancha walls to attack the Spanish cavalry in the streets. The Spaniards countered by dismantling the walls. After the war, Cusco masons were made to rebuild parts of the city from the fallen stones. This work, often mistakenly thought to be Inca, can be distinguished by its untidier appearance, the lack of harmony in the proportions of the blocks (whatever came to hand was used), and the fact that these hybrid walls, in deference to Spanish custom, are vertical. Curiously, it is on this work that one finds a plethora of snakes carved in low relief—as if the masons wished to show that their hearts were not in the postwar reconstruction for new masters, but rather in ukhu pacha, the underworld, with the amarus and the overturned order of the past.

Outside the market a battery of tourist stalls glows with the black-and-red reticulations of semiantique weaving, Runa heirlooms purchased from their owners in times of need by itinerant cholo pedlars, sold to mestizo shop-keepers at a handsome profit, and then resold to gringo tourists for fifty or a hundred dollars apiece. There is a complexity of symbolic design in the apparently geometric motifs: q'enqo mayu (zigzag river), sun, moon, potato flower, ch'aska ñawi (eye of the morning star), conch horns in rows like breaking waves, and of course amarus.

But I've come for more mundane items: a hat to keep the sun off my peeling nose, and an assortment of dried foods. The market building, which covers an entire block, is a lofty structure supported on thin iron columns like those of a Victorian railway station. The narrow aisles between stalls are all but blocked by heavy baskets and Runa women with scanty piles of produce spread around them. I wonder how it can possibly be worthwhile to sit all day beside a cloth on which are displayed a dozen stunted carrots.

All products of the same kind are grouped together; one moves through a succession of territories defined by their distinctive smells: coffee, chile peppers, maize, bananas from the jungle, cilantro leaves, onions. The meat section is a sight to behold. Butchers stand behind the stout eucalyptus logs they use as chopping blocks. Above them hang fly-trodden sides of beef, sheep, and llama. Forearms rivaling Popeye's wield glinting cleavers with the aplomb of samurai. The butchers are female—formidable chola matrons in flowing skirts, well-filled blouses, and trilby hats. Their speed is the intimidating thing: one feels that any moments wasted in selecting a cut of meat are likely to cost one as many fingers. I buy some ch'arki (dried meat—our word "jerky" comes from the Runasimi). Elsewhere I get dried, filleted bananas, oats for porridge, ch'uñu (dried potato), bread, and cheese. The cheese is a find—round, firm, and yellow, the way cheese should be; not like the shriveled, rancid objects usually offered, which resemble infected poultices, breed small worms if kept too long, and never fail to cause diarrhea. This one is labeled "Tilsit type, product of the national cheesemaking school, SAIS Tupac, Amaru, Ayaviri." The lettering encircles a portrait of the Inca. How many SAIS Tupac Amarus are there in Peru?

= 61 =

This morning I separated camping gear from the rest of my luggage and left the things I can do without in the care of Señor Kusi. He has the doggish expression of one who fears he is mistrusted but is in fact utterly reliable. I plan to spend the day in the ruins above Cusco, camp overnight on the edge of the puna, then hike across it to the remote ruin called Huchuy Qosqo, Little Cusco. From there I can descend to the Willkanota valley and catch a bus to Ollantaytambo.

I leave the city by a steep street on the puma's neck—a winding cobbled stairway, smoothed by centuries of bare feet, still proof against the invasion of the wheel. Yesterday's storm has left a small delta of mud and refuse at the corner of each block. Through smoky doorways one sees black kitchens, grubby children, dusty dogs; but some of the tall white walls conceal gardens, and from one a giant wachuma cactus thrusts itself among the electrical wires, an improbable yellow flower on its stem like a lapel carnation.

A drove of pack llamas appears with a rustle of dainty hooves, followed by an old woman in lampshade hat, muttering, carrying a stick. The llamas halt, shocked by my presence, avert their fine heads slightly, and watch me with feminine, disdainful eyes. The leader turns to face me, showing two buck teeth between mobile velvet lips. I stare back. Suddenly a cud of chewed grass and saliva strikes my cheek; and the llamas, having given their warning, continue their descent into the city.

The street ends at the concrete road that carries taxis up to the ruins. On the far side of the road a level terrace supports a seventeenth-century church, but above there's a much broader terrace retained by a magnificent wall of cellular masonry and full-length niches. This is Qollqanpata, Terrace of the Granaries, where Waskar built a palace that was later occupied by Paullu and Don Carlos Inca, quislings who defended Spanish interests against their independent kinsmen in Willkapampa. A modern villa overlooks the city from the Qollqanpata now, but a corner of the old palace still stands, pristine as a folly, in a eucalyptus grove.

From here the sagging roofs of Cusco look like tattered books open face-down on the ground; amid them the plaza bathes in a pink light radiating from the worn cameos of La Compañía. (I remembered to ask Señor Kusi about the name of the plaza: "Waqay Pata, señor. They say it has been called Waqay Pata, Plaza of Weeping, ever since the death of Tupaq Amaru.") It is possible with some imagination to make out the limits of the puma's body. Most noticeable is the Tullumayu, or, rather, the street of the same name beneath which it flows. Tullumayu, River of Bone: the puma's spine.

Above the city to the south there looms a bare hillside that seems, by some foreshortening effect, much closer than it really is. Sparse vegetation has been removed from the underlying scree in the pattern of a national shield and the words VIVA EL PERU. Over the shield are the insignia of the army regiment whose job it is to maintain the figure. Apparently it was created to disguise a hammer and sickle put up by radicals in the 1930s. Whatever the logic behind it, I find something offensive in this factitious assertion of Peruvian nationalism, in Spanish, above the center of the Runa world. But there is worse to come. As I climb higher, there arises on the hilltop immediately east of Saqsaywaman a forty-foot white concrete Cristo—a colossal apparition of Our Lord of the Chicano Dashboard.

A few hundred yards beyond the motor road, the footpath enters the small ravine of the Tullumayu. In these upper reaches the stream flows down an eroded channel where people come to wash clothes, throw rubbish, and relieve themselves. Remains of an Inca conduit show that the Tullumayu once knew tidier days. To the left appear fragments of the single wall that defended the escarpment of Saqsaywaman on the steep side overlooking the city. But as the ground starts to level out, the easternmost ramparts come into view—a tall trapezoidal gate and a wall more than two stories high made of stones the size of small cars. The Hatun Rumiyoq megaliths are small compared to these, but the fit here is just as exact.

$$=== 62 ===$$

SAQSAYWAMAN

I think the first photograph I saw of Saqsaywaman was in a *National Geographic*, and there was a caption that read "brooding majesty" or "awesome splendor" or some such. The early Spaniards were moved to similar phrases: "the eighth wonder of the world . . ."; "it will stand as long as the world exists"; "it is impossible to believe that these stones could have been raised by human hands; they are as big as small mountains . . ." (inevitably, the Devil was credited with lending a hand in its construction). All who try to describe the monument fall into what sounds like the wildest hyperbole; yet none of their descriptions do it justice. Saqsaywaman is too exceptional and, most of all, too alien to reveal itself in words. Many conquistadors voiced the unusual sentiment that the monument be preserved for posterity, and those who saw the movable parts dismantled swore that what remains is a shadow of what was.

Today one sees the three zigzag terrace walls that fortify the hill on its northern side. They form a triple sawtooth a third of a mile in length, rising to a total height of sixty feet; the walls overlook a broad, artificially leveled esplanade. The bottom terrace is made of enormous stones, up to twenty-five feet high and weighing between fifty and two hundred tons apiece. They are fitted in a style similar to that of Hatun Rumiyoq.

What strikes me most, walking below this wall, is the way the rough surface treatment matches the size of the blocks.

The stones bulge from their recessed joins like inadequately restrained bellies; some are almost as rough as when they left the quarries (hard limestone cliffs about a mile away), others show clear evidence of building techniques: knobs, holes, and grooves for the placement of levers, wedges, crowbars, and the piles of small stones on which they were supported during the final fitting. It is possible that further trimming of the faces was planned, but I think it more likely that the craggy finish was a deliberate foil to the uncanny precision of the joins: such contrasts between nature and artifice are the essence of Inca aesthetics.

The sun is higher now, and the furrowed joins frown in deep shade; the bulbous megaliths above me sail against a lightly dappled sky. The top of the wall is gapped like an old man's jaw where the Spaniards succeeded in knocking out a stone or two; I have the sensation of being swallowed by a geological formation as I enter one of the three narrow gates and climb to the upper terraces.

=====

Several chroniclers agree that the building of Saqsaywaman spanned the reigns of Pachakuti, Tupaq Yupanki, and Wayna Qhapaq, and occupied twenty thousand men for sixty years—figures that seem to me quite credible. Workers were levied by the mit'a during slack seasons of the agricultural cycle. Cieza wrote: "These Indians did not stay at the work always, but only a limited time; when others came they would leave and thus they felt the labor little." In this way the mit'a system avoided the lifelong slavery typical of Old World civilizations, but the constant rotation was not purely humanitarian: by bringing people to Cusco several times in their lives it encouraged the spread of Runasimi, acculturation to Inca ways, and an appreciation of the mighty capital as center of the world. The Incas knew that their empire had been preceded by *auqa pacha runa*, the "epoch of warring people"; the objective of their statecraft was clearly to forge a homogeneous nation from the

Peruvian diversity. Had this process not been truncated by the arrival of Europeans, it might well have prevented the political disintegration that overtook Wari-Tiawanaku and (probably) Chavín.

———

The top of Saqsaywaman hill is a waste of rubble covered by a low scrub of dryland plants. It is hot here when the wind drops, and my feet raise puffs of dust fragrant with sage. Cusco is now hidden by the brow of the escarpment; to the east the snowcap of Apu Ausangate rises like an iceberg on the horizon of a turbulent green sea; to the north, rock outcrops and rolling hills rise gradually to the puna. From time to time a breeze brings the heavy balsam of eucalyptus trees from the ravine of the Watanay. There were three towers here on the summit in Inca days. The largest was said to be five stories high, with two great windows overlooking the city and so many rooms that "one cannot see them all in a day." The size and quality of these buildings impressed most early observers even more than the terrace walls below. But the conquerors found their relatively small squared blocks only too useful for building the cathedral and their own houses.

One of the towers was round, and from its base issued an abundant supply of pure water whose source was "a secret of the Inca and supreme council." In 1934, the Peruvian archaeologist Luís Valcárcel uncovered foundations of Muyuq Marka, The Round Tower, and was able to confirm early accounts. From within the three concentric walls issue water channels radiating like the spokes of a wheel. How did the water get here? The tower is on top of a porous limestone hill more than a hundred and twenty feet above the highest surrounding topography. Valcárcel did not dig deep enough to find the subterranean pipes, but there's little doubt that the water was brought in by a pressure siphon. (Smaller examples elsewhere show that the Incas knew this advanced application of hydraulics.) With closely fitting stone conduits, it was possible to bring water from a mountain reservoir, send it underground at a point slightly higher than the base of Muyuq Marka, pipe it beneath the esplanade, and allow it to rise by its own pressure to the distribution tank. From there all points of the Saqsaywaman complex were supplied by gravity.

But not everyone is sufficiently impressed by this achievement: while I am here a party of tourists comes by; their guide (who has, I suspect, been reading Von Däniken) points out the complicated circular foundation: "This is the famous Calendar of Saqsaywaman. . . ."

———

There are many small rodents and birds in the scrub, especially tawny puku doves, who utter a mournful cry.

Saqsaywamanpi pukuy pukuycha,	Little puku dove in Saqsaywaman,
Imallamantas qanri waqanki?	Why are you crying?
Noqachu kanki waqanaykipaq,	You need not cry, you are not like me,
Mana mamayoq, mana taytayoq.	Without mother, without father.

High overhead circle the menacing, effortless shapes of hawks; occasionally one drops suddenly on a kill. I have been told that the name of the hill comes from these birds, that it means Hawk, Eat Your Fill, from *waman*, "hawk," and the verb *saqsay*, "to be sated." But there's an archaic word *saqsa*, meaning "royal"; Royal Hawk is probably a better translation.

The name, however, has very little to do with the physical presence of raptorial birds. In the scheme of Cusco, Saqsaywaman represents the puma's head; the zigzag ramparts are the big cat's jaws. Why then is the hill not called Puma's Head? The puma, a creature of the earth and night, is lower moiety. He therefore cannot represent something that is whole; to do this a composite being must be called into existence—the "bird-feline," a figure that first appears in Peruvian iconography on the carvings of Chavín. Waman, the hawk, is of the day and air, hence upper moiety. It is therefore fitting that the highest part of Cusco should include the name Waman, and there are those who go so far as to suggest that the zigzag walls represent not only a puma's fangs, but also the tail markings of the hawk.

There's an interesting footnote to all this: though he does not say so, it seems that the writer Felipe Waman Puma assumed the same combination of names for the same reason—to express symbolically that in his plea to the king he was representing the people of Tawantinsuyu as a whole.

=====

When one descends, the terraces look so shattered from behind. I become oppressed by a sense of the fragility of civilizations and the futility, perhaps, of civilization in general. I think of those who have starved in impregnable castles, been outflanked while waiting behind Maginot lines. Like all monuments to security, Saqsaywaman failed the Incas. Its first recorded use as a fortress came in 1536, when Manku Inka's forces made it their base for harrying the invaders in the city. But the Spaniards, well versed in European siege techniques, soon swarmed over the terrace walls with ladders. When Tupaq Amaru II invested Cusco two and a half centuries later, the fortress had already been garrisoned with native troops loyal to Spain. Again, the Inca's failure to hold Saqsaywaman cost him the siege and ultimately the war.

In pre-Conquest times, Saqsaywaman was regarded more as a temple than as a fortress; it was often called Inti Wasi, House of the Sun. Garcilaso adds that the monument was intended by the Incas mainly as an overwhelming statement of prestige: "the immense and majestic work was made more for admiration than any other end."

Whatever its military failures, it succeeds in this.

=== *63* ===

"Gringo! Where are you from? . . . What do you think of the fortress? Magnificent, no? Do you want to buy some marihuana?"

"No, thanks."

"Some cocaine?"

"Let me see it."

I have been sitting quietly for twenty minutes on the bald hemispherical hill that forms the north side of the esplanade. There is a series of steps here, carved from the rock, known as Kusilloq Hink'inan, the Monkey's Perch. The spot commands a panoramic view of the puma's jaws three hundred yards away, which seem to be holding this hill at bay or about to swallow it.

Five street-wise local youths have me marked for a gringo rube. One rolls up his shirt sleeve and shows me a copper forearm: "See, we are of the blood of the Incas. We can tell you anything you want to know about the ruins. Did you know that there's a tunnel from here to the sun temple? They say three university students went in one day—two were never seen again, but the third appeared weeks later, aged like an old man. He came out behind the altar in Santo Domingo with a golden corncob in his hand."

"When did this happen?"

"A few years ago, but now the tunnel has been blocked up." (Exactly the same tale was told to Squier in 1865.) The spate of mythological jive continues; it becomes evident (as Squier might have written) that my interlocutor has already been sampling his wares.

"Try some of this." I am handed a scrap of newspaper containing what looks like a small pile of crushed sugar—except that Peruvian sugar is always beige and this is sparkling white. I take a tentative sniff and feel almost instantly vigorous.

"How much will you buy?"

"Thank you, but I don't want any."

"Nice hat!" One of them grabs it from my head and tries it on. I realize for the first time how ridiculous I must look—it's a trilby made of bright pink denim. I wanted a blue one, but only the pink would fit. The hat is tried on by all five and reluctantly returned. I search for possible allies, but the only tourists are tiny figures on the fortress, and there are few left now that the day is at its hottest.

"Give me your pen!"

"I need it."

"Well, lend us some money. We're poor and we're thirsty, we want to buy some chicha."

"When will you return it?"

"Tonight. We'll be around the plaza—we're always there."

"Well, I won't be."

"That's all right . . ."

"I'm sure it is. *Kunan ripukusaqmi!*" The Runasimi ("I have to go now") has the desired effect. A few more questions, during which I intimate that I'm well connected in Cusco (a lie), and they leave.

———

Seen from Saqsaywaman, the hill on which the Monkey's Perch is carved looks like a lifeless planet half buried in the ground. At close quarters one sees that its folds of smooth rock have been fused to the texture of ceramic glaze. Some striations on the far side of the hill make ideal slides for children, and for these the outcrop is called Suchuna, Sliding Place. The name is apter than the ancients could have guessed: the formation was created by a geological process called a slickenslide. During the ice age, glacial pressures caused layers of rock to buckle and slide over one another. Friction generated enough heat to melt the strata in contact, and later erosion (or perhaps the Incas— Suchuna was an important wak'a) took away the overburden and revealed the glasslike surfaces. (The *Chariots of the Gods* school has a different explanation—Suchuna hill was melted when the extraterrestrials downed tools at the fortress and blasted off for home.) This material is extremely hard: centuries of weather have not dulled it, and the steps of Kusilloq Hink'inan are as sharp as the day they were cut.

The Suchuna is just one in a menagerie of fantastic rock outcrops: porous limestone weathered to the appearance of brain coral; boulders pierced with cracks and fissures; labyrinths of tunnels, open passages, and caves. All have been further elaborated by the Incas. Cracks have been enlarged to make winding corridors with smoothed walls, or opened out into caves provided with niches; any natural shape suggesting an animal is brought to life by subtly adding ears, eyes, or a tail. The complex extends for miles and must constitute one of the most remarkable collections of sculpture in the world.

These carved rocks, together with some springs and holy fields, were the principal points on the compass of radiating lines known as the seqe system, whose pivot was the high altar of the Qorikancha. The system integrated geography, social groups, and the heavens in a complex symbolic order. The wak'as were associated with specific families, lineages, and ayllus who maintained the shrines and performed rites in them. Those wak'as well placed for watching the sky were used as astronomical observatories, and were themselves thought of as earthly counterparts of stars and constellations. And in the recesses of the rocks were kept ancestral mummies. Numerous manifestations of the hanan/hurin duality—past/present, living/dead, heaven/earth, this world/underworld—were thus expressed in the wak'as; and the wak'as in turn were arranged according to the four suyus of the world and the moieties of Upper and Lower Cusco.

The rocks still have evocative names, some ancient, some betraying attitudes of the conquerors—Chinkana, The Labyrinth; Saqraq Sermunan, The Devil's Pulpit; Q'enqo, The Zigzag; Sayk'usqa Rumi, The Weary Stone. The last is a house-size boulder said to have stopped while on its way to the walls of Saqsaywaman: the stone became "tired," refused to move any farther, and, as is the custom of sacred rocks in the Andes, wept blood.

The shadows lengthen now as evening approaches; around me the oblique lighting brings more and more of the strange, half-natural landscape to life. I am looking at a small chamber—the rock-hewn foundation of a shrine whose walls have long ago been taken by Spanish priests and builders with a common interest—when I find a modern offering. On a circular bed of select coca leaves (*kuka k'intu*) lie an oddly formed potato and the pink arm of a plastic doll. Misshapen vegetables, like any peculiar manifestation of nature, have long been revered as talismans in Andean belief: perhaps the potato, with the wak'a's help, is intended to absorb sickness or deformity from a child's arm? The sight is unsettling—I have intruded on a private magical act.

I walk north toward Tampu Mach'ay, beyond which I plan to camp. The sun sets. Cusco is hidden in its valley, but the smooth swell of the dark hills is broken by the jagged wreck of Saqsaywaman. To the east, Apu Ausangate can be seen as a disembodied crown, purple in the last of day.

It is an hour's walk to Tampu Mach'ay. Dusk falls quickly, but before long the moon rises and lights my way to the water shrine. The light is sufficient to make out the wall with four dark niches standing like doors to the hillside and, below this, a Cyclopean terrace from whose base still flows a spring in a channel of Inca masonry. The water runs into a stone basin from two spouts; its steady plash is the only sound in the valley.

I camp higher up, in a meadow beneath somber cliffs. During the night a wind blows; twice it carries men's voices and the crepitation of many hooves.

In the morning there is a dusting of snow around the tent, and the ridge over which I must hike is completely white. But by the time I've made porridge the snow has steamed away in the sun.

According to my map I am at about thirteen thousand feet and must climb to fourteen. There should be a trail and a row of power-line pylons in the direction I want to go. The topography gives me no sight of these until I am almost upon them. The "pylons" turn out to be nothing but old railway rails stuck in the ground, most of them bent and leaning; from some hang copper wires soughing in the wind—relics of some development scheme long *fracasado*.

Sometimes on the hillside I can see stretches of Inca road, overgrown with sod but evident from the raised bed and constant grade. The modern trail keeps low, often sharing its right-of-way with a muddy trickle. Once the puna is reached the trail disperses and I have to pay close attention to the map.

I meet a llama caravan: about twenty animals driven by three Runa. They are as surprised to meet a gringo as I am to see such a fragment of the old Peru. They tell me they are carrying ch'uñu to exchange in Cusco for sugar, aluminum pots, and batteries—the typical consumer goods that reach even further into the Third World than Coca-Cola.

In a dimple of the puna half a mile to my right, Qoriqocha, Gold Lake, lies silver under a sky now white with a diffuse cloud layer through which the sun still shines brightly. From the lakeshore seven fields radiate, equal wedges on the slopes. One is in deep black furrows, another is spotted with the green of new potatoes; the rest are in various stages of returning to puna sod. This is *laymi* crop rotation, a traditional seven-year fallow cycle that minimizes erosion and controls the potato's chief predator, a nematode whose cysts can survive only six years. (When modern pressures force more intensive land use, the peasant finds himself increasingly dependent on fertilizers and pesticides, with predictable effects on his society and environment.) The square sods of the furrows show that the land has been worked by the Inca foot-plow, the *chaki-taklla*, a digging stick equipped with handles and a narrow blade. Communities share in this work, the men turning the sod in teams, women breaking up the soil with hoes. Other chores—for example, hilling the potatoes—are done in the same ceremonial way, with songs, offerings, and much drinking of chicha. Songs ensure a good harvest by making the field and its crop "happy." (*Hamank'ay*, or *amancay*, mentioned in the last line of the song, is the native Peruvian daffodil.)

Señor qollana, aysayapuway
Qori lampawan, qolqe kutiwan.

Q'omer pampachallapi
Aysayapuway, aysayapuway!

Ama mamachay mancharinkichu
K'ullu rumiwan tupayuspapas;
Ama mamallay mancharinkichu
Aqarap'iwan tinkuyuspapas.

Hoqta kutimusaq chaypachankiqa
Asusinas hina p'anchiyushanki;
Hoqta vueltamusaq chaypachankiqa
Hamank'ay hinachu t'ikayushanki.

Señor leader, hill me
With your golden spade, with your silver hoe.

In the green fields
Hill me, cover me!

Mother (potato), do not fear
When your roots touch stones;
Mother, do not fear
When you also meet the hail.

When I come back another time
You will be budding like the lilies;

When I return again
You will be flowering like the *hamank'ay*.

I leave the Qoriqocha basin by a ridge that leads into a wide pampa dotted with the dignified woolly figures of grazing llamas. The white cusps of the Willkanota and Willkapampa ranges support a vast sky, and at the far limits of the tableland there is a suggestion of the Willkanota valley.

I stop on a rock outcrop for lunch. While munching greedily on a sandwich of Tupac Amaru cheese I become conscious of the gentler feeding rhythm of the llamas. Most of the long necks are bent to the ground, but one or two are always lifted for a brief, wary perusal of the surroundings. As soon as one neck falls another rises, quickly but without haste, as if by a consensus of rotation. It is rather like watching the hammers on a piano.

The close-cropped puna is awash in places from last night's storm; tiny yellow-and-white flowers, smaller than daisies, are growing in the puddles.

———

At the rim of the puna begins the watershed of the ravine that will take me down to the ruins. Three black pigs are rooting in a bog, and the soil they have disturbed is intensively studied by several kinds of bird: sparrows, thrushes, caracaras, many gulls.

The sky clears; shadows are sharp again and getting longer. I follow the left bank of the ravine, passing remains of terrace walls and stone foundations overgrown with yellow broom. The soil changes from the black of the puna to a rust red. On the opposite bank is the settlement called Pukamarka, Red Town—terracotta walls beneath silvery roofs of ichu. A fine road—it must be Inca—comes up from the valley and enters the town after squeezing between a cliff and a huge boulder. Women are returning home with flocks of dirty sheep.

The map insists I must leave this ravine and traverse a bluff to the next after losing some two thousand feet. But there is no road, only a confused scribble of animal paths. Fortunately I meet an old woman. Her speech is hard to understand, but I follow the direction she indicates with puckered eyebrows and protruded lip—the Runa substitute for pointing.

Within an hour I pick up an ancient trail, well cut into the precipitous bluff. The Inca town appears suddenly, tiny, almost directly below: a thousand-foot jump would land me among the buildings.

The light is failing now. The path soon comes to a stream in the crease of the hillside. It would be wiser to look for a camping place here, and descend to the ruins in the morning. The stream bank is thick with bush—blackened *achupalla*, a spiky relative of the pineapple that Andean herders burn on sight, and cacti lurking behind the foliage of kinder plants. But suddenly the scrub thins out to reveal a magnificent and unexpected sight. The crease opens into a natural amphitheater stepped with tier upon tier of terraces. Water channels (now dry) and flights of steps lead from one to the next, and the whole complex is divided by a central aisle; down this falls the stream that once irrigated the hanging fields. Someone has cleared away the bush—I camp on soft grass, feeling like a lone spectator at an empty stadium.

———

65

HUCHUY QOSQO

This morning the world was enveloped in cloud. Only the terraces immediately above and below the tent were visible. But an hour later the cloud fell away, and as it retreated down the valley the Willkanota range appeared like a Chinese watercolor.

Little Cusco lies below me on a broad spur, a stepped city of shrimp-pink buildings arranged on terraces as wide as football fields. Tradition has it that an ousted Inca spent his days of exile here; if there's any truth to the story the ruler in question was probably Inka Wiraqocha. He appears in history as a peaceful mystic, dedicated to the cult of the supreme deity after witnessing him in a dream and taking his name. When the Chanka threatened the early Incas, Wiraqocha fled Cusco and left its defense to his son Pachakuti. After a victory in which the stones of the battlefield came to life and aided the outnumbered Incas, Pachakuti took the throne and the old man went into retirement. The modest size of Huchuy Qosqo does indeed suggest a royal residence rather than a town, and for a man like Wiraqocha the setting would have been ideal: overlooking the Willkanota, or Willkamayu, the Holy River, yet hidden from it; surrounded by superb views of the Willkanota range and the emerald cornucopias of tributary valleys that spill from between the mountain massifs. The Willkamayu, moreover, was considered the earthly counterpart of the heavenly Mayu, or Milky Way, and both rivers were the visible substance of Wiraqocha, the God.

The main building of Huchuy Qosqo is a square structure resembling a castle keep. The first twenty feet of its walls are of gemlike cellular masonry in bright pink stone. A ledge around the inside shows that a first floor rested halfway up the stonework. There is a well-preserved third story of adobe, relieved on the interior by generous niches; two of the niches are pierced with small windows. The Inca adobe bricks are smaller and better made than modern ones—a fact confirmed by their survival without protection from the weather. When one pictures this lofty building with paintings on its upper walls and roofed by a neat pyramid of thick thatch, it is not hard to form an idea of how the greater Cusco must once have looked.

Apart from one temple of fine masonry surrounding a votive rock, the other buildings are mostly of adobe or plastered field stone. But there is nothing mean in their proportions—great halls with rows of wide doorways command the broad terraces. In one hall the niches show traces of original stucco and paint, enough to indicate that the walls were once whitewashed and that a charcoal-gray stripe ran around them like a picture rail and entered each niche. This feature has been noted at several other sites, including the Qorikancha; it is the only clue I know of to the interior decoration of Inca buildings. It was perhaps such a line that Atau Wallpa chose as the height to which he would fill his prison with gold.

A lunch of bread and cheese, then the long descent to the valley bottom. An Inca road leads out of Huchuy Qosqo and over the neighboring spur. Acacia and broom are flowering here, but my eyes are arrested by the impossibly bright scarlet blooms of *aha kiska* cactus: the color vibrates with an intensity like that described by Aldous Huxley when writing of his mescaline visions.

Once over the spur all trace of Inca road disappears; I descend by a trail so steep that my feet are rammed into the toes of my boots. Two thousand feet of this before the going levels out beside the river. A track follows the bank of the Willkanota for some miles, and crosses on a bridge ancient in design but made of old steel rails and cables.

One enters the town of Calca by an avenue of magnificent *pisonays*, big as mature oaks, covered in crimson flames against leaves the color and sheen of holly.

A bus in the plaza is about to leave for Ollantaytambo.

=== *66* ===

OLLANTAYTAMBO, 9,200 FEET

The valley here is narrower and deeper than at Calca. Three-thousand-foot cliffs shut out the morning and evening sun, and shut in the hoarse roar of the rivers.

Dusk was approaching when the bus arrived last night, but the heights of Pinkulluna, immediately above the town, were still splashed with yellow light. Very high up, in places where one might expect to find the nests of shy and solitary birds, roofless Inca buildings perch like Tibetan monasteries on crags. The structures are long and narrow, rising in tiers, made of stones set in pastry-colored mortar. I wondered if the neat rows of black doorways suggested the name of their perch, Hill of the Flute.

Through Ollantaytambo runs the Patakancha River, canalized between walls of rough but solid Inca masonry. The hostel where I am staying is a mile from town, just before the confluence of the Patakancha and the Willkanota.

A bridge of eucalyptus logs leads to a door in a garden wall coped with aerial plants. Letters burned on a board say ALBERGUE ("inn"), and PLEASE KEEP THIS DOOR SHUT in English and Spanish. Unusually, for a rural Peruvian dwelling, no waft of feces attends the scent of the broom and passion flowers that grow against the simple whitewashed building.

It was dark when I got here; there was a welcoming smell of candles and kerosene lamps. I was shown a neat room with a ceiling of reeds, and a lliqlla decorating the wall. Through the glassless window poured the clamor of the rivers, but I was soon asleep and heard nothing except, once, the panting of a steam train in the night.

There is chatter around the breakfast table in several European tongues, but the only Spanish comes from a Frenchman who refuses to speak English. All seem to be hikers, either returning from the "Inca Trail" to Machu Piqchu or about to start it.

I shall wait until after the full moon, when the weather in the mountains is generally drier.

This hostel is known among backpackers as "the Canadians' place." Wendy and Randall, I discover, are from California (it is their partners—away at the moment—who are Canadian); before settling in Peru they saw much of South America, and their misadventures included a canoe trip down an Ecuadorian tributary of the Amazon.

"We were crazy," Randall admits. "No one travels on the river in the wet season. But we didn't know that, and the Ecuadorians were happy enough to sell us the canoes."

They survived, despite whirlpools, rapids, sudden rises in water level, and infected insect bites: Randall, an odd combination of cynic and optimist; Wendy, artistic, dark, with the long black hair and serene carriage of a Runa woman, and a California existentialism: "We don't own the hotel. The Peruvians could kick us out anytime. But that's just Zen to me. You know—an edge to life that you don't have when everything's secure."

———

The modest altitude allows a mixture of highland and tropical plants. In the garden there are peaches, figs, and palms; outside, by the river, eucalyptus, wachuma cactus, and wild kapuli cherries.

Kapuli ñawi cusqueñita	Little Cusqueña with dark eyes like kapuli,
Tus ojos tienen la culpa	Your eyes are to blame
Para amarte tanto.	For my loving you so.

Sutikitari qonqaymanchus,	If I could only forget your name,
Ese nombre tan bonito	That pretty name
Con que me engañaste!	With which you fooled me!

There are eagles and condors on the heights, hummingbirds in the valley. To the north stands two-thousand-foot Waqaywillka, Weeping Peak, whose glaciers do indeed resemble frozen tears.

A narrow-gauge railway joins Cusco to Ollantaytambo, continues to Machu Piqchu, and ends at the jungle town of Quillabamba. On the station platform behind the hostel I bought mangos, avocados, and bananas that came up on the morning train.

———

To the ruins. A short way along the path from the hotel one can see the main temple on a spur opposite Pinkulluna. A cascade of terraces hangs below it, not rigidly in contours, but draped on the terrain in concave sweeps like the walls of the Dalai Lama's Potala in Lhasa. The view is partly hidden by the ostrich feathers of pampas grass growing beside the river. Beyond, a wild rose grapples with a maguey. The maguey is doomed but not by the rose: it has sent up an asparaguslike stem thirty feet into the air—a single sexual act that culminates in death. A hawk is perching on this vantage point; he shifts from foot to foot as I pass, but doesn't fly away.

Apart from the modern plaza with its police station and mestizo shops, Ollantaytambo consists of Inca houses more or less continuously inhabited since ancient times. These buildings have fallen into a poor state over the years—doorways have been widened or walled up, windows hacked through walls; roofs of tin or tile (often both) have replaced the original thatch. Many old houses stand abandoned, while most of those in use have the forlorn look of railway carriages turned into gypsy dwellings. But there are streets that remain almost unchanged: straight, narrow streets provided with channels that in some parts of the town still carry fast-flowing water. And there are the same great enclosures as in Cusco, their Cyclopean walls broken by a single monumental door, the entrance to each kancha.

The original Inca plaza is on the north side of the Patakancha River, just below the ruins. It is called Mañay Raqay, Court of Apportionment, a name that perhaps refers to the distribution of lands and irrigation water. One side was destroyed when the church was built, but on the other three sides are tall walls of stone and adobe interrupted by imposing doorways at regular intervals. These were the Inca equivalent of colonnades—long corridorlike structures called kallankas. It was from buildings of this type at Cajamarca that the

Spaniards were able to charge on horseback when they ambushed Atau Wallpa.

A sign announces that UNESCO funds are paying for the modern plaza to be paved with cobbles and cement. Meanwhile these last Inca buildings of their kind are used as pigpens and corrals, their roofless walls abandoned to the weather.

=== 67 ===

The central doorway in the north kallanka still serves as the entrance to the temple complex. Wooden gates have been installed; they detract somewhat from the fine proportions of the trapezoid—nine feet high and six wide, capped by a granite lintel ten feet long. Beyond this gate one crosses a court bounded on either side by vertical crags, while opposite rises a flight of terraces ascended by a stairway. After climbing for some hundreds of feet, the stairway turns to the left and ascends five hanging walls of superb polygonal masonry. Each wall is made of larger blocks than the one below it: the scale of the architecture expands as one rises. The effect is immensely impressive. This crescendo is maintained to the summit of the hill, where stand six colossal megaliths more than twice the height of a man.

But before reaching the top, one walks below the wall of the fifth terrace, in which is set the finest of Inca monumental doors, the entrance to the temples above. The step and fallen lintel are in pink granite, the double-jamb sides and rest of the wall in gray; time has painted all the stones with splotches of orange lichen. The blocks are trimmed smooth, with only a gentle bulge and a nicely understated sinking of the joints. This reduction of the relief allows the shapes to be appreciated at close quarters (something not always possible at Saqsaywaman). The four stones that form the sides of the door, two to each side, are virtually symmetrical, and this symmetry is relinquished only gradually with distance from the door. An effective clustering of knobs calls attention to the contrast of symmetry and freedom.

The structures on the summit are very puzzling. It appears that the work was interrupted and altered several times, and the buildings were obviously never completed. Large blocks still lie propped on their working platforms of smaller stones. But the wall of six megaliths was finished, and it is done in a unique style. The blocks stand shoulder to shoulder like a phalanx of rectangular shields; each is about thirteen feet high and six feet wide. Between them narrow fillets, beautifully fitted, bulge as though squeezed by their massive neighbors. The base of each fillet is defined by a knob. Two of the "shields" show remains of extensive sculpture. One has the outlines of three creatures with their heads (smashed long ago) turned toward the viewer in high relief. These were probably pumas. The other has three zigzags, or stepped pyramid designs. Each "pyramid" consists of four levels and an apex—the classic expression of Andean cosmic order.

That there are three pumas and three "pyramids" is equally significant: tripartite division was also deeply rooted in the Inca worldview. In one origin myth the Incas emerged from three caves and founded Cusco with three ayllus; the world was composed of three levels: *hanaq pacha*, "heaven," or the upper world; *kay pacha*, "this world"; and *ukhu pacha*, the "inner" world, or underworld. Human society was divided into three kinship classes defined by "distance" from the ruler: *qollana*, the ruler and ruler's closest kin; *payan*, the people "in the middle"; and *kayau*, the people outside, or non-Incas. In the scheme of the empire, Upper Cusco was qollana, Lower Cusco payan, and the world at large outside the city, kayau. Intricate theoretical constructs reconciled the three-part division with the four suyus and with the seqe system, which was itself organized into the qollana-payan-kayau hierarchy.

The three classes were represented by white, black-and-white, and black respectively. Hence the name of the servant class in Inca society, who were not necessarily of low status but were drawn from the non-Inca peoples: the *yanakuna*. It means simply "the blacks," a term with no racial connotations in ancient Peru, where everyone was the same coppery brown. But it must have seemed an uncanny fulfillment of cosmic order when the conquering white men arrived with attendant Negro slaves.

= 68 =

The sun is fierce now on the summit but a fresh breeze is blowing. From the town three or four hundred feet below come shouts of children, the clatter of a truck, a donkey's bray. Bees are at work among the wild flowers—tiny magenta trumpets, some yellow-and-white daisies. The beards of aerial moss that hang from the steep rocks are beginning to revive with the rains, but in a few months only cactus will remain.

I climb onto the temple platform behind the six megaliths and find what

I believe may be an important clue to the meaning of the Ollantaytambo monuments. The great wall does not, as first appears, retain the platform. Behind the four middle stones is a narrow passage reached from above by a staircase. The backs of the megaliths have been given a facing of gray granite in the cellular style, while the other side of the passage—the original front of a votive rock round which the temple is built—is faced with a wall of rough stonework in which are three niches. This rustic little shrine seems to me to belong to an earlier, simpler temple that the builders of the megalithic wall regarded as too sacred to bury.

I think Ollantaytambo may be intimately connected with the Incas' beliefs about their own origins. Garcilaso mentions that the entrails of dead Inca rulers (removed in the embalming process) were kept in the temple at Tampu, the old name for Ollantaytambo. Other accounts say that one of the three founding ayllus of Cusco was called Tampu Ayllu, and that the ancient inhabitants of Tampu spoke not Runasimi, but a secret royal language used only at the Inca court. Little is known about this language, but it was apparently the ancestral tongue of the Inca "tribe."

The three "caves" from which the first Incas emerged were called Paqariq Tampu. *Paqariq* means "dawn," "birth," or "origin"; *tampu* is usually translated as "inn," but has the wider meaning "a place of lodging from which one sets out." There is a modern village called Paqaritampu to the south of Cusco (the opposite direction from Ollantaytambo); this is often assumed to be the place mentioned in the myth. But the seventeenth-century chronicler Bernabé Cobo was told by a grandson of Wayna Qhapaq that the first Inca and his sister-wife, after being created by the Sun and Moon in Lake Titicaca, traveled north seeking a place to settle. They came to the valley of the Tampu River (that is, the Willkanota, which rises halfway between Cusco and the lake) and traveled downstream to Paqariq Tampu. From this account it is clear that the "Origin Tampu" was on the Willkanota, and thus nowhere near the modern Paqaritampu. And, though there were countless tampus in the Inca Empire, the use of the simple name Tampu for the river and the town of Ollantaytambo suggests that here was the original destination of Manku Qhapaq and Mama Oqllo, founders of the Inca line. This version of the legend goes on to say that the pair *later* traveled to Cusco via the other (modern) Paqaritampu. Is this an attempt to reconcile two conflicting myths? Or does it reflect a moiety reversal necessary to establish the unifying principle—the first Inca—in both halves of the empire? A third chronicler, Pachakuti Yamki Sallqamaywa, a native writer of background similar to Waman Puma's, states that Manku Qhapaq's father and mother were called Apu Tampu and Pachamamachi, "Lord Tampu" and "Earth Mother." No doubt Inca theologians worked hard to reconcile this with the Sun and Moon parentage, but it, too, points to a connection between the early Incas and the people of Ollantaytambo.

The evidence is admittedly circumstantial, but if there is nothing to it, there remain two difficult questions: Why did the Incas keep the canopic relics of their rulers at Ollantaytambo? And why were they building here the most magnificent monuments outside Cusco itself?

———

Whatever may have been the relationship of Ollantaytambo and the first Manku, the town figured prominently in the career of Manku Inka II.

Pizarro tried to govern his immense prize through native puppets. He first gave the Inca "crown" (actually a headband, called *llautu*, with a fringe of scarlet vicuña threads) to Tupaq Wallpa, who soon died mysteriously, and then elevated a young prince, who took the name Manku Inka Yupanki, perhaps to symbolize the forlorn hope of a new beginning for the Tawantinsuyu. Manku was crowned at Cusco in 1534, and for a while he submitted to the insults and abuses of the conquistadors: when he failed to produce gold on demand they called him a dog, urinated in his face, and repeatedly raped his sister-queen and other wives. By 1536 Manku had had enough. He secretly summoned his generals and made the following speech, recorded later by his son, Titu Kusi:

> My brothers and sons: In the past few days I have called you here so that you may again see the new kind of people that have brought themselves to our country, which are these bearded ones who are here in this city.
>
> Because they told me they were wiraqochas, and appeared to be so in their dress, I commanded you to serve them as you would serve my own person, thinking that they were worthy people sent from afar by Tiqsi Wiraqochan. . . . But it seems to me that everything has turned out the very reverse of what I expected, because—know this, my brothers—these people have given me plenty of demonstrations since coming into my country that they are the sons not of Wiraqocha but of the Devil.

Manku escaped from Spanish custody and began what he hoped would be the reconquest of Peru. All Spaniards at large in the Tawantinsuyu were killed; there remained only the garrisons at Cusco and Lima. The Inca massed at least a hundred thousand men for the attack on his capital, and he tried everything—even setting fire to the holy city to destroy the invaders in its midst. The thick and ornate thatched roofs burned for weeks, releasing immense clouds of smoke, but the one building in which the Spaniards had barricaded themselves failed to catch. The Christians attributed this to miraculous intervention by the Virgin Mary, who was seen to decend from heaven and smother the flames with her skirts. However, Manku's son later recalled that the Spaniards had sent their black slaves onto the roof with buckets of water.

The Inca forces continued to besiege Cusco for eight months, but they gradually lost the initiative and were forced to disperse by Spanish sorties and the necessity of working their lands. In the meantime Manku made Ollantaytambo his headquarters. Work on the megalithic temple was suspended; instead, a defensive rampart was thrown across the valley, and the temple complex fortified by a perimeter wall. Here Manku brilliantly repulsed a massive Spanish attack. By now the natives were using captured European armor and weapons: Spanish prisoners were forced to make gunpowder for arquebuses in Inca hands, and Manku himself rode a horse into battle. The old superstitions that the Spaniards might be gods who carried the power of the lightning were gone. Before leaving Cusco the Inca had said to Hernando Pizarro: "What do you want? Is this the command of Wiraqocha, that you take by force the property and wives of everyone? That is not the custom among us. I tell you truly, you are not the sons of Wiraqocha but of Supay, which in our language is the name of the Devil."

The Inca held Ollantaytambo for over a year, but by 1537 many more white men had come to Peru and Manku had lost much of his force in daring raids into Spanish-occupied territory. In that year he decided to withdraw to the forested mountains beyond Machu Piqchu, and there he and his heirs resisted until 1572.

Manku's defenses are still here. The confusion in the construction of the temple must date from the late 1530s—it is hard to think of any other explanation for the haphazard inclusion of precisely cut megaliths in walls of clay and rubble.

The perimeter wall now serves to keep people without tickets from sneaking into the ruins.

$$=== 69 ===$$

Lunch in the Bahía Restaurant on the plaza, the "best" in Ollantaytambo. The only customers are a cholo couple already on their segundo and a mestizo drinking soup. A dog and three filthy toddlers are playing among bottle caps and crumpled paper napkins on the floor.

I glance at what the others are eating and decide on a fried-egg sandwich—the only alternative—and a large Cusqueña beer to wash it down. An electric fridge is displayed proudly by the door, and it isn't until the beer comes, warm, that I remember Ollantaytambo has no power: the refrigerator is the purest of status symbols.

Above my table there's a calendar showing a bathing beauty on the bonnet of a Hillman and, immediately next to this, a painting of the Last Supper.

=== 70 ===

Up at dawn to hike to the Inca quarries of Kachi Q'ata. There are still stars in the western sky but the tip of Waqaywillka is already pink. Half a mile upstream from the Albergue a rickety bridge crosses the Willkanota. It rests on a pier of Inca masonry in the middle of the river, which seems hardly touched by the assault of five hundred wet seasons. After crossing I have to double back downstream by a narrow path along the bank before climbing gently through a eucalyptus wood and a forest of giant p'atakiska, "biting thorn," a vicious barbed cactus that propagates by breaking off in chunks that stick to passing animals and people. Waqaywillka dominates the landscape, and the temple complex on the opposite side of the valley, so huge above the town, now seems distant and oddly small. A faint, intermittent line of greenery, drawn on the hillside as if by a pen short of ink, shows the course of the channel that once brought water from a distant torrent to the ruins.

After successfully negotiating the p'atakiska and rounding a bluff, I come upon the end of the great roadway built for hauling the stones from the quarry. It resembles a modern highway, being partly cut into the hillside and partly supported by a terrace; it climbs toward the quarries at a constant gradient and would be wide enough, if restored and cleared of brush, to carry two or three lanes of traffic. But it ends abruptly here, at the top of a steep scree down which the stones were slid to the riverbank at least a thousand feet below. From there the megaliths were dragged across the Willkanota (during the dry season) and the level fields of the valley floor to an enormous ramp, which can still be seen rising to the level of the great temple. I estimate the entire journey at four miles or more: two along the roadway from the quarries to here, and then another two from the river crossing to the ruins. Along the route, like abandoned cars, are occasional massive shapes—"weary stones" left when the work stopped. There is even one in the middle of the river. The Incas must have been planning a vast project: the quantity of stone in preparation and transit far exceeds that already raised at the building site.

Now, away from the rivers, I notice for the first time in days how their roar has made a luxury of silence. Silence, say the North American Indians, is the voice of the Great Spirit. I can hear the small sounds: dry leaves, the sudden shiver of the air when I surprise a dove, and crickets.

Ch'illik'utus qhawamuwan	The grasshopper watches me
Ruminanra ukhumanta.	From among the pebbles.
Imaynaraq rikumuwan	How does he see me
Huchuychallan ñawichanwan?	With his tiny eyes?

About a mile along the roadway some people have built huts and cattle corrals fenced by organpipe cactus. There is no one to be seen, but I have to drive off unfriendly dogs with stones. Here the road splits: a steeper section rises to a higher part of the quarry; the lower road continues as before, but there's a difficult stretch where a landslide has destroyed it. I pick my way on a narrow ledge cut into the cliff like a bookshelf and, because of my backpack, must crouch. Just beyond this is a small ravine and a spring of clear water (the cause, no doubt, of the slide). I have breakfast here: an orange and two slices of the banana bread that Wendy makes for the hotel guests. In the bushes are small green parrots, some finches, and a *siwar q'enti*, emerald hummingbird.

It is only a short walk from the spring to the bottom of the quarry. On the forty-five-degree slope of the mountain one sees a series of ramps separated by long screes. Ramps seem to have been built in areas where there were promising clusters of boulders. The rocks were dragged onto the ramps, roughly trimmed, and then slid down talus slopes, made partly of their own chippings, to the road at the bottom. At stages on the hillside, there are much larger working terraces, where extensive stone-trimming seems to have been done. One of these is thirty feet wide and more than a hundred paces long. On it sits a squared block measuring sixteen by eleven by six feet, which must weigh close to eighty tons.

There are small ch'ullpas dotted about the landscape, many of them perched like sandcastles on large rocks. They are mostly round, some four or five feet in height and diameter—just big enough to admit a doubled body. Tradition has it that these were the graves of laborers who died in the work, but I have seen no trace of bones, and neither did Squier a century ago. He noted their similarity to modern structures used for leaving offerings to saints. Whatever their purpose, the little towers look decidedly un-Inca; they are found elsewhere in the region unassociated with quarries, and in the upper quarry, where the work was just as intense, there are no ch'ullpas at all. I think their presence here is coincidental: they are probably relics of a local culture predating the Tawantinsuyu.

⸻

Reaching the upper quarry has not been easy. It was a climb of some two thousand feet up terrain that is either scree, threatening to slide at any moment, or bush, mostly dwarf acacia and p'atakiska. Twice the brim of my hat has saved my eyes from overhanging spines. Dry mint and sage crushed underfoot gave up a dusty fragrance in the heat.

The principle here is the same: seven ramps feed into a ravine. Stones slid down the ravine were stopped by a holding terrace built across it like a dam; this "dam" is the destination of the upper branch of the road.

Many granite blocks in various stages of preparation are waiting on the upper ramps; those that are finished sit on pedestals of small stones. J. Outwater, who studied the quarry some years ago, noted that the ramp surfaces are far from smooth; he suggested that the blocks traveled on rollers running along wooden rails. This would explain the pedestals—to raise the stones for the insertion of the rolling gear beneath. Hundreds of men would have been required on the steepest ramps, not to drag the stones, but to prevent them from running away. The gradient of the roadway clearly was designed to achieve the best compromise between labor and gravity. On this the surface is well prepared: rollers alone would have been sufficient.

I have lunch at the very top, immediately below the mountain cusp whose peeling vertical strata provided the Incas with their megaliths. A condor appears above me, closer than I have ever seen. (Is he warning me off or have his keen senses taken my corned beef for carrion?) I can see the bald head and Elizabethan ruff, and when he banks the sun flashes on the white feathers of his back as if on an airplane's fuselage. Then he catches an updraft and is gone over the peak, without a flap.

71

I descend a thousand feet and continue in a northwesterly direction. There are other things to see: the Door of the Wind, a curious stone tower whose silhouette stands out on the ridge that closes the north end of the valley, and a pampa where, according to Randall, there are Inca buildings and good camping.

On the saddle immediately to the north of the quarry I come across the remains of a water channel. Rock slides have hidden its course, but I presume it supplied the workers' camp. Water was also important in the stone-working techniques thought to have been used by the Incas. Rock was split by boring rows of holes, into which wooden wedges were driven; subsequent soaking caused the wood to expand and shear the stone. Thor Heyerdahl, of Kon Tiki fame, was given a remarkable demonstration of another simple but effective technique. Rows of Easter Islanders separated a partly finished statue from its matrix by pecking rapidly at the rock face with hand-held stone chisels: the stone was softened by repeated dousing. Marks on Inca stones indicate that pecking was the main finishing processs, but I've seen little evidence of it—or of boring—at these quarries. What I have seen today are long "columns" (probably lintels)—the largest is more than twenty feet long and only two feet thick—that seem to have been split like firewood. I don't want to add to the considerable body of ill-founded speculation on how such feats were done. One should keep in mind that the Incas, for all their bronze and precious metals, had an essentially Stone Age technology. Like ancient flint knappers, they possessed a practical knowledge of the possibilities of stone that far surpassed anything surviving in the modern world.

3:00 P.M.

Below on a spur there's a ruined town—dozens of crumbling stone houses arranged haphazardly on terraces. I would have missed it had shepherds not recently cleared the scrub.

The buildings are irregular, with rounded corners. Among them I find potsherds, and rocking querns for grinding, like those still used in Peruvian kitchens. The rough, irregular style of the place is very un-Inca, but the pottery fragments lying on the surface seem to be of Inca date. Was the town built by people brought here from another part of the empire to work in the quarries? Or was it perhaps a pre-Inca settlement later used as a billet for such workers? It would take a dig with good attention to stratigraphy to settle the issue.

The Incas were certainly here: lower down on the hill are several characteristically massive, orderly buildings of the imperium. But there's more—the entire hillside north of the quarry is stepped with ancient terracing, now so destroyed that in many places one hardly notices it. The retaining walls are low, made of flat stones laid in narrow courses; they look similar to the walls of the little ch'ullpas, and very different from the ranks of much larger Inca terraces that march boldly up and down the landscape elsewhere in the region. Whatever the chronology of all these works, the sad fact remains that these hillsides once supported a large population: where there was once a town and hundreds of miles of neat stone walls supporting irrigated topsoil, there are now only a few huts and a wilderness. And the hooves of European cattle belonging to the modern inhabitants are breaking down what is left of the terraces and scattering rubble over the precious strips of earth.

4:00 P.M.

It's a relief to reach the pampa almost a thousand feet above the ruined town: from below it is invisible and I was beginning to think I had missed it. At last a rim of yellow broom announced the brow of the hill, and a green lawn suddenly appeared as my eyes rose above the pampa's horizon. Above and to the south stands the granite cusp; to the north and west stretches the ridge that juts toward Waqaywillka like a headland, and from here one can see right through the Door on its crest. On the pampa itself there's a row of Inca buildings in a single block, and just below the mountain another group is raised imposingly on a high platform. Temples? Or, as Randall would have it, the headquarters of Inca "honchos"?

I pitch my tent. Horses are frisking on the grass; a chestnut mare cuts a fine figure chasing an errant foal, teeth bared, mane and tail streaming behind her.

The climb to Wayraqpunku, Door of the Wind, is easy; for the final stretch there's the luxury of an Inca road. The ruin is a square building of which three sides have fallen, leaving only the front wall with its impressive entrance. As one approaches, the peak of Waqaywillka is framed in this doorway and one feels one could step through onto the glaciers: by some trick of perspective the mountaintop appears level with the building. (In fact it is more than six thousand feet higher.)

Perhaps the Door was a shrine devoted to the cult of Waqaywillka. (*Willka*, incidentally, means both "peak" and "holy.") But it may also have been one of the signaling towers in the Incas' system of beacons. It was said that these could flash major news across the empire in a matter of hours.

From here the temple of Ollantaytambo looks scarcely higher than the town; the white peaks of Alancoma, Pitusiray, and Chicón have reduced Pinkulluna to insignificance. One can appreciate the extent of the valley floor—several square miles—and the fact that every inch of it has been leveled and stepped. The bottomland terraces are as accurately surveyed as rice paddies, and so broad that one is apt to notice only fields and miss that each hedgerow of broom and eucalyptus conceals a stone wall and a twelve-foot change in level. The formal landscape radiates from the town; the arrangement not only is beautiful (and perhaps symbolic), but also allows even distribution of the Patakancha's water over the whole valley by a system of canals as complex as the veins in a leaf.

Dusk floods terrace after terrace as the sun falls behind the mountains. Gaunt eucalyptus along the walls and ditches throw spears of shadow that are soon submerged. I can hardly see the creeping thing along the riverbank that is the evening train. But I hear its clatter and mournful howl—a howl answered by every dog on the hillside, who take it, no doubt, for the voice of the canine god. I return to the tent and light my stove.

8:00 P.M.

Supper: a freeze-dried curry brought from Canada; better than I feared. Afterward an almost full moon rises; a pale phosphorescence settles on the hills. In the chasm beyond the edge of the pampa, small clouds drift up the valley like ghostly ships; catching the moonlight, they seem illuminated from within. Waqaywillka, too, is lit that way, but the cusp behind me is dark, and the stars above it shine fiercely in a carbon sky. From where I sit, the rock wall looks like the rim of the world, and the idea comes to me that a person climbing up there and peering over would see only space.

== *72* ==

On the way back I spend too long rummaging in the quarries during the heat of the day. It is six o'clock when I reach the Albergue; I go straight to bed.

Maybe I have slept, maybe not; at any rate, I'm recalled from the borders of sleep by the unmistakable sound of a brass band: slowly it displaces the roar of the rivers, grows louder, and seems to position itself below my window like some perverse serenade. Again the sound brings to mind turn-of-the-century New Orleans: loose, rambling, yet solemn and almost funereal, but, as one's ears get used to it, with a compelling lilt that can only be Andean.

I dress, go downstairs and out into the darkness. The moon has not quite risen; there's a suggestion of *illa*, celestial glow, over Pinkulluna.

The band is playing at the end of a narrow alley behind the hotel (I am sure they do not notice me): fifteen musicians arrayed before a roadside shrine lit by dozens of candles—trumpets, cornets, trombones, a large drum, two saxophones, and three clarinets—all very sincere, very dignified, and very drunk. Some bottles of *trago* (raw spirit) manage to circulate without noticeably affecting the performance, passed from mouth to mouth like a sacrament; tears—or is it sweat?—roll down inflated cheeks in pure *enthousiasmos*.

The next day I learn that the music was part of the warmup for Qhapaq Raymi, Great Festival, a revival of the Inca summer solstice pageant. It is held early to avoid conflicting with Christmas.

The first event is a bullfight held in the Inca plaza. The Spanish custom has taken on a distinctly native identity in some parts of the Andes. Bulls, because of their horns, are associated with the Devil, and hence with ukhu pacha, the underworld. In the Ayacucho region the mythological role of the bull has blended with that of the amaru; supernatural bulls are believed to inhabit lonely tarns of the high puna. Wild bulls from the altiplano are preferred for fights. Such animals are not always killed, even though the inexpert and intoxicated Runa torero may well be fatally gored. Human blood spilled in these encounters is seen as payment to the earth for crops and livestock of the coming season.

Bulls are recognized also as symbols of Spain; in some regions there is enacted a bizarre contest, involving a condor, that turns the bullfight into a rejection of Spanish culture. The giant vulture is captured in a baited pit by a man who waits to grab the bird's feet as it lands. It is carried to the village, given alcohol and coca, and tied to the back of the bull, who of course tries to throw it off. The condor weakens the bull, tearing into his flesh with its beak and talons; toreros further vex him with prods and firecrackers. In these ceremonies, the bull is always killed—often dispatched with a final charge of dynamite—but the condor, totem of the Incas and the Sun, is returned victorious, inebriated, to his mountain crags.

The Ollantaytambo bullfight is a lighter affair. A professional torero, or *diestro* (dexterous one), as Peruvians call him, has been hired for the occasion, and the model for the ritual is Iberian. The diestro, a foppish, unwashed-looking little man in a wide hat, gypsy waistcoat, and tight trousers with a shiny bottom, appears: a polite smatter of applause. Then a roar of excitement as a black, shaggy, long-horned bull charges into the wooden enclosure and trots around looking for a way out.

An affable mestiza shopkeeper (from whom I bought tinned fish and a bottle of rum a few days ago) is sitting beside me: "It's the same animal as last year—a *bravo* from the puna. They're more dangerous the second time. They remember, you see."

The bullfighter seems to grasp this ugly fact: he stays as far from the bull as possible. Soon angry heckling comes from the crowd; he flaps his cloak; the bull charges. The dexterous one leaps the corral wall to safety. Shouts of "*Carajo*, get in the ring! . . . Fight the bull!" The diestro is shamed into a second attempt but within a few moments has leaped out again. This time a shower of orange peels, tomatoes, and one or two empty bottles follows him, along with yells of "*Maricón . . . sincojones . . . cornudo!*" ("Fairy . . . eunuch . . . cuckold!")—ultimate insults. At this the bullfighter turns to the crowd, shrugs, shouts that the bull is impossible, and stalks away toward the town. Several mestizo youths vault into the ring, eager to display machismo in front of the girls. But the *mayordomo* of the fiesta won't allow it, and the bull is driven into a roofless Inca building by a man on horseback. The mayordomo then announces that we will be entertained by a *banda filarmónica*; a metallic braying heralds the reappearance of the musicians I heard last night, evidently flagging from lack of sleep and surfeit of trago.

More Runa are arriving now, trickling down the steep paths from the heights, seating themselves on the higher terraces still vacant. The village mayors, *varayoqkuna*, are given the best spots. They sit regally holding their silver-tipped staffs of office (*vara*) before them, passing round shots of trago in tiny glasses. The "philharmonic band" dies away toward the modern plaza and is replaced by the not entirely dissimilar sound of panpipes and drums. An orchestra of sixteen pipers files into the square and forms a slowly rotating circle. The music, from the Lake Titicaca region, is played in an intricate arrangement of parts on panpipe sets ranging in length from a few inches to three or four feet. As the musicians revolve, different elements of the music are emphasized to the stationary listener.

The pipers make a wider circle and admit a concentric ring of a dozen dancers. These wear long feathered cloaks that extend into wings at the arms, and beaked masks with the white ruff of the condor. The plumage is black and white. Stretched across the diameter of the ring of dancers and held at the wingtips by two of them is a real condor whose wingspan is at least ten feet. The bird appears heavily drugged, possibly dead; shots of trago are poured down its beak from time to time. The pathetic dangling legs seem to keep time with the music as the dancers circle and sway.

"Barbarous, no?" says my neighbor with a delighted shudder.

"Do you think the condor is dead?"

"Just drunk. Afterward the *indios* will take him back where they caught him and set him free."

The fiesta ends with a band from P'isaq performing some of the music from the drama *Ollantay*. This verse-play tells of an illicit love between Ollantay, lord of Ollantaytambo, and Kusi Qoyllur (Joyful Star), daughter of Inka Pachakuti. Ollantay takes up arms against Cusco to secure his love. For ten years he fortifies himself, in open rebellion, at the town that bears his name. Eventually he is pardoned by Pachakuti's successor and allowed his bride, who has meantime been sequestered with the Chosen Women of the Aqllawasi.

It is now known that the play in its present form is not authentically pre-Conquest. On linguistic grounds, it can be dated to the eighteenth century, and the plot is suspiciously romantic. *Ollantay* was probably composed by a sympathizer of Tupaq Amaru during the renaissance of Andean culture that coincided with the revolt. But the drama is based on older traditions that may well contain clues to the history of Ollantaytambo. Whatever its dramatic shortcomings, *Ollantay*'s language is magnificent: the classical Runasimi that Tupaq Amaru is said to have spoken with great eloquence. A girl of fifteen, accompanied by a harp, two qenas, and two violins, sings a harawi in the soaring female falsetto of old Cusco. The wayno fugue (second verse here) is addressed to the *tuya*, a small dove that robs cornfields.

Qhechiprankunan	Her eyelashes,
Munay uyampi	Her beautiful face:
Kikin paqarin	On this same morning
Iskaymi inti	Two suns
Kikin ñawimpi	Will rest
Chaymi sayan.	In her eyes.
Ama pisqo mikhuychu	O bird, do not eat
Ñustallaypa chaqranta;	The fields of my princess;
Ama hina tukuychu	Do not destroy
Hillurina saranta,	Her delicacy, the maize.
Tuyalláy, tuyalláy!	O tuya, O my tuya!

73

There are some diesels on the Cusco–Quillabamba line nowadays, but the morning train is one of the old German steamers—the sort of machinery that gave rise to the Runasimi neologism *yana machu*, "old blacky."

Maypiñan yana machu?	Where's the yana machu?
Ña Santa Rosapiña,	Already in Santa Rosa,
Carretay	My carriage
Ña Kisakisapiña.	Is already in Kisakisa.
Sichus Rosalina	If, Rosalina,
Mana waylluwanki,	You don't love me,
Sichus Rosalina	And if, Rosalina,
Mana munawanki,	You don't want me,
Yana machu rakrawachun!	May the yana machu swallow me up!

Today is a bad day to travel because of yesterday's fiesta. The carriages are hideously crowded, and I find it impossible to get through the press of large baskets and larger women at the doors. Only those passengers with friends or relatives inside succeed in boarding—by being pulled in through windows. I ride on one of the little platforms over the couplings, less dangerous than it looks: there's a ladder to hold, and the maximum speed is twenty miles per hour.

At first the train runs on an Inca terrace beside the artificially straightened Willkanota, but once in the narrow gorge below the Ollantaytambo valley winds between boulders, below cliffs, and through countless tunnels. Its sinuous progress recalls Gregorio Condori's description of the first train he saw: "It is a black animal like a snake, made entirely of iron; and to move it opens its mouth where there is fire." In the tunnels I am showered with soot and ash. Fortunately we arrive within an hour at Kusichaka, where the "Inca Trail" to Machu Piqchu starts.

The footbridge across the river no longer exists—according to Wendy it was taken down by the man who now runs the *oroya* (a kind of bosun's chair hanging from a cable) and charges gringos fifty soles for the crossing. He must do well at the height of the dry season, when as many as sixty hikers a day "do" the trail. Today, thank God, there are only three besides myself. I set a slow pace that soon grants me solitude. It is already hot: at eight thousand feet, this valley is the lowest I have been for weeks.

Beyond a eucalyptus wood one comes to the Inca town of Llaqtapata. A British expedition has been digging here, with the eventual aim of restoring to use the ancient irrigation network. The trail now turns west to climb a small ravine hung with moss and posted with columnar cactus. Beside the stream there are broom thickets and little swards of grass cropped by sheep.

I reach Wayllabamba, the first and last inhabited settlement on the route, at noon. A scruffy place: the children have learned to beg for sweets;

two wolfish drunks search my equipment with their eyes and demand I hire them as "guides."

The view back down the valley is of glaciers framed in the vee of the ravine. The fringes of the snowfields are skirted by cloud, from below which issues the dark tangle of forest that gives the easternmost Andes a character like the volcanoes of Hawaii.

An hour beyond the village, signs of human activity—clearings, cow trails, and rough shelters for shepherds—start to give way to native cloud forest: gloomy stands of *chachakuma* and *kiswar*, the first with peeling red bark like an unraveling cigar, the latter pale, slender, and heavily festooned with moss. The woods have a fresh smell of leaf mold and wild mint that reminds me of hikes in the Canadian Rockies.

The trees thin out above twelve thousand feet, revealing a horseshoe, or cirque, of gray crags cupping an alpine meadow. This is Llulluch'a Pampa, named for the fleshy, broccoli-green plants that grow in the bogs of the watershed. I thought I would find some of the other gringos here; they must already have crossed the fourteen-thousand-foot pass, which I shall leave for the morning.

While pitching the tent, I see for the first time a *taruka*, an Andean dwarf deer. It's about the size of a spaniel and has a pair of miniature antlers.

Tarukatapas wik'uñatapas	The deer and the vicuña
T'aqarqanin tropanmanta;	I have snatched from the herd;
Chaychu mana t'aqarqoyman	So I should snatch away
Warma yanayta	My beloved
Taytamamanmanta.	From her mother and her father.

———

Supper is a disaster. In a fit of enthusiasm for the idea of local provender I bought at Cusco market quantities of ch'arki (dried meat) and ch'uñu, "freeze-dried" potatoes made by alternate exposure to frost and sun, and squeezing out the moisture. The ch'arki, despite its strong smell and scabrous appearance, is fine when added to a broth; but the ch'uñu has a frostbitten taste (much loved by sierra Peruvians) that I find impossible to acquire. A pity: the stuff is light and nutritious (it was a staple of the Inca storehouse system), and I have brought two kilos of it.

———

Next morning the ominously named Warmi Wañusqa (Dead Woman) pass looks deceptively close, but I find the last few hundred feet arduous. I have symptoms of lack of oxygen: pounding chest, confused thoughts, inability to speak simple sentences aloud to myself without mistakes. As soon as I rest at the top these troubles disappear. The pass is a narrow knife edge between two basins. There's a small apachita, to which I add a stone, and a mist spontaneously forming here that hides, then reveals, dark crags, bone icefields, and the dull green ichu moors behind.

So far there has been no trace of Inca road: the descent from Warmi Wañusqa is a muddy switchback worn into frost-slumped turf. One must drop four thousand feet to the floor of the basin, then zigzag wearily up the far side to the second pass. Halfway up the far mountainside appears the circular form of Runk'u Raqay, Round Court, a small ruin looking from here like a hat hung on a wall.

In the valley bottom there are spidery trees, again heavy with moss, but the climb to the ruin takes me up a trail bristling with achupalla.

Lunch at Runk'u Raqay: the last of my Tupac Amaru cheese. The ruin has two round terraces, superimposed like layers of a wedding cake, with a courtyard on the upper tier surrounded by apartments of rough stone. The buildings are standard Inca, but made to curve in conformity with their site. The courtyard opens to the south, commanding the whole basin and the first pass, which from here is nothing but a small chip in the mountain rim.

Two gringos trot up the hill with remarkable speed and are soon in the ruin, greeting me unbreathlessly in German accents.

"How long will you take to Machu Piqchu?"

"I reckon about a week."

"A week! We shall arrive Machu Piqchu . . . two days." And they leave with the neurotic energy of thoroughbred horses. Behind comes a third hiker; I take him for a tardy member of the same group, especially when he introduces himself as Wolfgang:

"No. I was behind you yesterday. I spend the night in Wayllabamba— very dirty place. I don't like. Those others just passed me, going very fast. Do you know they started from the train this morning? Good hikers, but I think they see nothing."

———

Wolfgang and I find the second pass, at only thirteen thousand feet, much easier than the first. Soon the going improves and I notice we are on the remains of an Inca step-road. Though the stone blocks are somewhat scattered and broken, they follow a route and gradient whose economy could only have been designed by a race of walkers. Near the top the clouds unveil the great icefields I saw yesterday; I recognize them now as the western slopes of Waqaywillka. The crest of the pass is a graveyard of boulders daubed with improbably brilliant white and orange lichens. Clumps of white heather and lu-pinlike plants with yellow blooms sprout from between the rocks.

The descent is gentle, the road well preserved. After an hour we sight the first major ruin: Sayaq Marka (Hanging City)—tiers of terraces, and neat gabled houses, draped on a headland jutting into rising cloud. As we enter the city so does the mist; for the rest of the day we see nothing of the new water-shed we have entered, nor any hint of our location in the landscape. There is only the immediate presence of stone walls, empty niches, roofless gables. It is utterly silent.

Wolfgang builds himself a small shelter of sticks and plastic. Despite the constant drizzle he turns down an offer to share the tent: "This is all I bring, so this is all I use." His food is equally stoic: a ten-pound bag of muesli. "I make this because it needs no cooking, but already I am hating it." It looks good to me—he agrees to swap some for a hot soup to which I add ch'arki and ch'uñu. Each prefers the other's provisions.

A storm breaks violently in the night. Hail that is deafening on the tent is followed by torrential rain; soon the groundsheet wells up and yields to the touch like a waterbed. I lie awake, relatively dry, wondering how long it will be before a bedraggled Wolfgang appears for sanctuary.

I find him in the morning, naked, huddled over a tiny fire that he has somehow managed to light. There is still a layer of hailstones on the ground.

"It was terrible. With first hail the plastic comes down in my face, then suddenly there is ten centimeters of water everywhere. Everything is wet, even my clothes, so I spend all night moving in order to keep warm."

"Why on earth didn't you come to the tent?"

"No. It's my own fault. This is all I bring"—he points to a sheet of plastic, now in shreds—"so this is all I use."

———

Wolfgang left after breakfast, anxious to get to Phuyupata Marka, the next ruin, where the Peruvian parks service has built some rudimentary shelters. I stayed on in Sayaq Marka and was rewarded when the weather cleared in the afternoon. The city hangs above a completely wild valley carpeted in cloud forest. The horizon, distant but marvelously clear when the sun came out, is a semicircle of white peaks: Sallqantay and Soray to the south, and a great chain that must be the Willkapampa range to the west.

I leave Sayaq Marka the following morning. The Inca road is superb. It drops down a long flight of steps, crosses a swamp on a causeway, traverses precipices on viaducts of solid masonry, and in one place pierces a headland by a tunnel cut through the rock. I arrive at Phuyupata Marka (City above the Clouds) at midday, stop to admire the Inca baths, then move on. There

are too many gringos camping here, too much rubbish and not enough architecture to persuade me to linger. Rather than go directly to Machu Piqchu I
shall make a detour to Wiñay Wayna; with any luck few will have bothered
to go there.

WIÑAY WAYNA

I remember this town, whose name means Forever Young, from my first visit
to Peru eight years ago. Like Machu Piqchu, it overlooks the Willkanota; I
climbed up from the railway then (the Inca Trail had not been discovered by
hikers in those days) and spent almost a week here. A few other gringos came
and went; I met one who was also from Canada, an anthropology student. A
year later we met again by chance in a Chinese restaurant in Calgary, and
have since become friends.

Today there are no gringos here, but their presence has had a devastating
effect on the ruins. (Perhaps one should never return to a place one has loved
so much, especially a place that one found unspoiled.) Eight years ago the
ancient town was intact. Archaeologists had cleared away the bush to reveal a
miniature Machu Piqchu on two levels: an upper (hanan) and a lower (hurin)
town, separated by an amphitheater of terraces but connected by a monumental flight of stairs, beside which is a row of baths or water shrines. In the
upper town are most of the temples—rectangular buildings like those of the
Qorikancha but of rougher construction, and a parabolic sun temple that
used to be Wiñay Wayna's crown. The curved wall was pierced by large windows, and through these windows lay a view of magical amplitude and depth,
a view extending from the river three thousand feet below to the peak of Waqaywillka ten thousand feet above, and in the foreground wild peonies growing on the temple walls.

Since 1971, half this wall of windows has fallen, and it is easy to see why.
The buildings of Wiñay Wayna are made of roughly trimmed granite blocks
set in a mortar of clay and lime. When the roofs rotted centuries ago, moss
formed on the mortar and thus sealed the walls from erosion. Thoughtless
gringos, however, have made campfires against the walls; the fires have killed
the moss "pointing" and allowed the heavy rains to wash the mortar from
between the stones. A year or two of this and the wall falls. In addition to the
portions already collapsed, there are many other places where the same thing
is about to happen; at every ominous bulge in the masonry one sees the tell-
tale soot of a gringo's fire. It is no exaggeration to say that in the last eight
years Wiñay Wayna has suffered more than in the previous four centuries.

Not all is disappointment. The lower town remains much as I remember
it—undergrowth has kept campers out. On the mountainside opposite this

sector there is a waterfall falling five hundred feet into the gorge over which part of the town literally hangs on its jutting rock foundation; and on the tip of the rock, facing the waterfall, is the largest window in the city, a window that can only have been made for contemplation. If one stepped through this window, one would fall as far as the water.

I must leave first thing tomorrow. My food is gone: gone, that is, except for the ch'uñu, which I still can't stomach.

MACHU PIQCHU

By leaving Wiñay Wayna at dawn, one can reach Machu Piqchu an hour or two before the tourist train arrives from Cusco.

Halfway between the two cities the Inca road is buried by an avalanche of loose rock chippings that must be crossed with caution—more than one hiker has slid to his death here. This scree, which can be seen for miles as a fresh white gash on the dark green landscape, is not a natural slide but the result of an ill-conceived scheme to build a luxury hotel on the knife edge of the mountain behind Machu Piqchu. The planned building was to have been linked to railway and ruins by a cable-car system. After blasting away thousands of tons of rock, and laying a water main that draws half the flow from the Wiñay Wayna waterfall, the builders discovered that the geological formation was unstable; work was abandoned. The "Lost City of the Incas" has temporarily been reprieved from looking like a ski resort, but the mess on the mountainside (luckily invisible from the ruins) remains.

"The Lost City of the Incas," "The Shangri-La of the Andes," "shrouded in mystery": the tangle of clichés and hyperbole grows thicker around Machu Piqchu than the cloud forest. Hiram Bingham must take much of the blame for this. When he "discovered" the ruins in 1911, he was not at all sure what the city was or why it existed. Chronicles make no mention of the place. Bingham was aware that the physical location did not fit well with what was known about Viticos and Willkapampa, the Incas' last strongholds, but as time passed and his fame grew, he became more and more convinced that Machu Piqchu was the capital of Manku, Titu Kusi Yupanki, Sayri Tupaq, and Tupaq Amaru. Ironically, Bingham himself penetrated Rosas Pata and Espiritu Pampa—less impressive ruins farther into Vilcabamba province, which modern archaeologists have now convincingly identified as the two last capitals.

But what was Machu Piqchu? And why was it unrevealed to the Spaniards? There were many turncoat Incas who must have known of its existence and, to judge from their other deeds, would have had no scruples about leading the invaders there. Paradoxically, I think the most likely reason that the now most famous of Inca cities remained hidden was because it was unimportant. It is relatively small—about four hundred houses—and extremely inaccessible; since Manku evidently did not occupy it for any length of time, there was no military or economic reason for its annexation by the Europeans. The large number of female skeletons found by Bingham has raised the idea that Machu Piqchu was a religious retreat to which the Chosen Women were removed when Cusco fell. Perhaps, but one must bear in mind that the sexing of ancient skeletons is not an exact science even today, much less seventy years ago.

Title deeds in Cusco and Lima show that the region known as "the Piqchus" was occupied for a while by Ecuadorian Indians loyal to the Spaniards. There is one reference to Manku harassing the area and burning "Indian houses." (Incidentally, *piqchu* or *pikchu* is the Runasimi word for the swelling of the cheek produced by habitual chewing of coca leaves. The name is often metaphorically given to prominent rounded mountains.) The Piqchus later became property of the Huadquiña hacienda, which still exists as a co-op, just a few miles downstream from the "lost" city. Most likely the owners of the hacienda did not know the extent of the ruins between the peaks of Wayna and Machu Piqchu (Old and New Peak), but they knew there were terraces up there with some agricultural potential: they rented these terraces for twelve soles a year to the Alvarez family, who were growing beans at Machu Piqchu when Bingham arrived.

———

Beyond the hotel excavation the Inca road reappears. After an hour's walk, I come to a flight of steps, and shortly a building on the very spur of the mountain. This is a gatehouse known as Inti Punku, Door of the Sun. When one enters there is no hint of the city around the corner, but as one leaves, there it is, stretched out on its saddle below, light stone walls and green planes beneath the erupting black tooth of Wayna Piqchu. It is now eight o'clock, small clouds are lifting from the houses, and the sun is lighting up the terraced lawns.

There are already too many unsuccessful descriptions of Machu Piqchu for me to attempt another. The photographic image of the city as seen from Inti Punku is well known: almost every travel brochure shows it. What is less well known is that one must frame one's picture carefully to avoid the hotel and its veranda roofed with lime-green corrugated plastic.

I wish I could report how I plunge, enraptured, into the ruins, how I ascend the sun altar, descend to the Cave of the Moon, scale thousand-foot Wayna Piqchu. But I do none of these things. Instead I make straight for the hotel restaurant and order bacon and eggs and toast and coffee; and when the elderly couple at the next table leave, I eat their toast, too.

Afterward, I visit those parts of the city that I missed eight years ago, and do climb Wayna Piqchu to see the terraces and temples perched up there; but as I climb down the tourist train arrives, fills the ruins with people, and empties them of magic.

= 75 =

I leave Machu Piqchu by the Hiram Bingham Highway, a precipitous gravel road that drops the two thousand feet from hotel to railway station. A microbus now plies the route once followed by the famous explorer, the lanky gringo on a diminutive mule whom local Runa dubbed "the man with six legs."

I catch a Peruvian (as opposed to tourist) train back to Ollantaytambo. This time I am able to find a seat—in the *especial*, or first-class carriage, among members of the Quillabamba élite: rich cholos (growers of coffee or perhaps cocaine), government officials, army officers. At the table across the aisle two middle-aged policemen and their wives are playing cards.

Fragments of Inca walls come into view beside the river from time to time: some terracing below Wiñay Wayna; the ruins of Torontoy (I've never visited those; the name intrigues me—it could be translated as My Toronto).

At the Albergue I meet Lindy and James, the real Canadians, just returned from their hike. It is now time off for Wendy and Randall. Hiking is a passion with James: he once walked from La Paz, Bolivia, to Santiago, Chile, living on stale bread and sardines, the only portable fare to be had in the whistle-stop towns that bead the railway through the Atacama desert. I can scarcely imagine a less appealing journey; but I forget to ask him, Why?

===

After two days of idleness, enjoying the Albergue garden and some books from Randall's library, I force myself to leave. The rains have not yet begun in earnest; I should take advantage of this by heading south to Lake Titicaca.

The afternoon train to Cusco. Opposite sits a well-dressed man in a corduroy jacket who dozes most of the way. Above him, on the hat rack, is a pile of fruit: oranges, peaches, bananas. The train crosses the pampa of Huarocondo, a wide, lush plain with terraces just apparent on the distant hillsides. Ragged Runa children who are supposed to be watching their parents' sheep and cattle run beside the slow-moving train. My neighbor wakes, opens the window, and throws fruit to the children, who fall on it like dogs. He seems a kindly man, but the deed is so ancien régime.

The train drops into Cusco by a series of switchbacks—reversing into sidings, throwing points, rolling down to the next level—in a motion like that of a falling feather. Beside the track are shanties of Cusco's poor. Small children board the train each time it stops, run shrieking through the carriages, and jump off when it brakes again.

There is a view of Saqsaywaman in twilight, then the lighted city, which seems a tawdry marvel after three weeks of country nights.

=== 76 ===

The bus south from Cusco passes a megalithic street corner on the edge of what was the Inca city and pulls into a PetroPeru station for the inevitable fueling stop. Above the driver's seat a sign says: DEMUESTRE SU CULTURA, TIRE LA BASURA POR LA VENTANILLA—"Be cultured, throw rubbish out of the window."

Beyond the suburb of San Sebastián, where some descendants of royal Inca ayllus still live, the bus snorts into the pastoral landscape of the Cusco valley: rich alfalfa fields, hedgerows of maguey and broom, the canary yellow of flowering *nabo*, a relative of rapeseed. The valley widens for several miles; ruddy green hills retreat and then close in again. Twenty miles from Cusco I disembark near some tall but tattered stone walls—the ruins of Pikillaqta, City of Fleas.

This site puzzled archaeologists for many years. There is a monumental terraced esplanade, and behind, a series of quadrangular compounds enclosed by high parallel walls between which there appear to have been wooden floors. The walls are rough and vertical, not sloping like those of almost all Inca structures. It has long been suggested that Pikillaqta might belong to the Wari period, but several excavations failed to reveal any occupational debris that might confirm this; other archaeologists argued that the complex was an Inca granary, or even an Inca garrison hastily built during the campaign against the Spaniards in 1536. But recent work has shown that the remains are in fact Wari; the scant deposits within the walls suggest that the empire of the Middle Horizon did not prosper for long in the Cusco valley. If Pikillaqta was a garrison, not merely a town, then one can argue that Tiawanaku and Wari, though sharing a common culture, were rivals for supremacy in the southern Andes. This view is also supported by the enduring ethnic boundary between Qolla and Qheswa (people of the altiplano and those of the valleys), which coincides with the continental divide, some hundred miles to the south.

About a mile from Pikillaqta, escarpments draw the valley to a narrow neck, and here the Incas have been active. They closed the valley with a great rampart, built across it like a dam, in which there are two gates—one used by the modern road, the other faced with fine masonry and known as the gate of Rumiqollqa (Stone Storehouse). The name is puzzling: possibly it derives from the nearby quarry, where the fine porphyry blocks for the kanchas of Cusco were obtained.

It's only a ten-minute walk to the quarry, but I search for an hour among cactus, thorns, and heaps of chippings only to find that the storehouse of stone is today largely bare. According to Squier and other writers, stones in various stages of preparation were common here in the past; but it seems that restoration work in Cusco, and the recent vogue for pseudo-Inca walls, have resulted in their disappearance.

It's a mistake to get off public transport between points. By noon two buses have passed me by—so full that they refused to stop—and now it is siesta time and the road is as empty as the ruins. I sit in the shade of a rock, severely parched after exploring the quarry, and resolve to flag down whatever comes next, be it public or private.

An ancient Dodge van approaches, slows, and stops fifty feet beyond me. I run after it, fail to notice the Ohio license plate, and am surprised to meet an elderly American whose face and neck have the lean, leathery appearance of a Galapagos tortoise.

Hiram (of all names) has the manner of a man who has lived long enough to form a generally low opinion of his fellow creatures, but not so long that hope has been completely defeated by experience. Hence his presence in South America: "Wanted to see this 'Third World' you keep hearing about. And isn't it just what you expected? Filth, poverty, communism. A great past, sure—long past—'beggars on golden thrones.' Seems to me I read a book called that. . . ."

"Stools."

"Yes, that's it: 'golden stools.' Ain't it the truth. I took this old panel truck off the lot—I own a used-car lot in Cincinnati, see. Hundred seventy-five dollars she cost me—I know a good one when I see it—and headed south. Walter, my son, he came with me as far as Ecuador, but then he got lovesick for his wife, the young fool. She's no good—a gold digger—about as mean, as mercenary, and as much fun in bed—what I hear—as a parking meter. But that's his problem. . . . That Cozo's an interesting place."

"Cusco?"

"Yeah. That Cozo's an interesting place. Those Incas musta bin something. But you know the trouble with this country? Latins. They move in: the neighborhood goes down—we got the same trouble in the States. . . ."

=== 77 ===

Not far from Rumiqollqa, the road emerges into the valley of the Willkanota, or Willkamayu, and crosses to the right bank of the river at Urcos. The valley opens, becoming a broad, fertile floodplain.

After two hours' driving, during which I receive dramatic monologues on Jimmy Carter ("He may be born again, but we'd all be better off if he hadn't been born the first time"), Hiram's wife ("I miss her cooking—you know what they say, 'Kissin' don't last, cookin' do' "), and socialism ("I got to admire England, England's the only country that ever went socialist and was able to vote 'em out"), we draw opposite the small town of Tinta, visible on the other bank as a cluster of low, mud-walled houses and thatched roofs with some patches of tin or tile.

Tinta and nearby Tungasuca: in the 1760s and 1770s, home and headquarters of the kuraka Tupaq Amaru.

———

During the mid-eighteenth century a remarkable change began in the power structure of colonial Peru. The Spanish Empire was in a period of economic decline, while the native population was beginning to recover from the plagues and disruption that had attended the Conquest. The colonial government was simultaneously onerous and corrupt; by 1750 several million Runa had died in forced labor in the mines of Potosí and Huancavelica. (Some estimates go as high as six million; two to three million is probably more realistic.) And for those who stayed in their homes there was the scandalous *repartimiento de mercancías*—the forced purchase at inflated prices of shoddy manufactured goods, sickly mules, or any items the stagnant Spanish economy wanted to foist on its colonies under the pretext of civilizing the Indians by drawing them into the market system. The repartimiento was exercised by *corregidores*, local "judges" whose privileges were so lucrative that candidates paid the Crown sums amounting to many times their prospective salaries for the right to hold the post.

As the colonial regime became more burdensome, Spanish culture lost, in Runa eyes, whatever prestige it may once have had. The old Tawantinsuyu assumed the proportions of a golden age—an image of the past much aided by the clandestine circulation of "Inca" Garcilaso's *Royal Commentaries* among the native aristocracy through whom the Europeans governed. Garcilaso's utopian vision of the Inca Empire, which he constantly compared with ancient Rome, fostered the inevitable conclusion that both had fallen to barbarian invasions: a conclusion supported by the aqueducts, roads, and terraces lying everywhere in ruins. His book, together with new liberal ideas percolating into the Andes from Europe, provided the ideological basis for movements aimed at "uprooting the European invader from our soil." There was a corresponding renaissance of Andean culture and its symbols. Portraits of Inca nobles from eighteenth-century Cusco show a return to native dress and royal insignia; ancient pageantry, semihistorical dramas such as *Ollantay*, and plays lamenting the Conquest were revived and encouraged.

The wave of insurrections began with a guerrilla war waged in the central Andes east of Tarma by one Juan Santos Atau Wallpa. This local chieftain eluded or defeated Spanish forces throughout the 1740s and 1750s. In 1750, twelve Inca nobles from Lima plotted to overthrow the viceroy in a palace coup. The plan was revealed to the authorities by a priest violating the secrecy of the confessional—neither the first nor last time that the Church acted as a spy network for the Crown: the same fate befell Bernardo Pumayalli Tampuwaqsu, the kuraka of P'isaq (near Cusco), when he planned an uprising early in 1780.

Meanwhile, José Gabriél Kunturkanki Tupaq Amaru, the lineal descendant of the last Inca ruler, had tried to seek relief for his people from the repartimiento and mit'a through legal channels in the Lima courts. At the same time he sought to have his ancient title confirmed against a spurious rival claim brought by the Betancourt (!) family of Cusco. Failing in both efforts, and with "eyes opened in Lima," as his wife Micaela Bastidas Puyuqhawa later said, Tupaq Amaru returned to Tinta and opened the rebellion by arresting and hanging the corregidor in November 1780.

Events moved quickly. On November 16 he issued his famous proclamation of freedom for all slaves. Two days later, at Sangarara, he defeated a

Spanish force sent from Cusco. He then invaded the provinces between Tinta and Lake Titicaca. Micaela, who bore arms herself, urged her husband to march on Cusco immediately, but he delayed until January 2, 1781, and thus seems to have lost the initiative. He made two attempts to invade the city, but finding it defended largely by native troops loyal to Spain, and loath to fight a bloody battle against fellow Runa, he opted for a siege. In this he was no more successful than Manku Inka two and a half centuries earlier.

There followed several months of skirmishing between Tupacamaristas, as the Spaniards called the rebels, and *pukakunkas*, "rednecks," as the Runa called the whites. Allied rebellions broke out in other parts of Peru, in Bolivia, and even as far north as Colombia. Some of these were mestizo in character, some even attracted support from criollos who would later pursue independence, but in the La Paz region there were wholesale massacres of whites by the Aymara under Tupaq Katari. Tupaq Amaru, an educated man with some Spanish relatives, had tried to avoid a race war, and had called on all castes to unite in building a new Peru. But as the conflict inevitably grew more racial, non-Runa sympathizers defected from the Inca's cause. In April, a mestizo named Francisco Santa Cruz betrayed Tupaq Amaru to the Spaniards; a week later, another betrayed Micaela Bastidas Puyuqhawa.

Tupaq Amaru was imprisoned at Cusco and repeatedly tortured by Visitador José Antonio de Areche, the "visitor" originally sent by the Crown from Spain to correct abuses in the government. The prisoner's arms were broken in the course of Areche's interrogations, but the Inca remained silent. He tried, meanwhile, to smuggle a note to allies, asking for a file with which to escape. This note survives in the Cusco archives—a pathetic, almost illegible scrawl written in the only ink available: his own blood. Again questioned under torture to reveal the names of his collaborators, Tupaq Amaru told Areche: "There are only two accomplices here—you and I. You the oppressor, and I the liberator. Both of us deserve to die."

Tupaq Amaru and his wife were killed in Cusco's Waqay Pata on May 18, 1781. After the lengthy executions, Areche gave the following order to scatter the remains of the Incas throughout the rebellious provinces (I quote only a small selection):

> *Distribution of the bodies, or parts thereof, of the nine principal prisoners convicted of the rebellion.*
>
> Cusco: The body of Tupaq Amaru, on Piqchu hill;
>   of his wife, the same with the head.
> Carabaya: An arm of José Gabriél Tupaq Amaru; a leg
>   of his wife.

Lampa: A leg of José Gabriél Tupaq Amaru; an arm
          of his son.
Tinta: The head of José Gabriél Tupaq Amaru; an
          arm to Tungasuca; another (arm) of Micaela
          Bastidas, to the same.

═ 78 ═

RAQCHI

A few miles beyond Tinta one comes to the small pueblo of Raqchi, where
the Incas built their largest covered temple. The modern village clusters on a
flight of ancient terraces; it is not until one has climbed these and crossed a
plaza in front of the tiny whitewashed church that one comes to the Inca
structure.

It reminds me of a ruined abbey or cathedral, but where the nave would
be in a European building there is a great central wall, still fifty feet high and
more than three hundred long, which formed the backbone of the temple and
supported the ridge of the gabled roof. One end wall still stands—this shows
the gable and indicates that the two sides of the temple were, as one might
expect, symmetrical. It is as if there were two temples, mirror images of one
another, back to back. They are connected, however, by ten wide doors, or
openings, through the central wall, and by small windows in the masonry
piers between the doors. There is little left of the outside walls but the foundations—enough to show that they were made of small square blocks (hence
their disappearance) and that the total width of the building was about ninety
feet. To support so wide a roof, eleven columns marched down the center of
each half. This is the only known use of columns by the Incas, and much has
been made of the uniqueness of the temple on this account. It *is* unique—
and was recognized as such by the Incas—but the authors of *Inca Architecture* have shown that the Raqchi temple was in fact a daring extrapolation
from a common Inca design in which wooden pillars served the same purpose. The surviving column and central wall are of finely cut masonry for the
first eight feet, with adobe above. In recent times they have been given a cop-
ing of Spanish tile to prevent further decay.

Adjoining the temple, at right angles to it, is an eight-hundred-foot row
of houses, arranged on a terrace with the same talent for symmetry and perspective evident in the main structure. In Squier's day, there were still traces

of purple paint in the niches of these houses; perhaps the adobe portions of the temple were painted the same rich color.

Behind the houses, and overgrown now with thorn bushes and enormous yellow-flowering wachuma cacti, are a hundred and twenty round storehouses standing in ten rows of twelve; each is twenty-seven feet in diameter and about fifteen high. Hiram, who has, as he says, a head as well as an eye for "figures," calculates a total capacity of about a million cubic feet.

There is now only an hour of daylight left, but we have time to see the water system at the foot of the volcanic hill half a mile to the west of the buildings. A spring flows through baths of finely cut stone before emptying into a large artificial lake halfway between the lava flow and the temple. The chill of evening is covering the lake surface with a fog, behind which the great wall rises like an apparition. Hiram has fallen silent; I can hear the cries of waterfowl and the splash of cattle drinking at the shore.

———

Several traditions assert that Raqchi was the temple of Wiraqocha, the Creator, built by Wiraqocha Inka at the dawn of Inca greatness. The design of the building is said to have been given by the god to the man in a dream.

The location is strange—far from Cusco, yet not quite at the source of the Willkamayu, where one might expect it. It seems the volcanic eruption occurred here within human memory; the subsequent appearance of a spring where there had once been heat would certainly have indicated a spot of great holiness. In Andean belief, it would represent a triumph of moisture (lower moiety) over fire (upper moiety)—a reversal appropriate to the Creator, a water deity whose name means Foam of the Sea.

After the Conquest, Wiraqocha and his coastal equivalent, Pachakamaq, became identified in the Runa mind with the Christian god. Evangelizing Spaniards generally went along with this syncretism, though it was later declared a heresy. Today, "wiraqocha" is used by Runa for "gentleman" or "white man," or simply as a substitute for "señor." But the old god remains in the myriad Taytachas (Little Fathers), the miraculous apparitions of "Our Lord" that inhabit the chapels of the Andes and are almost always associated with a rock or spring.

Wiraqocha had a special place in Inca legend. It was he who brought to life the stones of the battlefield in the struggle against the Chanka. And it is said that José Gabriél Tupaq Amaru came to the ruins of the Raqchi temple to implore the old god for a second gift of help against the Incas' enemies.

———

79

We camped after dark last night in a meadow by the roadside, Hiram in his panel truck and I in the tent. This morning an audience of curious but un-communicative Runa watched us get up, eat breakfast, and strike camp. Old vans are a commonplace to them, but nylon fabric, aluminum poles, and my miniature stove are marvels.

At the large market town of Sicuani, where Arguedas taught in the late 1930s while writing his first novel, *Yawar Fiesta*, the road crosses to the west bank of the Willkamayu. An hour later we pass through Maranganí, a town of eucalyptus trees and textile mills where blankets of sheep and alpaca wool are made.

The terrain continues its gradual rise to the divide.

LA RAYA, 14,200 FEET

La Raya must be the gentlest pass in Peru: railway and road cross it without the need for switchbacks or hairpins. But it is bleak and cold, and the wind blows incessantly. Beyond the pass lies the great altiplano, the home of the Qolla, or Aymara, people. Since the rise of the Incas, the Aymara language has receded before Runasimi as far as the lake, but the ethnic boundary re-mains in other things and especially in legend. Thus, Gregorio Condori:

> When the Inca was building Cusco, where our grandfathers lived, it was all pampa; there were no hills and the wind blew in like a raging bull, knocking down whatever houses and walls the Inca was building. So one day the Inca said to his wife:
>
> "*Carajo!* This wind won't let me work. I shall shut it in a kancha until I finish making Cusco."
>
> So the Inca went to La Raya to shut in the wind, but while he was rounding up the wind to capture it, Inka Qolla appeared—they say the wind belongs to Inka Qolla, because in the Qolla lands all is wind and pampa.
>
> Inka Qolla said: "Why are you shutting in my wind?"
>
> "To build my city," answered the Inca.
>
> "If you want to build your city I will let you enclose my wind for just one day; if you don't finish in that day, you will never fin-ish. . . ."

So the Inca tethered the sun, and in that way he lengthened the time of the day.

When he finished building Cusco, his wife suggested to the Inca: "You will have to build great embankments, because when Inka Qolla looses the wind it will blow again." And understanding this, the Inca made all the hills that surround Cusco, and these hills have existed ever since.

The Willkamayu rises at La Raya in the form of two springs: one hot, one cold; where they mix there is good bathing to be had. Steam is emanating from the ichu pasture a quarter of a mile from the road. Hiram and I take towels and find a pool where the temperature is just right. It's my first hot bath since Cajamarca; in spite of the wind and the muddy bank, it is superb.

Not until we emerge, parboiled and completely naked, do we notice three Runa shepherdesses who have gathered on a knoll twenty yards away for a view of wiraqocha flesh. Thinking it more decorous, I turn my back to them, but cannot help hearing peals of shrill laughter while bending down to pull up my pants.

———

Beyond La Raya there's an ascetic beauty to the altiplano that reminds me of southern Alberta in autumn: the same expanses of coarse brown pasture under a vast blue sky, the same presence of distant mountains on the horizon; except that here mountain chains are visible both to east and west, carrying the thirteen-thousand-foot plain between them, defending it from the jungle on one hand and the desert on the other.

One sees cattle and sheep, uncouth and lumbering beside the more numerous llamas and alpacas, whose graceful posture and large, liquid eyes might convince an extraterrestrial that they were the intelligent species on these reaches of the planet.

The scattered settlements are all alike—mud walls rising from mud streets; ichu roofs held down against the wind by hairnets of grass ropes from which hang heavy stones. But there is color—the shocking-pink sweaters and rainbow-colored lliqllas (here made of commercially manufactured cloth) on the stout and bowler-hatted Qolla women. The clashing scarlets, pinks, and crimsons seem to be the inventions of aniline dye companies, until one sees a cactus in flower or a qantu blossom, and recalls ancient ponchos that have a predilection for the same loud hues.

The next day we reach Juliaca, and for the first time since Sicuani can fill the tank of the Dodge from a gasoline pump. The plaza in front of the railway station is occupied by stalls selling alpaca woolens. Hiram buys a ch'ullu, which, when donned, changes him from a tortoise into a gnome.

From Juliaca the road is paved the forty miles to Puno, Peru's port on Lake Titicaca. Ten miles before Puno we turn off to see the ch'ullpas of Sillustani that stand above the shore of Lake Umayo. This road is also recently paved—another sign of the government's faith in tourism.

On the low hills that separate the two lake basins sits Hatunqolla, a small mud town that has seen better days. In Inca times Great Qolla was one of the most important centers of Qollasuyu, the southeast quarter of the Tawantinsuyu, and it had been a rival for power in the southern Andes before the sudden rise of the Incas. Shortly before the end of the fourteenth century, Hatunqolla's ruler attended the wedding of Wiraqocha Inka in a Cusco that was soon to become an imperial power. The Qolla chieftain arrived with a huge retinue, including even the gold-bedecked image of his local wak'a, and attempted to overawe the young Inca with a somewhat Teutonic speech in broken Runasimi:

Qam Qosqo Qhapaqa,	You, Lord of Cusco,
Ñoqa Qolla Qhapaqa.	I, Lord of Qolla.
Upyasun, mikhusun, rimasun!	Let us drink, let us eat, let us speak!
Ñoqa qollqe tiyakan,	I am surrounded by silver,
Chuqi tiyakan.	And by gold.
Wiraqocha Pachayachi much'aq,	Wiraqocha, World-Maker, I worship.
Ñoqa Inti much'aq.	The Sun also I worship.

SILLUSTANI

Some five miles beyond the town the road ends in a car park, below the promontory from which the burial towers of ancient Qolla nobles overlook the lake.

Lake Umayo, smaller by far than Titicaca, has an otherworldly character deriving from its resemblance to a crater. The water lies at the bottom of sheer cliffs, and from the center of the lake abruptly rises a flat-topped island whose height equals that of the surrounding land. It is as if the lake were an enormous circular moat excavated from the puna. The strange effect is enhanced this afternoon by a sky of steel herringbones and a single storm cloud hanging above the island.

The ch'ullpas are larger and quite different in most respects from those at Oxamarca. The largest is forty feet high and sixteen feet in diameter at the base; its bulk achieves preponderance by flaring outward as it rises, so that the diameter at the top is close to nineteen feet. Originally, this tower (like many of the others) was roofed with a hemispherical dome of solid masonry. Just below the base of the dome a simple cornice, like a broad, flat ring, circles the building.

The resemblance to a stylized phallus is obvious—supported by the multiple meanings of the word *ayllu*, in both Runasimi and Aymara: "clan," "ancestor," and "penis." But the point isn't belabored—some of the ch'ullpas, though keeping the same outline, are square in plan.

All have been rifled long ago. In some cases robbers were content to break into the burial chambers through the tiny doors at the base of each building; but in others the domes and parts of the walls were destroyed by the search for treasure. Cross-sections thus revealed show that the chambers are small in relation to the mass of the structures, and that only a few have a second chamber above. The interior fill is rubble, but the outer walls are of massive masonry as finely cut and fitted as that of Cusco.

Many of the towers date from pre-Inca times: it was the ch'ullpa builders who kept alive the art of precision stonework through the five or six centuries between the fall of Wari-Tiawanaku and the rise of the Tawantinsuyu. Spanish inquiries about the pre-Conquest mit'a in the Qolla region met with the answer: "We used to go to Cusco, to build houses for the Inca."

=== 80 ===

PUNO, 12,650 FEET

A fiesta was starting in Hatunqolla when we passed through this morning: a panpipe ensemble on one side of the plaza, a brass band on the other. Girls in bright costumes were dancing in the crossfire, but to which music I couldn't tell.

Hiram has left for La Paz and points beyond ("I hear a guy can get a real steak in Argentina"); he has dreams of shipping his van from Buenos Aires to South Africa.

This morning I went down to the wharf and booked a seat for tomorrow in an open boat to Takili Island.

Puno has improved: I've found a hotel with hot water and a restaurant with hot food.

Next morning at Puno docks—all kinds of tatterdemalion shipping: reed boats bearded with algae, a Peruvian navy gunboat that might have been salvaged from Scapa Flow, and the two old steamers, *Inca* and *Ollanta*. These were built at Grimsby, England, in the 1870s, shipped to Peru in pieces, brought over the cordillera on mules and carts, then assembled at the lakeshore. The insane project was, of course, the work of Henry Meiggs. And it succeeded—for a hundred years the steamers made nightly crossings to Bolivia, linking the two nations' rail systems. Now buses and a hydrofoil have reduced them to one trip a week. But the copper steam pipes are kept polished, and through the portholes of the *Inca*'s locked superstructure I get a glimpse of ornate brass and mahogany.

The boat to Takili is a forty-foot open launch powered by an old car engine and containing twenty-five passengers and two lifebelts. The lake has a reputation for turning ugly without warning; I am not reassured.

For an hour the boat negotiates shallow channels between beds of *totora*, the reed from which the slow but unsinkable native craft are made. We pass the "floating island" of the Uru, a people who live on an immense pile of rotting reeds. Their houses are of reeds, their boats of reeds, and they eat the roots of reeds. Apparently they have always preferred this life to domination by Aymaras, Incas, or Spaniards. But they haven't escaped modern tourists (who visit them by hydrofoil), and Seventh Day Adventist missionaries, who have attacked what is left of their culture and built the most prestigious structure on their island—a chapel of corrugated iron.

Beyond the Uru settlement the boat enters open water; for the first time the size of Titicaca (about the same as that of Lake Erie) becomes apparent. The eastern shore, some forty miles distant, is below the horizon, but tips of the snow-capped Carabaya range can just be seen. The near shore appears as a dark line along which countless heliographs are flashing—reflections from tin roofs. Southward, to the Bolivian railhead at Waki, the water stretches for a hundred and forty miles.

On board there are half a dozen gringos and some twenty Takileños, all men. When their island comes in sight—a hump of rock rising from the dazzling sheen of the water—they change from drab city clothes to the distinctive dress of Takili. This is a blend of sixteenth-century European garb with pre-Columbian accessories: black britches, white wool shirt, and small black waistcoat; floppy knitted ch'ullu like a brightly colored Victorian nightcap, and an exquisite woven *chumpi*, a belt up to ten inches wide decorated with intricate pallay designs.

Meanwhile I have been listening to Christine, who has just finished a two-year aid program among Bolivian Aymara; she has had some experiences of her own with Adventist missionaries.

"I was trying to develop commercial outlets for the Indians' alpaca products, and trying to promote alpaca in general because they don't degrade the environment the way sheep do. But the fundamentalists have a strong hold in those communities—they ban the rituals, the ceremonial drinking, the music, the dances, all the things that are the Indian culture. And worst of all, they ban llamas and alpacas because they're not biblical animals and are therefore 'unclean.' "

"Why do the Aymara listen to them?"

"They came in twenty or thirty years ago when there were terrible famines on the altiplano; they got their foot in the door with aid. Nowadays Indians looking for social mobility, wanting to become cholos, see a way out of the constraints and obligations of their communities. By becoming *evangelistas* they can avoid sponsoring the fiestas, and get out of the whole communal prestige system. They keep what they earn, become rich and more westernized. It boils down to personal profit at the expense of traditional Aymara values. More Adventists means more sheep, fewer alpacas, more erosion. It's very depressing."

But after three hours' sailing we dock at Takili's tiny jetty, and the serenity of the island lifts our mood.

= *81* =

TAKILI

After a few days, Takili, like all islands, becomes the world. There is no electricity here, no vehicles, horses, donkeys, or oxen, not even any dogs. "We don't like dogs, so we don't allow them here," my landlord, Domingo Marka, tells me, "but we keep cats because of mice."

Despite the European elements in Takili dress, and the fact that sheep rather than alpacas are the wool animal, the island is in many ways a survival of the pre-Columbian past. All the arable land is carefully terraced and worked only with the chaki-taklla foot-plow. The island is crisscrossed by a network of neat stone roads, uniform in width, contained between stone walls and ascending steep terrain in flights of stairs. Everything is tidy and clean. No animals are kept in the houses or house compounds (sheep have a separate kancha); people relieve themselves far off in the fields and bushes: there are no unpleasant smells.

Domingo Marka's establishment is typical. He has two houses, one for himself and family, the other used partly for storage and as lodging for occasional gringos. The buildings form two sides of a kancha whose other sides are six-foot stone walls with stone benches around the inside. One end of the kancha has a lean-to shelter in which pails, basins, brooms, and farming tools are kept. The kancha is swept every day.

The houses are of stone and clay with reed roofs. Inside my lodgings there is a raised adobe sleeping platform covered by a layer of reeds and thick weavings. Niches in the walls hold crockery and small kerosene lamps. For this I am charged forty soles (twenty cents) a night. By the door hangs Domingo Marka's prize possession: an ebony staff with silver pommel and bands—a *vara*, symbol of his office as varayoq ("he with the vara"), an elected community leader. I only hope some gringo doesn't take a fancy to it.

The island's eleven hundred inhabitants are organized in six ayllus and are self-governing. There are no non-Runa except for visitors and one schoolmaster, who teaches mostly in Runasimi. The "town," Takili Llaqta, is simply a ceremonial center—a square surrounded by a dilapidated church, a hall, a very basic restaurant, and a cooperative where the weavers sell their goods. The people's kanchas are scattered over the whole island, but none is more than two hours' walking from the *llaqta*.

It is weaving that links Takili to the outside world and draws the visitors. Takili work is prized for the fineness and uniformity of the hand-spun thread, for the consistency of the dyeing, the intricacy and complexity of the pallays. The woolen cloth is so tightly spun and woven that it is as smooth and stiff as first-class denim. Until a few years ago, Takileños traveled to Puno and Cusco to sell their cloth, but recently they decided to bring the buyers to them. The Takili people themselves own and operate the motor launches that carry the tourists.

How the sudden influx of frequently unwashed, unclothed, and willful gringos will affect the quiet, archaic culture of the island is hard to say. Almost all the visitors I talk to are sure that Takili's serenity won't last; but Domingo Marka is confident the islanders know what they are doing. He tells me that the Peruvian government once had plans to evict the inhabitants and turn the place into a penal colony, but the Takileños successfully fought the issue in the Lima courts, and have since had great confidence in their ability to contain threats from outside.

As yet there is no civil guard post here, no mestizo class to usurp the sovereignty of the Runa; but I fear it will take only one or two incidents between locals and tourists to attract the apparatus of the modern Peruvian state.

"Today there will be a fiesta. If you wish to come you may accompany me." I follow Domingo Marka down the step-road to one of the tiny harbors. On the way we pass a drab building he identifies as an Adventist chapel. How many have converted?

"About a hundred and fifty, mostly women. It is something I don't agree with. I am a Catholic."

"So am I," I say, secure in the knowledge that in the Andes *católico* means pantheist. (Like most of the important men, Señor Marka has a good command of Spanish; I haven't heard Takileños speak anything but Runasimi among themselves.)

The day is wonderfully clear. The crown of the island rises a thousand feet, and there I can make out silhouettes of the pre-Inca ruins I visited yesterday. Titicaca is calm, an electric blue with swaths of green indicating currents. On the horizon are the peaks of the Qallaway mountains, from here quite prominent, their snows reflected on the water among the images of scattered clouds that are also brilliant white.

The fiesta is to celebrate the launching of a new boat—a forty-foot clinker-built craft. When we arrive it is still sitting on the terrace where it was built, a long way from the water.

Women have spread a snake of white *unkhuñas*—ceremonial offering and eating cloths—over two terraces to form a "table" cloth several hundred feet long on two levels. A band of panpipers with two large drums is circling the boat. It seems every man is an amateur musician: several join the band for a while, then others take their places. At times there are as many as twenty-six players with a full range of instrument sizes. Between tunes, one prominent citizen or another—the master boatbuilder, the captains of the other boats, the varayoqs—make impressive but not overly long speeches in Runasimi.

The spirit of the gathering flags only once, when the ladies' choir of the Adventist chapel insists on singing a dreary Salvation Army song in Spanish, a language few, if any, women on the island understand. But immediately the panpipes and drums resume, and the intrusion seems forgotten.

(There is something odd about the status of women on Takili. They remind me of North African women: retiring, their faces often hidden behind head cloths. Even most of the weaving and the knitting of ch'ullus is done by males—no Takili man is ever without his knitting. All this is untypical of Andean culture. I assume that the men's control of shipping, and hence commerce, has eroded what are usually female preserves. Perhaps the women's marginal role accounts for the missionaries' success among them.)

At two the meal is served. Four hundred Takileños and about twenty gringos kneel before the cloth. Men come with large pots and ladle a broth of potatoes, *okas*, other native tubers, barley, and (alas) ch'uñu into each person's pottery bowl. The eating is hearty; after fifteen minutes second helpings are served. Afterward, quantities of chicha, soft drinks, and bottled beer are consumed; the band resumes. Then the launching.

Fifty sturdy Takileños surround the boat, turn it upside down, heave it onto their shoulders, and carry it the five hundred yards to the jetty. They set it in the water as easily as a toy, step the mast, fit the rudder and propeller. Ten others climb on board carrying an old Ford V-8 motor. Within an hour everything is connected and working.

The panpipe band—well lubricated, since they got the lion's share of the beer—gets into the boat, along with all the dignitaries. They cast off and sail triumphantly round the bay, a Peruvian flag at the mast, the popping of exhaust and breathy lilt of the ancient instruments blending and wafting back across the water.

I think, *This is how the Incas did things*, and for the first time feel hopeful about the future of Takili.

$=$ *82* $=$

COPACABANA

I return to Puno from Takili, and then resume my journey south. Eight hours by colectivo along the lakeshore, a brief exchange at the frontier ("Where's your visa, *señor*?" "The consul in Puno said I didn't need one . . ." "OK."), and I am in Bolivia: the most Indian nation in the Western Hemisphere, named after the most criollo of liberators.

Copacabana is a sort of Andean Lourdes, a place of large dismal hostelries with cell-like rooms catering to pilgrims from all South America. (I am able to get a room only by promising to be gone by the weekend, when thousands are booked to arrive from La Paz.) As soon as the sun leaves, the town turns gray and bitterly cold—nothing could be further from the association of the name (in the mind of the undevout) with the beach at Rio de Janeiro. And the hygiene of Copacabana makes Cusco seem immaculate: one must tread with great care to avoid the fecal offerings of incontinent faithful.

One wonders how many nightclubs around the world have named themselves after this cold and malodorous town; for this is the original Copacabana, a spot whose holiness far predates the cult of the "Christian" Virgin of the Lake. Qopaqhawana means "the clear blue vision" or "the place from which one sees the clear blue." In pre-Conquest times there was a temple here "of vast renown among the gentiles"; in the temple stood a translucent blue stone, carved in the form of a woman's face, which was said to grant visionary powers. I would guess that the figure was probably a representation of Mamaqocha, "Mother Water," the female counterpart of Wiraqocha.

During Inca times, the cult of Qopaqhawana was eclipsed to some extent by that of the nearby islands, Titicaca and Koati. According to the principal Inca origin myth, Manku Qhapaq and Mama Oqllo—brother and sister, husband and wife, children of the Sun and Moon—descended to earth at these isles, which consequently are also called the Islands of the Sun and Moon. But the old lake goddess survived the fall of the Incas in a way that the cult of sun and moon did not. Within a few years she discarded the clear blue stone for the blue robes of Mary, Mother of God.

The Catholic miracle of Copacabana is suspiciously similar to that of Guadalupe in Mexico. At Guadalupe stood the ruins of the Aztec temple to Tonantzin, "Mother of the Gods." Scarcely a decade after the Conquest, a baptized Aztec named Juan Diego came before the bishop of Mexico and displayed his humble cloak, on which had miraculously appeared (while he happened to be in the neighborhood of Guadalupe) a painting of the Virgin and a spray of roses out of season. At Copacabana in 1582, one Titu Yupanki, a local noble of Inca descent, received a nocturnal visit from the Virgin that also resulted in a miraculous painting—but no roses.

Theologians have recently voiced doubts about these miracles; there has been talk that the bishops involved, overcome with "an excess of zeal," confected them to "deceive the Indians." But there's no more willing mark than the double agent. The miracles were clearly mutual deceptions from which everybody profited: the Spaniards achieved "conversions," and the Indians ensured the continuity of worship at the two most important shrines to female deities in the New World.

———

I go to the bay to look for a boat to the islands. A tourist launch goes every day, but does not stop long enough for one to see the major ruins. I am directed to a Señor Puma, whom I find busy with the innards of an outboard motor. His plump face and prominent ears would need only the addition of whiskers to suggest, if not his namesake, at least a large and amiable house cat. We strike a bargain for all day tomorrow.

A little farther along the bay is a chainlink fence with a sign showing a skull and crossbones and the words MARINA DE BOLIVIA. On the other side of the fence are some buildings, a jetty, and two old gunboats. I have within my gaze the entire navy of Bolivia—the country has been landlocked since losing its ocean corridor in the War of the Pacific.

Copacabana's central plaza contains some odd concrete imitations of local Inca sculpture, and a fine stand of native trees and shrubs, among them the qantu, at present flaming with its trumpet-shaped crimson Flower of the Inca. The north side of the square is bordered by Nuestra Señora de Copacabana's precinct and basilica, a graceless concoction of Moorish and Baroque architecture covered in gaudy paint and tiles. I decide to spend the rest of the day elsewhere, and content myself with Squier's description of the Holy of Holies:

> The spangled velvet veil was slowly withdrawn, and the *milagrosa imdgen* . . . revealed to our heretical eyes. It is an elaborately dressed figure, scarcely three feet high, brilliant in gay satins, and loaded with gold and jewels. Its head is a mite in comparison with the blazing crown that it supports, and its face is delightfully white and pink. . . .

Copacabana is surrounded by hills, which quickly lift one above the town and tawdry shrine to reveal superb views of the lake and distant peaks. The hills are rocky and wild and have many vestiges of ancient sculpture, including the Inca's Gallows, a trilithon made by uniting two natural rock spires with a lintel.

Between the south side of the town and the water there is a steep crag, perhaps four hundred feet high, ascended by a stairway of recent origin. Landings at regular intervals represent the fourteen Stations of the Cross. I was expecting to find a concrete crucifix at the summit, and am surprised to stumble on an altogether more lively gathering. About twenty or thirty Bolivians—middle-class people of both sexes from La Paz—are drinking heavily from beer bottles and haggling with vendors who sell (besides drink) toy trucks, cars, and models of bungalows made of colored plastic. All this in the shadow of three large crosses, on the far side of which are small stone chambers filled with sputtering candles. A minor cleric, evidently deep in his cups, is reciting blessings over the toys handed to him by purchasers; beer is poured over the truck or house and it is placed among the candles for a length of time apparently commensurate with the amount of beer or money that has accrued to the padre.

Turning from the bibulous worshippers to the lake, I have a view of water and sky, equally blue, and of parts of Titicaca Island, especially the extraordinary rock ridge, resembling the spine of a dinosaur, that forms its western side. Immediately below me, at the foot of the crag, the water is so still and clear that one can see the rocks receding many fathoms into its depths.

I return to the town and, passing through a secondary plaza where buses park, see several new trucks caparisoned with paper streamers and floral rosettes. Some intoxicated mestizos are drinking, singing, and solemnly splashing beer over the vehicles' wheels. Chola women approach with more flowers and more beer; then a priest—similar in deportment to the one on the hill—gives the necessary blessing. The men pile into the trucks and drive off at high speed through the streets, blowing horns and shouting. The ceremony is uncannily like a Canadian wedding, but it's clear that the ritual in the plaza, and those on the hill, are designed to invoke the protection of the Virgin of the Lake over newly acquired property. If one can bring one's vehicle to Copacabana, so much the better; but if not, or if one has a house to bless, coverage is effected by use of the plastic models.

83

Señor Puma has an eighteen-foot launch, powered by outboard, with a partial cabin over the bow and midships. He says nothing as we rapidly leave Copacabana behind and pass over the submerged section of the dinosaur's skeleton—the strait separating Titicaca Island from the shore. It is still cold, and the water, so clear and deep, seems black, lifeless, even sinister. I think of the giant toads that live in the lake and are said to grow up to fifteen inches long. Soon the sun is burning as fiercely as the wind chills—an Andean duality, I reflect in discomfort, that resulted in the Qolla invention of the freeze-dried potato.

Today is the Southern Hemisphere midsummer solstice, the ancient Qhapaq Raymi: a good day to see the Incas' *paqarina*, their place of origin or "dawning," and to end this narrative.

ISLAND OF THE MOON

The other name for the island, Koati, is apparently an Aymara corruption of *koyata*, "of the queen"; it was here that Mama Oqllo, sister and wife of Manku Qhapaq and daughter of the Moon, was believed to have descended to earth. The island is a dark, bald ridge shaped like a Brazil nut floating on the water. As we approached we could see sparse reddish soil clinging to the vestigial contours of ancient terracing.

Koati at first was forbidding, but on reaching the north side the boat entered a crescent bay that simultaneously catches the sun and excludes the prevailing wind. Puma, trousers rolled above the knees, jumps into a foot of water and pulls the boat to shore.

"Up there"—he points—"you will find the ruins."

There are four broad terraces sweeping down almost to the water. Each is a hundred feet in depth, and three hundred wide. The walls, of fine masonry, rise about ten feet. On the topmost terrace, and right against the hill, stands the building known as the House of the Chosen Women or the Temple of the Moon.

The best description of the complicated structure is given by Squier, who saw it when more was standing. It had an upper story with prominent gable ends (now completely gone), and reminded him of Elizabethan architecture. Like a country house of that period, the building surrounds three sides of the upper terrace, the open side facing the lake. The walls are indented with doors sunk in large corbel-vaulted porches that resemble somewhat the *ivans* of mosques. The construction is of rough stone in clay mortar, but enough stucco remains to give an idea of the smooth, painted finish the building once had. In the middle of the long central wing are two open alcoves whose back walls are ornamented in the same way as the doors. According to tradition, a life-size silver woman and golden man stood here and gazed over the terraced gardens, the lake, and the twin crowns of the Andes: the great peaks of Illimani and Illampu, which rear above the far shore and are reflected in the water.

Despite the unusual style, there is no doubt the building is Inca—an Inca architecture influenced perhaps by the Tiawanaku ruins, by the use of corbeling in the Qolla ch'ullpas, and by similarly vaulted sod houses like those one can still see today in the region of Huancané.

———

Señor Puma wants to leave—he's noticed an approaching cloud and says there is much more to see on the larger island.

When we are halfway between Moon and Sun, the storm reaches us. Huge raindrops, then hail, spatter the boat like grapeshot. I give my rain jacket to Puma, who must stay with the outboard, and retreat under the cabin roof. In minutes the sheen of the lake is lashed into four-foot waves topped with whitecaps. We begin to bob and yaw so violently that I have to emerge from shelter and sit on the windward gunwale to trim the craft. It is about a mile to the nearest land, but if the boat sank, swimming would be impossible. Parts of Titicaca are more than a thousand feet deep, and the water keeps to a constant fifty degrees Fahrenheit, cold enough to induce early cramp.

No sooner have these thoughts become preoccupations than the storm passes; the water does not settle immediately, but when the sun reappears, the lake changes its character from that of the North Sea in January to the Mediterranean in July.

=== *84* ===

TITICACA ISLAND (ISLAND OF THE SUN)

We land at the southeast tip, only a short walk from the Pillku Qayna, Colored Ruin, or Inca's Palace.

Of the almost complete two-story building drawn by Squier only a shaky bottom level stands; of the painted stucco that once covered it there isn't a trace. As at the Moon Temple, there are many corbel-vaulted rooms, and the two principal apartments have a similar view of the mountains across the lake. Adolph Bandelier, who ransacked the islands in the 1890s, held the opinion that these two buildings were dedicated to the cult of the snow-capped peaks. But the weight of semihistorical evidence argues in favor of their traditional associations; there is, anyway, no reason why worship of the sun and moon would exclude adoration and admiration of the finest apus in the Andes.

We touch briefly at Puma Punku, the landing stage visited daily by the tourist boat from Copacabana. A copious spring flows down a channel descending a flight of Inca terraces and waters a park of cedar and eucalyptus trees at the bottom. But the so-called Fountain of the Incas is a disappointment: "improvements" made by the local hacendado in the eighteenth century have completely butchered the ancient work.

Señor Puma now takes me to the bay of Ch'alla, where the hacienda buildings stand. From there, he explains, I will be able to walk to the remains on the north side of the island, including *the* Titicaca, the sacred rock of Manku Qhapaq.

Ch'alla looks like a small bay on the Aegean coast of Yugoslavia—it has the same clear water, rocky shore, and sense of calm antiquity. But when the motor falls silent I hear young girls' ululating voices and a wild snoring of panpipes. Puma will be happy to wait here for me until I return: he enjoys fiestas.

The people are dressed very differently from those of Takili. The men are wearing flannel slacks, shirts, manufactured sweaters (many bright pink), and felt fedoras. Sandals made of motor tires are on their feet, and, because it is hot, ponchos are carried folded over one shoulder. The women have the classic bowler hat of the Aymara, full blouses, fuller skirts, and stocky brown calves showing beneath countless petticoats; in outline they look like stout Christmas trees. But today is fiesta; many are dressed in elaborate and expensive costumes bought or rented for such pageants. There are men got up as "Incas," smothered in buttons and medallions, like pearly kings; others are wearing devil masks representing the seven deadly sins—these are depicted as lascivious Spaniards with pink papier-mâché faces, or by extremely ornate headdresses like those one might expect to see in Bali or Bangkok: horns, ears, lightning bolts, bulging eyes made of painted light bulbs, interlocking Chavinoid fangs. The women's dancing costumes are closer to their everyday wear, but the blouses are tighter about the chest, the skirts shorter, the petticoats more numerous—well calculated to display the robust figure of the Aymara adolescent, and all in a collage of pink, yellow, gold, green, silver, and crimson.

I have some difficulty getting through the fiesta and decline countless invitations to get drunk. On the far side of the settlement a young boy appears; he offers to guide me to the "ancient things" for two pesos.

The path—less well kept than those on Takili but probably ancient— leads onto the hillside above the hacienda and through a grove of brilliant qantu trees in bloom. This side of the island is exceptionally warm: there are even small green parrots in the bushes and some plantings of maize. The air smells of flowers and wild herbs. The path rises to skirt a bare ridge; here the boy shows me two marks in the bedrock: the "footprints of Manku Qhapaq"—outlines made by veins of iron ore. Squier was shown the same things, and remarked, "They are rather large for those of even so mighty a personage as the Inca Yupanqui, being more than three feet long. . . ."

I pay the boy; he leaves after pointing out a ruin he calls the Chinkana and the path to the sacred rock. The Chinkana is unlike any in the Cusco region: it has no hewn tunnels or bizarre carvings, merely narrow winding passages that were once roofed with stone slabs, and that lead to rows of small rooms and an inner courtyard. Squier and Bandelier are probably right in thinking that this was the house of the Chosen Women who wove cloth and made chicha for the rites associated with the rock.

The remains on these islands are puzzling in their unimpressiveness. Though the Temple of the Moon and Pillku Qayna were once fine-looking buildings, they were built cheaply by Inca standards. There is even an account that the priests of the islands upbraided Tupaq Inka Yupanki for neglecting their cult, and that the buildings and Chosen Women were installed only after these complaints. It also seems that traditions of pilgrimage to the rock predate any Inca activity in the area. Perhaps the association of the first

Incas with Lake Titicaca was a fiction designed to unify Cusco history with the older legends of Wiraqocha, Qopaqhawana, and the birth of the sun itself, which was said to have appeared on Titicaca Island after a period of darkness at the creation of the world. Or perhaps the Incas embellished Cusco, their Rome, at the expense of this, their Holy Land.

———

The view from the Chinkana ruins is enchanting. The far shore of the mainland can just be seen as a twinkle of tin roofs in the heat haze. Half a mile from here stand several bald rock islands inhabited only by black cormorants. The bay below is also empty of human settlement and has a shingle beach that looks good for bathing. I decide on a dip before starting back toward the rock. The bay is a sun-trap; though I can bear the icy water for only a minute, I steam dry in the hot, thin air in less.

A large gray eagle is combing the hillside as systematically as any aerial photographer, catching the updraft from the warm bay, making pass after pass over the slope, each time some ten yards farther up. The whole flight is made without one flap of his wings. At last he reaches the ridge and is gone over the sacred rock.

The rock, like the buildings, is relatively unimpressive—merely a sandstone cliff about two hundred feet long and twenty-five feet high. It has none of the seats, steps, or adornments that one might expect from the Incas: nothing but a terraced esplanade in front of the sheer face. Yet this is the rock whose Aymara name, Titi Qaqa, Rock of the Cat, has named island and lake. And this is the rock the Inca dynasty regarded as its paqarina, its place of dawning. It was said that Mama Oqllo and Manku Qhapaq, after descending on their respective islands, united here before traveling to Cusco. In the version of the legend that has them emerging later from three caves at Paqaritampu, the journey was made underground; in another version, Manku carried a golden rod, which sank of its own accord into the fertile soil where now stands the Qorikancha. Whatever may have been the historical facts, the Incas pictured their divine ancestors beginning here a mission to rule the known world.

From the top of Titi Qaqa one has a view of much of the island and the lake, and of the mountain rim beyond. My own journey has brought me in reverse through the itinerary of the Incas' brief and brilliant career to this enigmatic starting point—from their twilight at Cajamarca to their mythic dawn. It is tempting to imagine what might have been if the Spanish Conquest had failed; but, regardless of short-term political events, the diseases (and eventually the economics) of the Old World would have fallen hard on the New. Millennia of isolation had created an imbalance that was certain to be the ruin of the less populated and biologically more vulnerable hemisphere.

I think of what Titu Kusi Yupanki, son of the second Manku, wrote while he ruled the Willkapampa remnant of the Inca imperial enterprise:

> All the people were gathered in the four parts of the world, which we called according to our custom: Antisuyu to the east, Chinchaysuyu to the north, Kuntisuyu to the west, and Qollasuyu to the south. This we conceived standing in Cusco, which is the center and capital of all the earth. And my ancestors there in the center called themselves Lords of Tawantinsuyu—which is to say, Lords of the Four Parts of the World—for they thought there could surely be no more world than this. . . .

Afterword

When this book went to press in the early 1980s, reports of an obscure guerrilla group calling itself Sendero Luminoso, the "Shining Path," had just started to come out of Peru. The uprising began with a burning of ballot boxes near Ayacucho on the 199th anniversary of Tupac Amaru II's execution. Other deeds were more bizarre: dogs, identified as Deng Xiaoping and other "traitors," were hanged from lampposts. Dynamite was lobbed into the embassies of the USA and China, and the Soviet Union's cultural centre, all on the same day; not even the CIA thought Sendero was the work of foreign powers. Yet the Shining Path would dominate Peruvian life for a decade.

The movement declared itself to be "ethnic and cultural," and Peru to be "a fundamentally Indian republic," but otherwise kept silent, cultivating an air of mystery. Its leader, a philosophy professor of mestizo background named Abimael Guzmán, became known in Runasimi (Quechua) as Puka Inti, the Red Sun, and the word pachakuti ("upheaval, overthrow") emerged from mythology to be shouted on the streets. For a while it seemed that Guzmán was casting himself in the role of Inkarí, the once and future king who would lift five centuries of oppression.

But during the course of the 1980s the movement's true nature became clear. Guzmán was no Inca but an extreme Maoist, and his ruthlessness with peasant lives soon earned him comparisons with Pol Pot. After the jailing of Osmán Morote, an anthropologist in Sendero's leadership, the movement dropped its Andean messianism and shifted its appeal to the Lima slums and cocaine jungles.

By 1990 roughly half of Peru's territory was under Shining Path control, and much of the country had suffered atrocities—from the army and police as well as Sendero. A smaller Marxist group, named for Tupac Amaru, was also active. In ten years 20,000 died, most of them civilians. Sendero's near-success stemmed from the raising of hopes by Velasco's reforms, followed by the dashing of those hopes (especially in the Andes) and a return to bankrupt politics in Lima. Everything had been tried: army rule, various bits of Right, Left and Centre, even a chaotic APRA regime in the mid-eighties.

The watershed election of 1990 was contested by two amateur politicians: Mario Vargas Llosa, the well-known criollo novelist; and Alberto Fujimori, an obscure agronomist of Japanese descent. The urbane Vargas presented himself abroad as a champion of democracy, a Latin Václav Havel. Peruvians, however, were aware that he fronted for parties of the far Right and the old white elite. Parts of his "Freedom Movement" had even opposed universal suffrage at the last Constituent Assembly, hoping to exclude "illiterates," i.e. Indians. Despite a war chest one hundred times greater than Fujimori's, Vargas lost.

Once in power, Fujimori implemented monetarist policies similar to those Vargas had advocated. But largely because he was an outsider and non-white, often portraying himself as a surrogate Indian, or "Chino," he enjoyed far more room for manoeuvre. He also forged a symbiotic alliance with the head of military intelligence, a powerful and sinister figure with the Conradian name of Vladimiro Montesinos, whose ruthlessness proved a match for Sendero's. Suspected rebels were jailed without due process; many were kidnapped, murdered and "disappeared" by security forces.

In 1992, Fujimori pulled off an autogolpe, or self-coup, suspending Congress and ruling by decree. Wags changed his nickname from Chino to "Chinochet," but many Peruvians winked at his methods when Abimael Guzmán was captured and put on show like a caged beast later that year. The Shining Path went into decline and never recovered. The Tupac Amaru Revolutionary Movement was dealt a similar blow in 1992, and finished off in '97 with a bloody end to a hostage-taking at the Japanese ambassador's Lima residence.

Once the threat of revolution faded, many Peruvians became alarmed by the brutality and corruption of their regime. In the 2000 elections, Fujimori changed the constitution to allow himself a third term, and rigged his victory. The triumph was short-lived. In November, Vladimiro Montesinos was caught on video, apparently in the act of bribery. Both men quickly lost their local and international backers. Fujimori was overthrown by a revived Congress while on a visit to Japan, and Montesinos fled the country. An interim president has been installed until new elections can be held.

The man who should have won the 2000 campaign, and may win the next one, was yet another charismatic outsider, named Alejandro Toledo. A former shoeshine boy with a United States education, he made much of his being a cholo, someone of indigenous looks and modest background, like most Peruvians. Toledo was vague on policy but drew enthusiastic crowds shouting *Chino no! Cholo sí!*

If there is cause for hope after twenty years of great suffering, it is that Peru's racial and cultural divide is now openly recognized and talked about. Native Peru has a new sense of its identity; the words Indian and cholo are not seen as the insults they once were; public life is no longer the exclusive preserve of whites and would-be whites. It seems that Peru may, for the first time ever, be ready to elect an Indian. Such an outcome would not end centuries of ethnic oppression overnight, but it could prove comparable, symbolically, to the election of a black president in South Africa.

Ronald Wright
Ontario
January 2001

CHRONOLOGY

Prehistory

30,000–15,000 B.C.	Man populates Americas from Asia.
15,000–11,000 B.C.	Hunter-gatherers in Peru at Piki Mach'ay cave near Ayacucho.
10,000–2000 B.C.	Preceramic Period. Peruvians develop fishing, herding, horticulture, and agriculture. Sedentary villages established in parts of coast, mountains, and jungle. The domestication of beans, squash, potato, maize, guinea pig, llama, and alpaca lays the economic foundation of Peruvian civilization.
2000–900 B.C.	Initial Period. Appearance of ceremonial architecture at Kótosh in northern highlands.
900–200 B.C.	Early Horizon. Cultural influence of Chavín de Huántar spreads over most of Peru. Paracas culture on south coast.
200 B.C.–A.D. 600	Early Intermediate Period. Local cultures such as Nasca, Moche, and Cajamarca I flourish.
A.D. 600–1000	Middle Horizon. What are now Peru and Bolivia fall under control or influence of Wari and Tiawanaku.
A.D. 1000–1438	Late Intermediate Period. Rise of Chanka confederacy and kingdom of Chimor. Beginnings of the Incas in the Cusco area.
A.D. 1438–1532	Late Horizon. The Tawantinsuyu, or Inca Empire, establishes sway over most of modern-day Ecuador,

Peru, and Bolivia, half of Chile, and the northwest corner of Argentina.

Inca Period (chronology after John Rowe)

1438–1471	Pachakuti Inka Yupanki defeats Chanka, takes Inca throne, and founds the empire. Controls Andean area from Ayacucho to Lake Titicaca. Begins rebuilding of Cusco as an imperial capital.
1471–1493	Tupaq Inka Yupanki succeeds Pachakuti, expands empire to central Chile, northwest Argentina, northern Peru, and Ecuador. Defeats Chimú and incorporates elements of Chimú organizations into Inca state.
[1492	Spaniards defeat last Moorish enclave of Granada. Columbus reaches Hispaniola.]
1493–1525	Wayna Qhapaq Inka succeeds Tupaq Yupanki. Reconquers rebellious Chachapuya (Chachapoyas), subdues Ecuadorian coast, and fixes northern frontier at Anqasmayu River in southern Colombia.
[1509	Henry Tudor crowned King Henry VIII of England.]
[1521	Cortés conquers the Aztecs of Mexico.]
1525	Wayna Qhapaq, his designated heir Ninan K'uychi, and at least a third of the empire's population are killed by a plague, probably European smallpox, brought by the Spaniards to Panama and Mexico and spreading ahead of them through South America.
1526	War of succession breaks out between Wayna Qhapaq's sons, Waskar and Atau Wallpa. Pizarro sails down Pacific coast and intercepts an ocean-going Inca raft. Three of the sailors are captured and taken to Spain; one, Felipe Wankawillka, will serve as interpreter at Cajamarca.
1532	Atau Wallpa's forces capture Waskar Inka. Francisco Pizarro captures Atau Wallpa Inka at Cajamarca.
1533	Death of Atau Wallpa.

Colonial Period

1534	Manku Inka Yupanki crowned in Cusco as puppet Inca.
1536	Manku rises against Spaniards, lays siege to Cusco and Lima.
1537	Manku withdraws to Willkapampa (Vilcabamba), where he establishes the Neo-Inca state. Paullu Inka made puppet in Cusco.
1537–1548	Civil wars and power struggles among the conquistadors. Manku makes frequent raids against the Spaniards and their collaborators.
1544	Manku murdered in Willkapampa by Spanish outlaws. Regents rule Neo-Inca state in trust for Manku's young son Sayri Tupaq.
1557	Sayri Tupaq crowned Inca in Willkapampa.
1560	Death of Sayri Tupaq. His brother, Titu Kusi Yupanki, succeeds to Inca throne.
1571	Death of Titu Kusi. Succeeded by half-brother Tupaq Amaru.
1572	Tupaq Amaru captured, brought in chains to Cusco, and executed. End of Neo-Inca state.
1585–1615	Waman Puma (Felipe Guaman Poma de Ayala) writes his *Nueva Corónica y Buen Gobierno*, a critique of the Conquest and Spanish rule.
1742–1761	Juan Santos Atau Wallpa wages a guerrilla war in the central Andes.
1750	Lima *kurakas* plot to overthrow Spanish viceroy and restore Inca rule.
1780	Last great Inca revolt led by Tupaq Amaru II (José Gabriél Kunturkanki Tupaq Amaru Inka).
1781	Tupaq Amaru captured, and executed in Cusco.
1781–1783	Rebellion continues under Andrés Tupaq Amaru and Tupaq Katari.
1783	Suppression of the revolt. The remaining Inca aristocracy are executed, exiled, or stripped of power and titles. Runa language, dress, customs, etc., banned by Visitador Areche.

Republican Period

1821	San Martín declares Peru independent, abolishes Indian tribute.

1825	Creation of Bolivia from what had been High Peru.
1826	Bolívar made president of Peru. Indian tribute re-established.
1879–1883	War of the Pacific: Chile, Peru, and Bolivia. Peru and Bolivia lose.
1911	Hiram Bingham makes Machu Piqchu known to outside world.
1920	Recognition of Indian communities included in the Peruvian constitution by President Leguía.
1930	Emergence of APRA (Alianza Popular Revolucionaria Americana) as radical political and intellectual force.
1945	APRA compromises in return for sharing power.
1963–1968	First term of President Fernando Belaúnde Terry.
1968	Belaúnde ousted in military coup.
1968–1975	General Juan Velasco Alvarado heads revolutionary military government. Radical reforms.
1975	Velasco, now ill, ousted by his prime minister, General Francisco Morales Bermúdez.
1976	Velasco dies.
1976–1978	Military government becomes more conservative. In a climate of worsening economic crisis, Constituent Assembly is convened to draft a new constitution as a preparation for civilian rule.
1980	Elections held under new constitution. Fernando Belaúnde Terry elected to second term. His government adopts monetarism and swings to the right. Economy continues to deteriorate.

NOTE ON RUNASIMI PRONUNCIATION

Almost all Runasimi words are stressed on the penultimate syllable. If a suffix is added the stressed syllable moves accordingly. In words of more than three syllables the first syllable is also stressed. Thus: *llaq*ta (town); *llaq*ta*ta* (to the town); *llaq*ta*man*ta (from the town).

Sound values of the new alphabet are approximately as follows:

a,e,i,o,u	Similar to vowels in European languages such as German or Spanish. In Runasimi there is little distinction between *i* and *e*, and between *o* and *u*. Both *i* and *e* are closer to the short sounds of English (as in *hit, get*) than to the Spanish.
au, aw	Interchangeable. Both represent the same *au* sound, as in German *Auto*.
ch	As in English *chair*.
ch'	Explosive *ch*.
chh	Aspirated *ch*.
h	As in English.
k	As in English.
k'	Glottalized *k*.
kh	Aspirated *k*.
l	As in English.
ll	As in Castilian Spanish. Similar to *lli* in English *million*.
m, n	As in English, but less readily distinguished.
ñ	As in Spanish. Similar to *ny* in English name *Sonya*.
p	As in English.

p'	Explosive p.
ph	Aspirated p. In Cusco region this sound approaches English f.
q	Guttural fricative similar to North German ch in Achtung.
q'	Q with glottal stop.
qh	Aspirated q.
r	Softer than in Spanish; somewhere between the r of Spanish and that of British English.
s	As in English sit.
sh	As in English shine.
t	As in English.
t'	Explosive t.
th	Aspirated t. Not like either th sound of English.
w	As in English.
y	As in English.

In Runasimi words of Spanish origin or influence, the letters b, d, f, g, and v may occur. These are either pronounced as in Spanish or changed to w, th, ph, q, and w respectively. Older orthographies often used u, hu, or gu to represent w (guaman, huayno), or hispanicized the sound to b or v (Viracocha, or the particularly hideous Atabalipa for Atau Wallpa). The older systems are especially weak in the area of the sounds q, q', qh, k, k', kh—all were merely written as c, although cc was sometimes used for q, q', and qh. Similarly, tt was sometimes used in the Cusco region for t'.

The glottalizations and explosives become less emphasized as one proceeds northward from Cusco, and are more emphasized to the south. This is probably due to Aymara influence. Another major difference between the speech of Cusco and Ayacucho is the change of sh to chk in verbal forms. Thus: rimashan (he is speaking—Cusco); rimachkan (he is speaking—Ayacucho). A third variant, rimasian, is also found in the Cusco region.

GLOSSARY

Note on Runasimi spelling

I have tried to follow the new standard alphabet approved by the Peruvian Ministry of Education and published in a series of grammars and dictionaries in the mid-1970s. Thus, Huayna Capac becomes Wayna Qhapaq, Viracocha becomes Wiraqocha, Atahuallpa becomes Atau Wallpa, and so forth. The word "Inca" is a special case: when it is used as an English word I write it Inca; when it occurs in a Runasimi context or as part of a name I use the new spelling (for example, Tupaq Inka Yupanki). "Tupaq" is another problem. The Andean scholar John Rowe has argued convincingly that the original form of this title was Tupa or Thupa, and that Tupac or Tupaq appeared during the eighteenth century as a result of a mistake made by Garcilaso de la Vega and copied by his readers. Be that as it may, the latter usage (with either c or q) has become standard in Peru.

Place names are also difficult. When both a Runasimi and a hispanicized form are in use I have preferred the former, but I have not followed this rule to the point of converting internationally known names. Thus Cusco remains Cusco, although the Runasimi spelling Qosqo is also used today.

Plurals in Runasimi are formed by adding the suffix *-kuna*, but in most cases I make do with the English *-s*.

AQLLAKUNA.	The "Chosen Women," sometimes called Virgins of the Sun. They were in some ways like nuns, but their duties included brewing beer, weaving cloth, singing and dancing at ceremonies, and serving in the tem-

ples. They were also a source of wives and concubines for the Inca aristocracy. The male equivalent of the *aqllakuna* were the YANAKUNA (see below).

AMARU.
Large serpent, especially the mythological serpent of the underworld, associated with the lower moiety in the Andean duality (see HANAN *and* HURIN).

APACHITA.
Cairn, pile of stones and chewed coca wads built up over the years by Runa travelers at mountain passes.

APU.
Lord. Title of the highest Inca nobility, still applied nowadays to the sacred mountains.

AUQAY PATA.
One of the names of Cusco's main plaza in Inca times. Usually translated "Square of Warriors." Other variations of the name are Wak'ay Pata, "Holy Square," and Waqay Pata, "Square of Weeping."

AYLLU.
Can mean, depending on context, community, clan, family, ancestor, penis, or set of bolas stones. I use it mainly in the first two senses.

CARAJO.
Spanish expletive used also in Runasimi. Literally, penis.

CEQUE.
See SEQE.

CHAKA.
Bridge, especially rope suspension bridge of Inca type.

CHAKI-TAKLLA.
Foot-plow, Andean digging stick with handle, footrest, and wide blade.

CH'ARKI.
Dried meat, source of English word "jerky."

CHIFA.
Chinese restaurant.

CHINKANA.
"Place in which one becomes lost." Maze or labyrinth hewn from rock, or building of similar design.

CHOLO, -A
Person at intermediate stage of acculturation between Runa and mestizo. Peruvian Spanish from Runasimi *chulu*, hybrid.

CHUCHA.
Vulgar Spanish word for vagina.

CH'ULLPA.
Burial tower or sepulcher.

CH'ULLU.
Characteristic knitted cap with earflaps worn by Runa. Spelled *chullo* in Andean Spanish.

CH'UNU.
Dehydrated potato made by alternate exposure to frost and sun. Spelled *chuño* in Andean Spanish.

COCA.
Plant or leaves of cocaine-bearing shrub *Erythroxy-*

lon coca. Chewed in leaf form by Runa and used extensively in rites and rituals. From Runasimi *kuka.*

CORREGIDOR.
Judge, especially of colonial period. Colonial *corregidores* were responsible for gathering taxes, tribute, and *mit'a* levies, and were famed for their corruption and rapacity.

CRIOLLO.
Literally, creole. In Peru this means white persons of European descent, the upper class.

ENCOMENDERO.
Holder of early post-Conquest feudal land grant from Spanish Crown. *Encomenderos* were supposed to protect and evangelize the Indians under their control in return for receiving tribute in labor and kind. Most were conquistadors; abuse of their privileges was common.

GRINGO.
Foreigner, especially North American, or Peruvian with pale skin and European features.

HACENDADO.
Owner of hacienda.

HANAN *and*
HURIN.
Upper and lower, the two moieties, or halves, of the Andean duality. Similar in concept to the Chinese *yin* and *yang,* the division may be literal or symbolic. Mountains, man, day, sky, sun, and present are *hanan,* upper; coast, jungle, woman, earth, water, night, and the past are *hurin,* lower. Cusco, and indeed the whole world, were divided into *hanan* and *hurin;* the division was based on various criteria, including topography, kinship, and mythology, and could be reversed under certain conditions.

HARAWI.
In Inca or modern Runa music *harawi* is an epic poem, a solemn ritualistic song, or a sad love song. The genre became blended with Spanish elements to form the *yaraví,* a sad romantic song very popular among mestizos in the last century.

ICHU.
Coarse, spiky grass found at high altitude in the Andes. Staple grazing of llamas, alpacas, and vicuñas; also used for thatch.

INDIGENISMO.
Indianism or indigenism, an intellectual, literary, and political movement originating toward the end of the nineteenth century. *Indigenistas* sought to glorify the native past, but were often naive in their

understanding of Runa culture; they were influential in formulating early APRA ideas. An opposing movement, *hispanicismo*, glorifies the traditions of Spain and the conquistadors.

INKA.

Inca, often translated as "King" or "Emperor," loosely and inaccurately applied to ancient Peruvians as a whole. Modern Runa gave ethnologist J. M. Arguedas the following definition: "*Inka* is the original model of all things." This is probably the fundamental meaning—archetype.

INTI.

The sun as celestial body. When given religious significance, the sun is known today as Tayta Inti, "Father Sun." In Inca times there seem to have been three aspects of the solar deity: Qhapaq Inti, "Almighty Sun," a spiritual entity thought to inhabit but be distinct from the physical sun; P'unchaw, the sun as resplendent "Day"; and Inti Wawqi, "Sun Brother," the totemic relative of the Inca royalty.

JALCA.

See SALLQA.

KAMAYOQ.

"He with command," a title given to many types of Inca official, e.g., *Chaka Kamayoq*, "Overseer of Bridges."

KANCHA.

Enclosure, compound, or courtyard. Characteristic architectural pattern of Inca and modern Runa settlements. Houses and other buildings are built against the inside of a four-sided perimeter wall, usually with a single entrance.

KHIPU.

Quipu, mnemonic device consisting of knotted and colored cords, the Inca substitute for writing. Modern studies have shown that Inca *khipu*s used a base-ten, place-system mathematics that included the concept of zero. The extent to which nonstatistical information could be recorded is not understood. An excellent book is *Code of the Quipu* by Marcia and Robert Ascher (see Bibliography).

KILLA.

Moon or month.

KUMPI.

Very fine cloth woven from vicuña wool by the Chosen Women; figuratively, anything fine.

KURAKA.

Important official in the Inca administration, often a local ethnic leader of proven loyalty. The Spaniards continued to govern the Indians through the *kurakas* until the great Tupaq Amaru revolt of 1780, in which many *kurakas* took part.

KUSI PATA.

"Square of Rejoicing" or "Recreation Square," the lower half of the main plaza of Inca Cusco. Part of it survives today as Plaza Regocijo, a translation of the old name; the rest is occupied by the Hotel Cusco and a block of shops.

LIMENO, -A.

Inhabitant of Lima. Thus, *cusqueño*, inhabitant of Cusco.

LLAQTA.

Runasimi for nation, town, or people. Encompasses all meanings of Spanish *pueblo* and *patria*.

LLIQLLA.

Shawl worn by Runa women. Often doubles as a carrying cloth.

MARICON.

Vulgar Spanish word for male homosexual.

MINK'A.

Reciprocal agreement in which a person invites others to work for him in return for providing food and drink; a work bee. The beneficiary is usually obligated to return labor when called upon. (Also known as *ayni*, though this has a slightly different meaning in some areas.) Hence Andean Spanish *minga*.

MIT'A.

A turn, period, or season; labor by turns. Under the Incas the *mit'a* was a labor tax by which the state enlisted workers in return for providing a measure of social security. Under the Spaniards the *mit'a* became forced labor in the mines, so onerous that it is known to have killed several million people and depopulated large areas of the Andes.

PACHA.

Runasimi word encompassing concepts of space, time, world, and universe.

PACHAKUTI.

Literally "world turning over." Cataclysmic event separating eras in time. The founding of the Inca Empire was seen as the beginning of a new era, and the Inca ruler responsible took Pachakuti as his name. The Spanish Conquest was also seen as a *pachakuti*, in the sense of a great disaster; Waman Puma mourned it as a "world in reverse" because *hanan* and *hurin* had been overturned and the Spaniards had failed to institute a new order that was just or made sense.

PALLAY. Adornment, ornament; the Runasimi word for the elaborate patterns and motifs in Andean weaving.

PAMPA. Runasimi for a plain or flat area of any size. The adjective for flat.

PAQARINA. Place of origin or dawning. Most ancient (and many modern) Andean ethnic groups and *ayllus* considered a particular rock, cave, spring, mountain, or other natural feature as their *paqarina.*

PATA. A terrace, level, or town square. Also a Runasimi adverbial suffix for "above" or "on top of."

PUEBLO JOVEN. "Young town," euphemistic name for *barriada,* slum or shantytown.

PUNA. The high-altitude intermontane plains, usually above twelve thousand feet. Characteristically treeless and covered in *ichu* grass. Also called *sallqa.*

P'UNCHAW. Runasimi for day; the name of a sacred image of the sun as Day.

QANTU. *Cantu buxifolia* Juss. Also called *Flor del Inca,* "Flower of the Inca," a bush bearing tubular crimson flowers. Of religious significance to the Incas, it became a symbol of Runa identity in the colonial period, and remains so today—Runa often wear it in their hats.

QENA. Quena, end-blown notched flute of pre-Columbian origin, still very popular in the Andes. The number of fingering holes may vary, but most *qenas* have six along the top and one below, operated by the thumb.

QOLLQA. Granary or storehouse; also a name of the Pleiades.

ROCANROL. Rock and roll.

RUNA. Person, people, mankind in general; The People—native Andeans, as opposed to *cholos,* mestizos, and whites. I use "Runa" in preference to "Indian."

RUNASIMI. Literally, "Mouth of the People," the language commonly known as Quechua. Runasimi was the lingua franca of the Inca Empire, and perhaps of earlier empires; it is spoken today by about ten million people in Peru, Ecuador, Bolivia, and parts of Chile and Argentina. John Rowe has pointed out that Quechua has become derogatory in some contexts, and has suggested calling the language Inca.

However, there is evidence that the Inca royalty may have spoken a secret courtly language called Inca, distinct from Quechua. I have followed Gasparini and Margolies and other recent authors in adopting the term Runasimi, which is what most speakers of the language call it.

SAIS. Sociedad Agrícola de Interés Social, "Agrarian Society of Social Interest," a cooperative landholding structure devised by the land reform architects to try to reconcile conflicting claims on former hacienda lands from estate serfs and surrounding free Runa.

SALLQA. Synonym for the *puna* zone. As an adjective it means wild or uncivilized, because the *sallqa* is considered a wilderness region. The word becomes *jalca* in Andean Spanish.

SAN PEDRO. *Trichocereus pachanoi*, a large columnar cactus with hallucinogenic properties, used by shamans. The association with Saint Peter is interesting—he is the keeper of the keys to heaven. In Runasimi the San Pedro is called *wachuma*.

SELVA. The Amazonian jungle, also called *montaña* and *yunga* in Andean Spanish. *Yunga* comes from the Runasimi *yunka*, lowlands.

SEQE. Line or alignment. The Incas believed that a complex system of *seqes* radiated from Cusco.

SIERRA. Literally, a saw, hence a jagged mountain range. In Peru *sierra* is the general term for the highlands.

SIRVINAKUY. A hybrid word meaning mutual service: the Andean custom of trial marriage, also called *watanakuy*, "a year together."

SOL. "Sun," the Peruvian unit of currency.

SOROCHE. Altitude sickness. From Runasimi *suruchi*.

SUYU. Region, division, or direction. See TAWANTINSUYU.

TAMPU. "A place from which one sets out," government posthouses built at intervals of a day's journey along Inca roads. Hence Andean Spanish *tambo*.

TAWANTINSUYU. Name of the Inca Empire. Literally, "The Unity of Four Parts," often translated as "The Four Quarters of the World."

TAYTACHA. "Little Father," a name applied in the Andes to God and miraculous images of Christ.

TRAGO.

Raw cane alcohol, consumed both ritually and convivially by Runa.

TUPU.

A brooch, often in the form of a spoon, used by women to fasten the *lliqlla* shawl. Also an Inca measurement of land, still used today. A *tupu* takes into account topography and fertility, and is therefore not a fixed area.

UKHU PACHA.

Literally, "the inner world." The Andean underworld, which has acquired a few traits of the Christian hell, but is primarily thought of as the abode of the overturned order of the past and all things *hurin.*

USNU.

Platform located at the center of Inca plazas and used as throne, altar, and observatory. A seat or axis of symbolic order.

UTA.

Leishmaniasis, a wasting disease whose symptoms resemble those of leprosy. Called *espundia* in Spanish.

VARAYOQ.

A hybrid word meaning "he with the staff of office." Title of the mayor of a Runa community.

WACHUMA.

See SAN PEDRO.

WAK'A.

Huaca, holy place or thing, tutelar deity. Natural rocks, caves, springs, etc., may be *wak'as,* as may places where carvings or buildings are found. On the coast, *huaca* is applied to ancient temple mounds, and the Spanish derivative *huaco* to artifacts, especially pots. A looter of archaeological sites is called a *huaquero.*

WAMANI.

Protective spirit inhabiting mountain peaks, high passes, springs, etc. Synonymous in some respects with *wak'a* and *apu.*

WAYNO.

Folk tune and dance characterized by pentatonic melodies, duple time, and ingenious lyrics employing assonance and repetition. Very popular among Runa, *cholos,* and Andean mestizos. From Aymara *wayñu,* lover or love song. Spelled *huayno* in Andean Spanish.

WIRAQOCHA.

Viracocha, Andean creator god associated with water, white, the Milky Way, periphery, and *hurin,* the lower moiety. "Wiraqocha" literally means "foam of the sea" or "sea (or lake) of fat"—fat being considered a life essence. The name was applied to the Spaniards because they came from the sea, the periphery of the Inca world, and were white-skinned. Today, "wiraqocha" is used in Runasimi as the equivalent of "mister," "sir," or "gentleman," and has more to do with a person's rank than his color.

YANAKUNA.   The servant class in Inca society, literally, "the helpers" or "the blacks." The latter meaning comes from the association of the color black with people who had no kinship with the Inca ruler. The *yanakuna* were the male equivalent of the *aqllakuna*, though their tasks were mainly secular. They were not necessarily of low status; some scholars see them as the beginning of an upwardly mobile "middle class."

SOURCE NOTES

References by author and date are to entries in the Bibliography. Translations are mine unless otherwise stated. Almost all of the songs and poems have been abridged and the spelling standardized.

I am grateful to Antonio and Miguel Angel Sulca of Ayacucho for the words to the traditional songs on pages 92, 119, and 140; and to Toribia Chávez, formerly of Abancay, for those on pages 76, 143, and 179. The songs on pages 153 and 162–63 are from Benavente Díaz's collection *Charango y quena* (Cusco: Editorial de Cultura Andina, 1976). The poem by Porfirio Meneses on page 97, and the songs on pages 112 and 113, appeared in *Runa* magazine, published monthly during 1977 by the Instituto Nacional de Cultura in Lima. Unreferenced songs were collected by me.

R.W.

Page

3–4   "It consisted of four rooms": Jérez, in Zárate, 1968, p. 94, trans. J. M. Cohen.

4   "There are [coming]": Waman Puma, 1936, p. 381.

6   The selection from *Atau Wallpa Wañuy* is in Lara, 1947, pp. 193–94.

7   "Atahuallpa was so intelligent": Alonso de Guzmán, in Zárate, 1968, p. 129, trans. J. M. Cohen.

7   "The Governor then spoke": Jérez in Zárate, 1968, p. 130, trans. J. M. Cohen.

20   "San Pedro has great power": Sharon, 1972a, pp. 130, 124.

53–54   "The Indians were many": Wachtel, 1971, p. 104.

54   "There used to be": Cieza de Léon, 1959, pp. 325–26.

57   My main source on the Cerro de Pasco Corporation is Lindqvist, 1973, pp. 178–82.

64   "A fortress with five blind walls": Estete, in Zárate, 1968, p. 113, trans. J. M. Cohen.

65   My main source on William Grace is Lindqvist, 1973, pp. 162–74.

67   "gaining fortunes": Gow, 1980, p. 29.

75   "The Wamani is really our second God": Ossio, 1973, pp. 222–23.

77   The Runasimi quotations are from *El Comercio*, February 19, 1975, Lima.

82–83   Much of this information on Julio César Tello is from a public lecture given by Dr. M. Chávez Ballón in Cusco, April 11, 1980. See also *Runa* #3 (June 1977), pp. 2–17, Lima: Instituto Nacional de Cultura.

101   Dr. William Isbell of the State University of New York at Binghamton has been excavating recently at Wari; he has various publications on the period and site. See William H. Isbell, 1977, 1978.

106   "All his life": Waman Puma, 1936, p. 18.

108   "You should consider": Waman Puma, 1936, p. 915.

108   "I offer, firstly": Waman Puma, 1936, pp. 948–49.

115   "The influence of Spain": Squier, 1877, p. 543.

130   "Does your heart not pain you": Waman Puma, 1936, p. 319.

130   "Inca Wanakauri": Waman Puma, 1936, p. 451.

131   "This is the reason": Valcárcel, 1977, p. 131.

132–33   "I remembered what my uncle Gumercindo once told me": Condori Mamani, 1977, p. 30.

145   "The whole palace was painted": Murúa, quoted in Hemming, 1970, p. 434.

146   "Over this skeleton dome": Squier, 1877, pp. 394–95.

150–54   For a collection of modern studies and early descriptions of these ruins, see Ministerio de Educación, 1970.

157–58   My source for the information on *laymi* is Brush, 1980.

158   "*Señor* leader, hill me": Kauffman, 1976, pp. 336–37.

162   "We were crazy": See Randall, 1980a, 1980b, for Robert Randall's own account of this river journey.

167   "My brothers and sons": Yupanki, 1973, pp. 38–39.

168   "What do you want?": Yupanki, 1973, pp. 36–37.

177   There are various editions of *Ollantay*, all differing somewhat in wording and spelling. One currently in print is *Ollantay* (Lima: Edi-

torial Universo, 3rd ed., 1980). It contains the "original text" in a poor choice of orthography, a Spanish translation, and a ghastly "adaptation for the modern theater."

178   The *yana machu* song is from Condori Mamani, 1977, p. 31.

190–91   *"Distribution of the bodies"*: Valcárcel, 1977, pp. 184–87.

193–94   "When the Inca was building Cusco": Condori Mamani, 1977, p. 19.

195   The Qolla chieftain's speech is in Pachakuti Yamki, 1968, p. 296.

203   "The spangled velvet veil": Squier, 1877, p. 323.

209   "All the people were gathered": Yupanki, 1973, pp. 39–40.

BIBLIOGRAPHY

Alegría, Ciro. 1935. *La serpiente de oro*. English edition, *The Golden Serpent*, trans. Harriet de Onís. New York: New American Library, 1963.

———. 1941. *El mundo es ancho y ajeno*. English edition, *Broad and Alien Is the World*, trans. Harriet de Onís. London: Merlin Press, n.d.

Allen, Catherine. 1981. "To Be Quechua: The Symbolism of Coca Chewing in Highland Peru." *American Ethnologist* VIII, 1:157–71.

Arguedas, José María. 1941. *Yawar fiesta*. New edition. Buenos Aires: Editorial Losada S.A., 1974.

———. 1949. *Canciones y cuentos del pueblo quechua*. Lima: Editorial Huascarán.

———. 1958. *Los rios profundos*. New edition. Buenos Aires: Editorial Losada S.A., 1978. English edition, *Deep River*, trans. William Rowe, 1973.

———. 1964. *Todas las sangres*. New edition. Lima: Ediciones Peisa, 1973.

———. 1971. *El zorro de arriba y el zorro de abajo*. Buenos Aires: Editorial Losada S.A.

Arguedas, José María, and Ruth Stephan. 1957. *The Singing Mountaineers*. Austin: Univ. of Texas Press.

Ascher, Marcia, and Robert Ascher. 1981. *Code of the Quipu*. Ann Arbor: Univ. of Michigan Press.

Bandelier, Adolph F. 1910. *The Islands of Titicaca and Koati*. New edition. New York: Kraus Reprint, 1969.

Bastien, Joseph William. 1978. *Mountain of the Condor: Metaphor and Ritual in an Andean Ayllu*. St. Paul: West Publishing Co.

Benavente Díaz. 1976. *Charango y quena*. Cusco: Editorial de Cultura Andina.

Blanco, Hugo. 1972. *Land or Death: The Peasant Struggle in Peru*. New York: Pathfinder Press.

Brush, Stephen B. 1980. "The Environment and Native Andean Agriculture." *American Indígena* XL, 1:161–72, México D.F.

Bushnell, G.H.S. 1963. *Peru*. London: Thames & Hudson.

Castaneda, Carlos. 1968. *The Teachings of Don Juan: A Yaqui Way of Knowledge*. Los Angeles: Univ. of California Press.

Cieza de León, Pedro de. 1553. *The Incas of Pedro de Cieza de León*, ed. V. W. von Hagen, trans. Harriet de Onís. Norman: Univ. of Oklahoma Press, 1959.

Cobo, Bernabé. 1653. *Historia del Nuevo Mundo, I–II*. In *Obras del P. Bernabé Cobo*, BAE XCI–XCII. Madrid: Ediciones Atlas, 1956.

Condori Mamani, Gregorio. 1977. *Autobiografía*. Ed. Ricardo Valderrama and Carmen Escalante. Cusco: Centro de Estudios Rurales Andinos "Bartolomé de las Casas."

Crosby, Alfred W. 1972. *The Columbian Exchange: Biological and Cultural Consequences of 1492*. Westport: Greenwood Press.

Cusihuamán, Antonio. 1976. *Diccionario quechua: Cusco-Collao*. Lima: Ministerio de Educación.

———. 1976. *Gramatica quechua: Cusco-Collao*. Lima: Ministerio de Educación.

De Mille, Richard. 1976. *Castaneda's Journey: The Power and the Allegory*. Santa Barbara: Capra Press.

Dobyns, Henry E., and Paul Doughty. 1976. *Peru: A Cultural History*. New York: Oxford Univ. Press.

Flores Galindo, Alberto, ed. 1976. *Túpac Amaru II, 1780*. Lima: Retablo de Papel Ediciones.

Franck, Harry A. 1917. *Vagabonding down the Andes*. New York: The Century Co.

Garcilaso de la Vega, El Inca. 1616. *Royal Commentaries of the Incas, I–II*, trans. Harold Livermore. Austin: Univ. of Texas Press, 1966.

Gasparini, Graziano, and Luise Margolies. 1977. *Arquitectura Inka*. English edition, *Inca Architecture*, trans. Patricia Lyons. Bloomington: Indiana Univ. Press, 1980.

Gow, Neil. 1980. "Golden Age of Guano." *South American Explorer*, 6:27–32.

Guardia Mayorga, César A. 1959. *Diccionario Kechwa-Castellano, Castellano-Kechwa*. Fifth edition. Lima: Editora Los Andes, 1971.

———. 1973. *Gramatica Kechwa*. Lima: Ediciones Los Andes.

d'Harcourt, Raoul, and Marguerite d'Harcourt. 1925. *La Musique des Incas et ses Survivances*. Paris: Geuthner.

————. 1959. *La Musique des Aymara sur les Hauts Plateaux Boliviens*. Paris: Société des Américanistes.

Hemming, John. 1970. *The Conquest of the Incas*. London: Macmillan.

Isbell, Billie Jean. 1978. *To Defend Ourselves: Ecology and Ritual in an Andean Village*. Austin: Univ. of Texas Press.

Isbell, William H. 1977. *The Rural Foundations for Urbanism*. Urbana: Univ. of Illinois Press.

Isbell, William H., and Katharina Schreiber. 1978. "Was Huari a State?" *American Antiquity* XXXXIII, 3: 372–89.

Izumi, Seiichi, and Toshihiko Sono. 1963. *Excavations at Kótosh, Peru*. Tokyo: Kadokawa Publishing Co.

Izumi, Seiichi, and Kazuo Terada. 1972. *Excavations at Kótosh, Peru: Third and Fourth Expeditions*. Tokyo: University of Tokyo Press.

Kauffman, Christopher. 1976. "Variation in the Music, Song Texts and Instrumentation of the Papa Aysay Ceremony in Chinchero, an Indigenous Highland Community in Southern Peru." Unpublished Ph.D. thesis. Bloomington: Indiana University, Dept. of Folklore.

Kauffmann Doig, Federico. 1969. *Manual de arqueología peruana*. Fifth edition. Lima: Ediciones Peisa, 1973.

Kendall, Ann. 1973. *Everyday Life of the Incas*. New York: Putnam's.

Lamb, F. Bruce, 1971. *Wizard of the Upper Amazon: The Story of Manuel Córdova-Rios*. Boston: Houghton Mifflin.

Lanning, Edward P. 1967. *Peru Before the Incas*. Englewood Cliffs: Prentice-Hall.

Lara, Jesus. 1947. *La poesía quechua*. Reprint. México D.F.: Fondo de Cultura Económica, 1979.

Lathrap, Donald W. 1968. "The Tropical Forest and the Cultural Context of Chavín." In *Dumbarton Oaks Conference on Chavín*, pp. 73–100. Washington, D.C.

León-Portilla, Miguel. 1964. *El reverso de la conquista: relaciones aztecas, mayas e incas*. México: Editorial Joaquín Mortíz.

Lindqvist, Sven. 1973. *Land and Power in South America*. Harmondsworth, England: Penguin.

Lowenthal, Abraham F., ed. 1975. *The Peruvian Experiment: Continuity and Change under Military Rule*. Princeton; Princeton Univ. Press.

Lumbreras, Luis G. 1968. "Towards a Re-evaluation of Chavín." In *Dumbarton Oaks Conference on Chavín*, pp. 1–28. Washington, D.C.

————. 1977. "Tello y su tiempo," *Runa* 3:4–5. Lima: Instituto Nacional de Cultura.

Mariátegui, José Carlos. 1928. *Siete ensayos de interpretación de la realidad peruana*. Thirteenth edition. Lima: Biblioteca Amauta, 1968.

Mason, J. Alden. 1957. *The Ancient Civilizations of Peru.* Harmondsworth, England: Penguin.

Ministerio de Educación Pública, Perú. 1970. *Saqsaywaman No. 1.* Cusco: Patronato Departamental de Arqueología del Cusco.

Moisés, Rosalio, J. H. Kelley, and W. C. Holden. 1971. *A Yaqui Life: The Personal Chronicle of a Yaqui Indian.* Lincoln: Univ. of Nebraska Press, 1977. First published as *The Tall Candle.*

Murra, John V. 1956. "The Economic Organization of the Inca State." Unpublished Ph.D. thesis, Univ. of Chicago.

―――. 1975. *Formaciones económicas y políticas del mundo andino.* Lima: Instituto de Estudios Peruanos.

Ossio, Juan M. 1970. "The Idea of History in Felipe Guaman Poma de Ayala." Unpublished B. Litt. thesis, Oxford University, Dept. of Anthropology.

―――. 1973 (ed.) *Ideología mesidnica del mundo andino.* Lima: Edición de Ignacio Prado Pastor.

Outwater, J. Ogden, Jr. 1959. "Building the Fortress of Ollantaytambo." *Archaeology* XII, 1: 26–32.

Pachakuti Yamki Sallqamaywa (Pachacuti Yamqui Salcamayqua), Joan de Santacruz. 1613. *Relación de antigüedades deste reyno del Perú.* In *Crónicas Peruanas de Interés Indígena,* BAE CCIX. Madrid: Ediciones Atlas, 1968.

Pease, Franklin. 1972. *Los ultimos Incas del Cusco.* Second edition. Lima: Ediciónes P.L.V., 1976.

―――. 1978. *Del Tawantinsuyu a la historia del Perú.* Lima: Instituto de Estudios Peruanos.

Philip, George D. E. 1978. *The Rise and Fall of the Peruvian Military Radicals, 1968–1976.* London: Univ. of London Press.

Prescott, William H. 1843. *History of the Conquest of Mexico.* 1847. *History of the Conquest of Peru.* Reprinted in one volume. New York: Random House, The Modern Library, n.d.

Randall, Robert. 1980a. "Tales of the Tiger, Part One." *South American Explorer* 6:4–12.

―――. 1980b. "Tales of the Tiger, Part Two." *South American Explorer* 7:4–12.

―――. 1982. "Qoyllur Rit'i, an Inca Fiesta of the Pleiades: Reflections on Time and Space in the Andean World." *Bulletin, Institut Français des Etudes Andines* (Paris) XI, 1, 2:37–81.

Reichlen, Henry, and Paule Reichlen. 1949. "Recherches archéologiques dans les Andes de Cajamarca." *Journal de la Société des Américanistes de Paris,* N.S., XXXVIII.

―――. 1950. "Recherches archéologiques dans les Andes du haut Utcubamba." *Journal de la Société des Américanistes de Paris,* N.S., XXXIX.

Rowe, John H. 1946. "Inca Culture at the Time of the Spanish Conquest." *Handbook of South American Indians* II:183–330.

———. 1976. "El movimiento nacional Inca del siglo XVIII." In *Tupac Amaru II, 1780*, ed. Flores Galindo, op. cit., pp. 11–66.

Sharon, Douglas. 1972a. "The San Pedro Cactus in Peruvian Folk Healing." In *Flesh of the Gods*, ed. Peter T. Furst, pp. 114–35. New York: Praeger.

———. 1972b. "Eduardo the Healer." *Natural History* LXXXI, 9:32–47.

———. 1978. *Wizard of the Four Winds: A Shaman's Story*. New York: The Free Press.

Spalding, Karen. 1974. *De indio a campesino*. Lima: Instituto de Estudios Peruanos.

Squier, Ephraim George. 1877. *Peru, Incidents of Travel and Exploration in the Land of the Incas*. Reprint. New Haven: Peabody Museum; printed by AMS Press, New York, 1973.

Stevenson, Robert. 1968. *Music in Aztec and Inca Territory*. Berkeley: Univ. of California Press.

Tello, Julio César. 1960. *Chavín: Cultura matríz de la civilización andina*, rev. T. Mejía Xesspe. Lima: Univ. de San Marcos.

Urton, Gary. 1978. "Orientation in Quechua and Incaic Astronomy." *Ethnology* XVII, 2:157–67.

Valcárcel, Carlos Daniel. 1977. *Túpac Amaru*. Lima: Universidad Nacional Mayor de San Marcos, Publicaciones.

Wachtel, Nathan. 1971. *The Vision of the Vanquished: The Spanish Conquest through Indian Eyes, 1530–1570*. New York: Barnes & Noble.

Waman Puma de Ayala, Felipe (Phelipe Guaman Poma de Ayala). 1615. *El Primer Nueva Corónica y Buen Gobierno*. Facsimile edition 1936. Reprint 1968. Paris: Institut d'Ethnologie.

Webster, Steven S. 1980. "Ethnicity in the Southern Peruvian Highlands." In *Environment, Society and Rural Change in Latin America*, ed. D. A. Preston, pp. 135–54. New York: John Wiley & Sons.

Werlich, David P. 1978. *Peru: A Short History*. Carbondale: Southern Illinois Univ. Press.

Whitten, Norman E. 1976. *Sacha Runa: Ethnicity and Adaptation of Ecuadorian Jungle Quichua*. Chicago: Univ. of Illinois Press.

Wilder, Thornton. 1927. *The Bridge of San Luis Rey*. New York: A. & C. Boni.

Woodcock, George. 1959. *Incas and Other Men*. London: Faber & Faber.

Yupanki, Titu Kusi (Titu Cusi Yupanqui). 1568. *Relación de la Conquista del Perú*. Lima: Ediciones de la Biblioteca Universitaria, 1973.

Zárate, Agustin de. 1555. *The Discovery and Conquest of Peru*, trans. J. M. Cohen. Harmondsworth, England: Penguin, 1968.

Zuidema, R. T. 1964. *The Ceque System of Cusco*. Leiden: E. J. Brill.

Index

Abancay, 119–22
Alegría, Ciro, 34
Andahuaylas, 117–19
APRA (*Alianza Popular Revolucion-aria Americana*), 21–22
Apurimaq, 124–26
Arguedas, José María, 68, 117–19, 121, 193
Atau Wallpa (Atahuallpa), 3, 5
Ayacucho (Huamanga), 98–102, 106–13

Baños del Inca, 3
Bastidas Puyuqhawa, Micaela, 189–91
Bingham, Hiram, 183, 184, 185
Blanco, Hugo, 43
Bolívar, Simón, 61, 77–78, 79
Bridge of San Luís Rey, 125–27
Bullfights, 175–76

Cajamarca (Qashamarka), 3–21
Cajamarca culture, 15
Castaneda, Carlos, 17–21
Celendín, 24–26, 32–34
Cerro de Pasco, 57–58
Chavín de Huántar, 81–86
Chavín Horizon, 14
Chiclayo, 1

Chimbote, 66–68
Chimú, 2, 64
Condori, Mamani, Gregorio, 132, 193
Copacabana (Qopaqhawana), 201–204
Cortés, Hernán, 5
Cuauhtémoc, 5
Cumbe Mayu (Kumpi Mayu), 9–12
Cusco (Qosqo), 127–56

FOCEP (*Frente Obrero, Campesino, Estudiantil y Popular*), 43

Garcilaso de la Vega, El Inca, 146
Grace, William, 65, 67
Guano, 66–68

Hatunqolla, 195–96
Hatun Rumiyoq Street, 134
Haya de la Torre, Victor Rául, 22, 60
Huánuco (New), 44–46, 54–56
Huánuco (Old; Wanuku), 48 ff.
Huarás, 77–79, 81
Huchuy Qosqo, 160–61

Inca's Seat, 8–9
Inca Trail, 178–83

Inkarí, 131
International Petroleum Company (IPC), 62

Jequetepeque River, 2

Koati Island (Island of the Moon), 204–205
Kótosh, 45–46
Kuélap, 37–39
Kusilloq Hink'inan, 154–55

La Chocta, 31–32
La Raya Pass, 193–94
La Unión, 48–49
Leimebamba, 35–36
Lima, 60–63

Machu Piqchu, 183–85
Mama Oqllo, 136, 202, 204, 208
Manku Inka Yupanki (Manco II), 168
Manku Qhapaq (Manco Capac), 136, 202, 204, 206–208
Mariátegui, José Carlos, 101
Mayu ("The River"; Milky Way), 116
Meiggs, Henry, 59, 67, 197
Mexico, 5–6
Mink'a (minga), 10
Missionaries (Seventh Day Adventist), 197–98
Mit'a, 10
Mochica, 2, 12–13
Morales Bermúdez, Francisco, 23
Moyobamba, 40–41
Music, 90–93, 111–12

Ollantay (drama), 177
Ollantaytambo, 161 ff.

Otusco, 15–16
Oxamarca, 28–33

Pacatnamú, 2
Pachakuti Inka Yupanki (Pachacuti), 125, 134–36
Pachakuti Yamki Sallqamaywa, Juan (Joan de Santacruz Pachacuti Yamqui Sallcamayhua), 166–67
Panpipe music, 176, 200–201
Paqariq Tampu, 166
Paracas, 13–14
Paramonga, 64–66
Pikillaqta, 186
PIP (Policía de Investigaciones del Perú), 72–74
Pizarro, Francisco, 5, 7
Population, decline of, 53–54
PPC (Partido Popular Cristiano), 43
Puno, 196–97

Qollqanpata, 149
Qorikancha (Coricancha), 135–36, 142–45
Quarries (at Ollantaytambo), 169–74

Radio Tawantinsuyu, 138–40
Ransom Room (at Cajamarca), 6–8
Raqchi, 191–92
Rimaq Tampu (Limatambo), 127
Rumiqollqa, 187
Runasimi (Quechua), 17, 77–78, 93–97

SAIS (Sociedad Agrícola de Interés Social), 80–81
San Martín, José de, 61
San Pedro (wachuma cactus), 19–21
Saqsaywaman (Sacsahuaman), 150–54
Sayaqmarka, 181
Saywite, 122–24

Seqe (*ceque*) system, 8, 156
Sillustani, 195–96
SINAMOS (*Sistema Nacional de Apoyo a la Movilización Social*), 80–81
Squier, Ephraim George, 114–15, 126–27
Suchuna (Rodadero), 155–56
Sucre, Antonio José, 100–101
Sucre (Peru), 26–27
Sulca, Antonio, 109–12

Takili (Taquile), 198–201
Tampu Mach'ay (Tambo Machay), 156–57
Tarapoto, 41–42
Tawantinsuyu, 14–15, 51–52
Tello, Julio César, 82–83, 86
Tingo, 36–39
Tingo María, 42–43
Tinta, 188
Titicaca, Lake, 196–209
Titicaca Island (Island of the Sun), 206–209
Titu Kusi Yupanki (Titu Cusi), 133, 167, 209
Tlaltelolco, 5
Tullumayu, 150

Tupaq Amaru I, 130–31
Tupaq Amaru II, 56–57, 131–32, 188 ff.

Uru, 197

Velasco Alvarado, Juan, 22–23, 62–64, 88

Waman Puma (Felipe Guaman Poma de Ayala), 4, 76, 106–109
Wanakauri, 130
Wari (Huari), 101–104
Wari-Tiawanaku Horizon, 14
Willkapampa (Vilcabamba), 100, 183
Willka Waín, 79–80
Wiñay Wayna, 182
Wiraqocha (Viracocha), 123–24
Wiraqocha Inka (Inca Viracocha), 160, 192

Yanakuna (*yanacona*), 165
Yin and *yang*, 123
Yungay, 76
Yuraqmarka, 71–72